Introduction to Health Economics

Second edition

Edited by Lorna Guinness and
Virginia Wiseman

Open University Press

Open University Press
McGraw-Hill Education
McGraw-Hill House
Shoppenhangers Road
Maidenhead
Berkshire
England
SL6 2QL

email: enquiries@openup.co.uk
world wide web: www.openup.co.uk

and Two Penn Plaza, New York, NY 10121-2289, USA

First published 2005
Reprinted 2006, 2007, 2008, 2009, 2010
Second edition 2011

Copyright © London School of Hygiene & Tropical Medicine 2011

A catalogue record of this book is available from the British Library

ISBN-13: 978-0-33-524356-3
ISBN-10: 0-33-524356-8
eISBN: 978-0-33-524357-0

Library of Congress Cataloging-in-Publication Data
CIP data applied for

Typeset by RefineCatch Limited, Bungay, Suffolk
Printed and bound by CPI Group (UK) Ltd, Croydon, CR0 4YY

Fictitious names of companies, products, people, characters and/or data that may be used
herein (in case studies or in examples) are not intended to represent any real individual,
company, product or event.

The *McGraw-Hill* Companies

Dedications

For John, Thomas and Theo
                    LG

I would like to dedicate this book to my parents, Kaye and Don, for their enduring support. I also dedicate it to my children, Franklin, Myrtle and Rose who have always reminded me of the importance of play as well as work. Finally, to my husband, Steve, who has the patience of a saint.
                                            VW

Contents

The editors

Lorna Guinness (PhD) is a lecturer in health economics at the London School of Hygiene & Tropical Medicine where she has worked in teaching and research since 2001. Prior to this she was working as an economist at UNAIDS in Geneva. She works on the economics of health care in low-income countries including contracting out health services and the economics of HIV/AIDS. She is currently also a visiting research fellow at the Australian Centre for Economics Research in Health at the Australian National University, Canberra.

Virginia Wiseman (PhD) is a senior lecturer at the London School of Hygiene & Tropical Medicine where she conducts research in the fields of economic evaluation, demand analysis and equity of access to health services. Much of this research has been in the area of malaria control in sub-Saharan Africa. She has 20 years' experience as a health economist and has been responsible for teaching health economics on the distance learning programmes for LSHTM since 2001.

Acknowledgements

This second edition has been fully updated and revised by editors Lorna Guinness and Virginia Wiseman. Open University Press and the London School of Hygiene & Tropical Medicine would like to acknowledge the invaluable contribution of the authors of the previous edition of this textbook, David Wonderling, Nick Black and Reinhold Gruen, as well as others who laid the foundations for this new work. Reinhold Gruen originally wrote chapter 9 'The changing world of health care finance' (which has now been updated by Lorna Guinness) and chapter 11 'Private health insurance' (since updated by Sachiko Ozawa). A number of activities, diagrams and short passages of text have been retained from the first edition.

The editors and authors would like to thank Alec Miners, Tazio Vanni, Arnab Acharya, Rosa Legood and Stephen Jan for their exhaustive reviews of the chapters and exercises; Richard Smith for reviewing the entire book; Nicki Thorogood and Ros Plowman for their reviews and support throughout the preparation of the book; Dominic Forrest and his team for seeking out copyright permissions; and Mylene Lagarde, Sachi Ozawa, Jo Borghi, Shunmay Yeung, Kristian Hansen and Damian Walker for their authorship of individual chapters.

We would also like to acknowledge UNICEF for their kind agreement to publish extracts and exercises developed for the LSHTM/UNICEF short course 'Health Policy and Financing: Achieving Results for Children'.

Open University Press and the London School of Hygiene & Tropical Medicine have made every effort to obtain permission from copyright holders to reproduce material in this book and to acknowledge these sources correctly. Any omissions brought to our attention will be remedied in future editions.

We would like to express our grateful thanks to the copyright holders for granting permission to reproduce material in this book from the following sources.

Anderson G and Squires D (2010). Measuring the U.S. health care system: A cross-national comparison. *Issues in International Health Policy*, 1412 (90): 1–9. By permission of The Commonwealth Fund.

'A Handbook for the Economic Analysis of Health Sector Projects' by the Asian Development Bank in 2000. By permission of the Asian Development Bank.

http://bookcoverarchive.com/

Borren P and Sutton M (1992). Are increases in cigarette taxation regressive? *Health Economics* 1: 245–53. Reproduced by kind permission of John Wiley & Sons Ltd.

CIVITAS (2009). Markets in Health Care; the theory behind the policy, http://www. civitas.org.uk/nhs/download/Civitas_Markets_in_healthcare_Dec09.pdf

Colombo F and Tapay N (2004). Private Health Insurance in OECD Countries: The Benefits and Costs for Individuals and Health Systems, *OECD Health Working Papers*, No. 15, http://dx.doi.org/10.1787/527211067757

Donaldson C, Gerard K *et al.* (2005). *The Economics of Health Care Financing. The Visible Hand.* By permission of Palgrave Macmillan.

Drummond M, O'Brien B *et al.* (1997). *Methods for the Economic Evaluation of Health Care Programmes.* By permission of Oxford University Press.

Fox-Rushby J and Cairns J. *Economic Evaluation.* Open University Press: Berkshire, England.

The Global Samaritans (Figure 13.1)

Green M (2007). *The Economics of Health Care.* London, Office of Health Economics.

Jacobs B, Price NL and Oeun S. (2007) Do exemptions from user fees mean free access to health services? A case study from a rural Cambodian hospital. *Tropical Medicine and International Health* 12(11): 1391–1401. Reproduced by kind permission of Wiley and Sons Ltd.

McIntyre D, Muirehead D and Gilson L (2002). Geographic patterns of deprivation in South Africa: informing health equity analysis and public resource allocation strategies. *Health Policy and Planning* 17(Suppl): 30–39. By permission of Oxford University Press.

Mills A and Ranson K (2010). Design of health systems. In: MH Merson, RE Black and Mills A, *International Public Health.* Reproduced by kind permission of Jones and Bartlett Learning, UK.

Murray C and Frenk J (2000). A framework for assessing the performance of health systems. *Bulletin of the World Health Organisation* 78(6): 717–31. By permission of the World Health Organisation.

Palmer S and Torgerson DJ (1999). Definitions of efficiency. *BMJ* 318: 1136.

Simon JL, Larson BA, Zusman A and Rosen A (2002). How will the reduction of tariffs and taxes on insecticide-treated bednets affect household purchases? *Bulletin of the World Health Organisation* 80(11): 892–9.

Smith RD (2006). Trade in health services: current challenges and future prospects of globalisation. In: AM Jones (ed.) *Elgar Companion to Health Economics*, chapter 16. By Permission of Edward Elgar.

Wensing M, van den Hombergh P *et al.* (2006). Physician workload in primary care: What is the optimal size of practices? A cross-sectional study. *Health Policy* 77: 260–67. By permission of Elsevier Press.

Introduction

Cigarette consumption among the young, access to anti-retroviral therapy for AIDS patients, the increasing prevalence of obesity, rising health care costs and international shortages of key health care workers are just some of the challenges facing public health policy-makers and practitioners at the start of the twenty-first century. Economics has a central role to play in helping resolve these problems.

This book will introduce you to economic techniques that can be used in public health. It will help you understand the specific features that distinguish demand for health care from demand for other goods and services. It will provide insight into the economic methods that are being used to promote public health policies, analyse health care delivery and shape health sector reforms. You will be better able to make use of information on the economic evaluation of health care interventions and you will better understand the strategic debates on the use of market elements to improve health service performance and the use of financial strategies to promote the health of the public.

As you read through this book, you will soon discover that economists like their jargon and that they do not always agree with each other! You will also discover that there is often a gap between theoretical concepts and political implementation. Moreover, economic policies that work in one country don't necessarily work in a different cultural context. This book does not shy away from such issues; instead emphasis is placed on evoking a critical understanding of issues by describing different views held on the subject, rather than imposing a single view. Throughout this book effort has been put into presenting relevant empirical evidence on each topic and providing case studies and examples that help to demonstrate how economic advice works in practice in low, middle and high income countries.

If you don't have a background in economics you may find the language economists use and the way they explain their theories challenging. Don't panic. This book tackles economic issues from first principles and has been designed for students who have no previous knowledge of economics. A certain amount of economic theory is indispensable to understanding the strength and limitations of economic concepts as applied to health and health care. Wherever possible, we have tried to visualize complex economic concepts by using graphs rather than equations and by giving examples from a wide range of regions and health care settings. Lists of key terms also help to clarify new concepts and terminology. If you don't understand something, don't worry. You may proceed and come back to the problem later. You will find plenty of case studies and some self-assessment exercises to guide you through difficult issues and allow you to compare and contrast what you have learned with your own experience.

Why study health economics?

You may ask yourself what economics has to do with health and health care. Should health and health care, as fundamental concerns, not have an absolute priority? You may, however, already know the answer. Resources are inevitably scarce and choices have to be made about their allocation. Health economics, as you will see in this book, is about the optimization of health relative to other activities and making choices to employ resources in a way that improves health status and service delivery within the limited resources available. Although economics is a relatively old discipline, its systematic application to the health sector is fairly new. It is only during the last 30 or 40 years that health economics has established itself as a sub-discipline of economics and gained influence in the health sector.

Managers and policy-makers rely increasingly on economic analysis. Economic thinking has gained in its influence on decision-making and economic ideas have fuelled health sector reforms. These changes are part of a larger process of public sector reform since the 1980s, which has been shaped by economic ideas. In pursuit of these reforms, multilateral agencies, such as the World Bank, have been aiming to redefine the relationship between the state and the private sector, to promote slimmer government services and an increased engagement of the private sector. A growing number of countries are using economic techniques to prioritize health services and to evaluate new health care technologies. The pharmaceutical industry has started to provide information on cost-effectiveness as this may provide a competitive advantage in promoting their products. But you should be aware that for most health care interventions, information on effectiveness and efficiency is not available. Health economics is still a developing discipline which is increasingly gaining acceptance of its methods.

Equity is another important area of economic analysis because of its usual prominence as a policy objective, its comparison with efficiency objectives and the implications it has for the allocation of resources. For instance, economists (as well as others) have shown that while imposing user fees can address the problem of consumer moral hazard by deterring the frivolous use of health services, this often comes at a high price by imposing heavy burdens on poorer groups. Another example is the use of 'weightings' within resource allocation formulae to reflect the higher health needs of particular population groups such as indigenous people or rural vs. urban populations. Almost all the chapters of this book will have something to say about equity.

Structure of the book

This book follows the conceptual outline of the 'Introduction to health economics' module taught at the London School of Hygiene & Tropical Medicine. The original edition was based on the materials presented in the lectures and seminars of the taught course, which had been adapted for distance learning. This revised edition places a greater emphasis on the practical application of economic theories and concepts to the formulation of health policy and planning. This is principally achieved through the extended use of new examples, case studies and activities. For instance, in Chapter 17 ('Promoting equity and the role of government'), case studies are presented from South Africa and Cambodia to illustrate how policies have been designed to address vertical equity concerns in these countries. Similarly, in Chapter 16 ('Economic evaluation and decision-making), new examples show how the results of economic evaluations have been used by groups such as the National Institute for Health and Clinical Excellence (NICE) in the UK and by the Copenhagen Consensus Project to set priorities on health care spending. The book also provides an update in terms of current thinking. Some important policy shifts have taken place since the first edition was published in 2005: the rise of performance-based funding in health care, increased evidence about the impact and cost of achieving universal health care coverage and the growing impact of globalization and international trade on the health sector are just a few examples. The book introduces some completely new chapters covering topics such as macroeconomics and health, provider payments and countering market failure.

The book is structured around a simple conceptual framework. It starts by introducing you to economics and goes on to consider the concepts of supply, demand and markets. You will then learn about how health systems can be financed. Next we consider how health care interventions can be evaluated using economic analysis and how such economic information can be used in policy-making. Finally, you will look at the issue of equity and the economic argument for the role of government in health services.

The six sections, and the 17 chapters within them, are shown on the book's contents page. Each chapter includes:

- an overview;
- a list of learning objectives;
- a list of key terms;
- a range of activities;
- feedback on the activities;
- a summary;
- references and a list of suggested further reading.

The following briefly summaraizes the book as a whole.

Economics and health economics

Chapter 1 defines economics as well as a range of key concepts commonly used by economists. Health economics is then introduced along with examples of the type of policy questions that this sub-discipline can help to address. In Chapter 2 you will learn about the macroeconomics of health and health care including the relationship between trade and health and health systems.

Demand and supply

This section provides the foundations for exploring how individual markets function, how market forces operate in health care and how they influence output and price for health services. It starts by considering the concept of demand in Chapter 3 and then goes on to explore the measurement of demand and the notion of price elasticity of demand in Chapter 4. You will start to explore the concept of supply in Chapter 5 by looking at production and the inputs to production. In Chapter 6 you will look at the costs of production.

Markets

Your attention will then turn to the interaction of demand and supply and the concept of markets in Chapter 7. This chapter focuses on markets and the conditions under which markets operate well. You go on to learn the reasons for market failure in health care in Chapter 8.

Health care financing

Chapter 9 provides a framework for assessing health care financing systems. It looks at the different sources and uses of funds and provides a brief history behind health systems development. In Chapter 10 you will explore the different methods of paying health care providers and how these might influence health care delivery. You then go on to look at private health insurance (Chapter 11) and the topic of achieving universal coverage (Chapter 12).

Economic evaluation

The penultimate section starts with an exploration of the key concepts behind economic evaluation, the different possible economic evaluation techniques and their uses (Chapter 13). Methods to determine the costs of health care interventions are discussed in Chapter 14 and the methods to determine the benefits of health care interventions are explored in Chapter 15. The final chapter in this section provides an overview of how economic evaluation is applied in practice.

Equity and the role of government

The final chapter begins by describing the relationship between equity and equality and exploring a number of different ways in which equity has been conceptualized and applied in health care. Potential trade-offs between equity and efficiency are considered, along with the pros and cons of government intervention in the health care sector.

A variety of activities are employed to help your understanding and learning of the topics and ideas covered. These include:

- reflection on your own knowledge and experience;
- questions based on reading key articles or relevant research papers;
- analyses of quantitative and qualitative data;
- key terms for each topic defined at the beginning of each chapter for easy reference.

SECTION 1

Economics and health economics

Key concepts in health economics

Virginia Wiseman

Overview

This chapter provides an introduction to the discipline of economics and to the sub-discipline of health economics. You will learn about the type of questions that economics is concerned with and some of the key concepts that it uses, particularly as applied to health and health care. If you have not studied economics before, this chapter will introduce many expressions and concepts that may be new to you. If you have problems fully understanding these concepts initially, don't worry! You will find that they are brought up throughout the book in different contexts and in relation to different types of problems. Ultimately what we expect is that, as you progress through the book, so does your understanding of these concepts and their applicability to 'real world' health issues.

Learning objectives

After working through this chapter, you will be able to:

- explain what economics is and the problems that it seeks to solve
- define and apply a number of fundamental economic concepts
- explain why economics is applicable to health and health care

Key terms

Efficiency. A general term used to describe the relationship between inputs and outputs. It is concerned with maximizing benefits with the resources available, or minimizing costs for a given level of benefit.

Goods. These are the outputs (such as health care) of a production process that involves the combining of different resources such as labour and equipment. Goods (including services) are valuable in the sense that they provide some utility (see below) to individual consumers. They are termed 'goods' as they are desirable, as distinct from 'bads' which you will read about later!

Health sector. Consists of organized public and private health services, the policies and activities of health departments and ministries, health-related non-government organizations and community groups, and professional associations.

Health services.   The range of services undertaken primarily for health reasons and that have a direct effect on health, including health care programmes such as health promotion and specific disease prevention and treatment.

Marginal analysis.   An examination of the additional benefits or costs arising from an extra unit of consumption or production of a 'good'.

Market.   A situation where people who have a demand for a good come together with suppliers and agree on a price at which the good will be traded. A necessary condition for properly functioning markets is a system of property rights to ensure that people can participate in good faith.

Opportunity cost (economic cost).   As resources are scarce, an individual, in choosing to consume a good, in principle, chooses the good which gives him or her the greatest benefit, and thus forgoes the consumption of a range of alternative goods of lesser value. The opportunity cost is the value of the benefit of the *next best* alternative.

Resources.   These represent inputs into the process of producing goods. They can be classified into three main elements: labour, capital and land. Different goods would generally require varying combinations of these elements. Resources are generally valued in monetary terms.

Utility.   The happiness or satisfaction an individual gains from consuming a good. The more utility an individual derives from the consumption of a good, all else being equal, the more they would be willing to spend their income on it.

Welfare (or social welfare).   The economic criterion on which a policy change or intervention is deemed to affect the well-being of a society. In general, this is assumed to be determined by aggregation of the utilities experienced by every individual in a society.

Types of economic problems in the health sector

The health sector consists of organized public and private health services (from surgery to health promotion programmes to dentistry), the policies and activities of health departments and ministries, health-related non-government organizations and community groups, and professional associations (WHO 1998). Those responsible for determining and managing different areas of a health sector are typically forced to consider questions such as:

- At what level should hospital fees be set?
- Are taxes on cigarettes a useful way of promoting health through reducing the prevalence of smoking?
- Which is the more effective method of increasing the take-up of health services: price controls or subsidies?
- How should doctors be paid?
- Which treatments are the most cost-effective for people with HIV?

You would probably agree that all of the above can be seen as economic problems. But what is economics and how would you define it?

Economics is the study of *scarcity* and the means by which we deal with this problem. Because resources are essentially limited, choices need to be made about how they are to be used. Economics, as a discipline, is concerned largely with how we make these choices in the context of scarcity. One of the key assumptions generally made in economics is that individuals will make these decisions *rationally*. This means that given good information they will choose to do things, such as utilize health services that will be in their best interests, where 'best interests' is defined as maximizing their *utility* given the resources they have at their disposal.

There are four specific questions that are the primary concern of economics:

- What goods are being produced and in what quantities? (For example: what types of malaria prevention measures are being implemented and how much of each type?)
- How are these goods produced? (What resources are required to produce these malaria prevention measures?)
- How is society's output of goods divided among its members? (Who has access to these measures?)
- How efficient is society's production and distribution? (Can we get the same amount of protection from malaria using fewer resources? Would an AIDS awareness campaign be a more effective use of resources than malaria prevention?)

What is an economy?

'The economy' refers to all the economic activities and institutions within a defined area (usually geographically, related to the political borders of a nation state). So you might refer to the performance of a specific national economy, or the global economy, or perhaps a regional economy.

'Resources' are items within the economy that can be used to produce and distribute goods. Resources can be classified as labour, capital and land:

- labour refers to human resources, manual and non-manual, skilled and unskilled;
- capital refers to goods that are used to produce other goods – for example machinery, buildings and tools;
- land generally refers to all natural resources, such as oil or iron ore.

Most resources are not, in themselves, useful to us as individuals but they can be combined to make something that is useful. This process is called production, and goods are the result of combining resources in the production process. *Goods* are either consumption goods, which are then used to directly satisfy people's wants, or else they are intermediate goods, which are goods used to make other goods. In economics the term *utility* is used to describe the satisfaction provided by the consumption of goods by individuals while *welfare* is the sum total of utility experienced across all individuals within a society.

Goods are either products that you can hold or touch (e.g. a drug) or else they are services that happen to you (e.g. a consultation). There are two essential characteristics that distinguish different goods:

1 *Physical attributes* – an ice cream and a cup of tea are clearly different commodities because they require different manufacturing techniques and because they satisfy different wants.

2 *Context in which the good is consumed* – for example:
   a. *The time* in which the good is available – an ice cream that is available on a hot summer's day is a different good from one available in the cold midwinter.
   b. *The place* where the commodity is available – a cup of tea available in a fashionable café is a different good from tea that is sometimes sold at a petrol station.

There are three ways in which individuals can benefit from the ownership of a good. Most immediately, it can be consumed (or used) and thus utility directly derived from it. Taking paracetamol is an example of such consumption because it increases utility by relieving the pain of a headache. Likewise, the use of a non-disposable good (i.e. not designed to be thrown away after use) such as a walking stick provides direct utility for an individual in terms of improved mobility.

The second benefit individuals can derive from (some) goods is their investment value. Although goods provide utility when consumed, goods themselves can also be used as inputs into a production process. For instance, apples might be the output from farm production and consumed immediately, or they can also be used as input into the production of apple pies or cider. People invest because they expect the good to be worth more in terms of its contribution to the production of the final product than its immediate utility. Often, an investment entails a risk such that the end return may be smaller than was expected at the time of investment.

The third benefit derived from a good is exchange value. If you do not invest or consume a commodity then you can sell it and potentially purchase other goods.

Figure 1.1 illustrates the different ways of using a resource (consumption, investment and exchange). Whichever route is taken, the result will be increased utility for the owner of the resource. The route chosen by the owner should depend on which one yields the largest increase in utility for them.

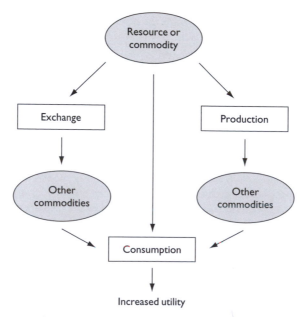

Figure 1.1 Alternative uses of a resource

What is a market?

In economics, the term 'market' is used to describe any situation where people who demand a good come together with suppliers. For it to be a market the buyers and sellers do not have to physically meet – for example, most obviously, trading on the internet can involve networks of individuals in all parts of the world who will never meet. Importantly, a necessary condition for properly functioning markets is a system of property rights to ensure that people can participate in good faith. This means that the transactions made between parties are somehow enforceable and that there are certain understood rules about how people behave in terms of providing information, making payment and delivering goods.

The amount of money that is exchanged for a good is the price. You will find in this book that the price is influenced by the number of suppliers in the market and the amount of money they are prepared to accept. The price is also influenced by the number of buyers in the market and the amount of money they are prepared to pay. Individual consumers or households are usually thought of as being buyers, while firms (or businesses) are associated with supply. However, this is not true in the cases of markets for resources and markets for intermediate goods. For example, in the labour market, households will supply and firms will demand labour.

Figure 1.2 shows a simple model of the flow of commodities, resources and money between households and firms. Households own resources (labour, land, shares in capital) and supply them to firms in return for money (wages, rent, interest and profit). Firms turn resources into goods and supply them to the households, again, in return for money. Households that supply more resources will receive more money and therefore will be able to consume more commodities.

This, essentially, describes markets – that is to say, markets that involve only firms and individuals buying and selling goods. In reality, most markets also have some kind of government intervention. Such intervention in the market might involve levying taxes, fixing prices, licensing suppliers or regulating quality. Alternatively, the government might decide to take control of demand for a commodity and prohibit private demand, or it might decide to take over supply entirely and prohibit private supply. On the other hand, a government might make laws that are intended to 'free up' market forces and

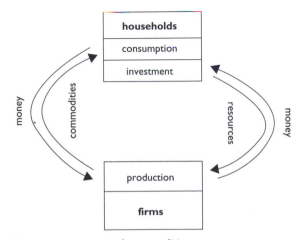

Figure 1.2 The flow of money, resources and commodities

make markets more easily accessible. Ultimately, as mentioned earlier, markets are generally also underpinned by some form of state intervention through the legal system to uphold a system of property rights.

In some economies, the government plays such a large role that markets as such scarcely exist at all. Such systems are referred to as command or centrally planned economies. Because of the difficulties involved with planning a whole economy and the problem of trying to motivate workers and managers, command economies have rapidly diminished in number over the last 50 years or so. Almost every country in the world today has a mixed economy, a system in which market forces and central planning both play a role. We will return to the topic of markets in Chapters 7 and 8. For now, try refreshing your memory with the following activity.

Activity 1.1

1 What is a resource, how are resources classified and what are the three ways of employing a resource?
2 In Table 1.1 match up the terms with their definitions.

Table 1.1 Some economic terms and their definitions

1 Subsistence economy	a A system where exchange takes place without the use of money
2 Global economy	b The economic activities and institutions around the world
3 Barter economy	c An exchange economy with little government intervention
4 Mixed economy	d An economy with an absence of exchange
5 Command economy	e A market economy with substantial government intervention
6 Market economy	f An economic system where resource allocation decisions are directed by the state

Feedback

1 Resources are inputs into the process of producing goods. They can be divided into three categories: land (including all natural resources and minerals), labour (all human resources) and capital (man-made resources used as aids to further products, e.g. equipment). A resource can be employed in one of three ways: consumed, invested or exchanged.
2 The terms can be matched up to the definitions as shown in Table 1.2.

Table 1.2 Some economic terms and their definitions (solution)

1 Subsistence economy	d An economy with an absence of exchange
2 Global economy	b The economic activities and institutions around the world
3 Barter economy	a A system where exchange takes place without the use of money
4 Mixed economy	e A market economy with substantial government intervention
5 Command economy	f An economic system where resource allocation decisions are directed by the state
6 Market economy	c An exchange economy with little government intervention

The building blocks of economics

Now that you have some idea about the problems that economists seek to solve and the ways economies function, you will learn about some of the most important concepts employed by economists. However, before reading further, you may like to bear in mind a statement made by Professor Gavin Mooney, a leading health economist.

I have sometimes suggested when teaching [health economics] that if any of the participants fall asleep during my lecture and awaken conscious that I have asked a question but that it has gone unheard, then the best response is to mutter something about *opportunity cost* and the *margin*. This has something like a 50 per cent or higher chance of being at least partly right.

(Mooney 1994: 27)

Scarcity

Economics as a discipline exists because resources are scarce and the wants of human beings are such that the resources available now or for any foreseeable time are insufficient to meet all our wants.

Because resources are scarce, choices are involved in both production and consumption. If we use resources to produce hospitals then fewer resources are available to produce other desirable goods such as public health clinics. If we use more of our income through purchasing health insurance then we have less income to purchase education. The production and consumption processes then come together to ensure that we produce the 'right level' of both hospitals and clinics so that we do not produce an excess number of hospitals and leave unmet wants for clinics. In other words, we want the quantity supplied to match the quantity demanded. The importance of scarcity is reflected in the following quote.

Economics is not just a 'bag of tools' but it is also a set of ideas (a discipline) which together represent a coherent body of knowledge and of thinking. Economics as a discipline takes its life blood from the fact that resources are scarce in that they are never seemingly adequate to meet all human needs and wants. This is true in many walks of life. It is certainly true of health and health care.

(Mooney and Shiell 1996: 1)

Choice and opportunity cost

These two concepts are the most important in economics. Since we cannot have all we want, then choices must be made. We all have to make choices on a daily basis. This might be about how we spend our income, how we earn our income, how we spend our time, etc. But why do we have to make choices at all? There are two basic reasons. First, our income is finite and second, given all the goods we would like to consume, our income is insufficient to finance them all. We must make choices about how best to spend our limited income. 'Best' here refers to the way that will give the individual most satisfaction or utility or maximize the population's gain in *social welfare* (or simply welfare).

Choices involve trade-offs. More hospitals means fewer clinics. More holidays means fewer cars or clothes. The *opportunity cost* (also known as the economic cost) of any good (including service) is the satisfaction or benefit forgone in not being able to use the resources involved to obtain some other good which is also desirable and provides satisfaction. Table 1.3 illustrates the relevance of this concept to the health sector by looking at the impact of increasing the number of inpatients on the number of outpatients that can be treated – i.e. the opportunity cost of treating inpatients in terms of outpatients. For example, the opportunity cost of treating 5,000 inpatients is 50,000 outpatients.

Table 1.3 Illustration of opportunity cost: options for expenditure in a year

Inpatients treated ('000s)	Outpatients treated ('000s)	Opportunity cost of treating inpatients in terms of outpatients forgone
0	50	0
1	45	5
2	42	8
3	20	30
4	15	35
5	0	50

It is important to note that opportunity cost may involve something other than goods with money prices. Spending a day in the hospital waiting room may involve forgoing a day at work (measured in wages lost). But it might also involve forgoing a day in the park with your family. Time is scarce and its cost can be measured both in terms of lost income but also lost leisure time, or indeed utility. Just because there is not always a money price involved (as in the case of leisure time) this does not mean time is of zero value or that there is no associated cost.

The margin

Marginal refers to 'the next unit'. It might be a health service deciding whether to expand an immunization programme or a doctor choosing whether to work an extra day. The reason why this is relevant is that, in making decisions, our interest is essentially on *change* in costs and benefits rather than their totals. Decisions are rarely made on an 'all or nothing' basis; instead they often tend to be made at *the margin*: if marginal benefit (the change in benefit) is greater than marginal cost (the change in cost), we go ahead; if marginal benefit is less than marginal cost, we do not.

One phenomenon which is generally observed is that the marginal benefits of most goods tend to diminish as the consumption of those goods increases. This is otherwise known as *diminishing marginal utility* and is intuitive – the first ice cream will generally be more enjoyable than the second, which in turn will be more enjoyable than the third and so forth. Health programmes also tend to experience diminishing marginal benefits as we will see in the next activity. After completing this activity, the importance of the concept of marginal analysis (including diminishing marginal benefits) and its relationship to efficiency should become clearer.

Activity 1.2

1 Consider Table 1.4 that includes data on screening for colon cancer. Complete Column 3 (additional cases detected) and Column 6 (marginal cost per case). We have started the process for you.
2 Broadly speaking, why might screening exhibit diminishing marginal benefits as is the case here?
3 What is the most 'efficient' number of screening tests to conduct?

Table 1.4 Screening for colon cancer

Number of tests	Total number of cases detected	Additional cases detected	Total cost ($)	Average cost per case ($)	Marginal cost per case ($)
1	65.946	65.95	77,511	1,175	1,175
2	71.442	5.4956	107,690	1,507	5,492
3	71.90		130,199	1,810	
4	71.938		148,116	2,059	
5	71.94172		163,141	2,268	
6	71.942		176,331	2,451	

Source: Neuhauser and Lewicki (1976)

Feedback

1 Table 1.5 presents the completed table. Additional cases detected were 71.9004 – 71.4424 = 0.4580 for the third test and 0.000028 for the sixth test. The marginal cost per case was found to be over $47 million ($176,331 – $163,141)/0.00028) for the sixth test.

Table 1.5 Screening for colon cancer

Number of tests	Total number of cases detected	Additional cases detected	Total cost ($)	Average cost per case ($)	Marginal cost per case ($)
1	65.946	65.95	77,511	1,175	1,175
2	71.442	5.4956	107,690	1,507	5,492
3	71.90	0.458	130,199	1,810	49,146
4	71.938	0.038	148,116	2,059	471,500
5	71.94172	0.00372	163,141	2,268	4,038,978
6	71.942	0.00028	176,331	2,451	47,107,143

Source: Neuhauser and Lewicki (1976)

Note: The results differ slightly from the original article due to rounding errors

2 Screening, for example, twice as frequently could theoretically double the number of cases detected but this is rarely observed in practice. Put simply, as you expand screening, it is harder to detect additional cases. It is also possible – if the screening tool was, say, painful, uncomfortable or associated with an increased risk of mortality – that expanding coverage to include otherwise healthy people could have an overall detrimental impact on health.

3 This example shows that the cost per additional case identified mounts rapidly with the number of additional tests. Ultimately it is *rational* for a policy-maker to continue to fund a programme when marginal benefit exceeds marginal cost but to stop once they eventually become equal. In this instance as marginal benefit diminishes. In this instance, this would mean stopping at two tests as 'pursuing such a screening program to the last degree of perfection is inefficient' (Shepard and Thompson 1979: 540).

In summary, marginal analysis is about getting the most value out of the resources used and in practical terms entails measuring the costs and benefits of expanding or contracting an activity, programme or service.

Efficiency and equity

In setting economic objectives, most health care systems will want to pursue both efficiency and equity. *Efficiency* is a general term used to describe the relationship between inputs and outputs; which in turn can be valued respectively in terms of costs and benefits. Efficiency is concerned with maximizing benefits with the resources available, or minimizing costs for a given level of benefit. In health care, benefits may be interpreted as health gains, although health services produce a range of benefits including less tangible things like information and reassurance. There are a number of different types of efficiency and we will explore each of these in detail in Chapters 5, 6 and 7. Here is a short list summarizing them.

- *Technical efficiency:* where a given output is produced with the least inputs (i.e. minimizing wastage). Also known as operational efficiency;
- *Economic efficiency:* where a given output is produced at least cost. Also known as productive efficiency;
- *Allocative efficiency:* where the pattern of output matches the pattern of demand;
- *Pareto efficiency:* the point at which no one can gain without someone else being made worse off.

Every level of a health system faces questions about efficiency. For example, there are several ways in which hospitals might seek to improve the efficiency of their operations including:

- length of stay could be reduced;
- staff productivity could be increased;
- equipment could be fully utilized and maintained regularly;
- over-prescribing of drugs could be avoided;
- drug ordering and storage could be managed properly to avoid wastage and pilfering;
- nurses could replace doctors when appropriate;
- low-cost equipment could replace staff when appropriate;
- day surgery could replace inpatient stays.

If you have worked in a hospital, perhaps you have already experienced or attempted some of these measures. Were they successful? Implementation might be difficult, although some measures will be harder to enforce than others. To encourage the efficient use of resources, hospitals should collect financial data and managers should be trained to carry out cost analyses. There is also a need for staff to be aware of the financial constraints of the hospital if implementation is to be effective.

Equity is another important concern of economists as well as of health services. Equity is about the distribution of benefits as opposed to their maximization (as in efficiency). In Chapter 17 we go into the finer details of how equity has been defined and applied in the health sector. At this point, it is worth noting three things. First, equity usually has something to do with fairness and justice. It is subjective, as it will mean different things to different people and different communities. Second, *equity* is different to *equality*. Equity is about fairness but this may or may not mean the equal sharing of a good or service. It may for example be deemed fair that a disadvantaged group in society receive a greater share of resources. Third, equity and efficiency are often conflicting objectives. For instance, it may be efficient to fund health services concentrated in a small number of large centres but more equitable in terms of access to services to fund a larger number of dispersed, smaller services.

Activity 1.3

Try to answer the following questions without referring back to the text.

1 What terms are used to describe the satisfaction gained from consuming a good?
2 Explain the concept of *opportunity cost* and its relevance to public health.

Feedback

1 'Utility' is the word most often used by economists to refer to the happiness or satisfaction gained from consuming a good or service. The terms 'welfare' and 'social welfare' are in turn the aggregate utility of a population. 'Quality of life' and 'well-being' are other commonly used terms with roughly the same meaning. It is important to note that the core of economic theory is dependent only on the assumption that people can differentiate between states that have higher or lower utility (it is not necessary to be able to measure utility).
2 Because resources are limited, choices have to be made on how to best allocate these finite resources among investments. For governments, investment choices have to be made between alternative public services. Examples of investment choices include: between malaria prevention and malaria treatment programmes; or, more broadly, between TB, malaria and HIV programmes; or even more broadly between education and housing programmes. Choices involve opportunity costs. These costs refer to the benefits of the second best investment that are forgone as a result of using resources in the first best investment. For example, if the alternative investments in malaria were ordered according to the benefit that they generate, from highest to lowest, the first alternative might be malaria treatment and the second might be malaria prevention. If all the available resources were committed to the malaria treatment programme, the opportunity costs would be the benefits of the malaria prevention programme.

Categorizing the discipline of economics

Like any academic field, economics has a number of sub-disciplines, defined either by the types of questions that are examined or by the methods that are used – health economics being one of them. Two other important categorizations of economic thought are as follows.

Microeconomics and macroeconomics

Microeconomics is concerned with the decisions taken by individual consumers, households and firms and with the way these decisions contribute to the setting of prices and output in various kinds of market ('micro' implies small scale); in other words, individual decision-making units. This is the focus of most of this book.

Macroeconomics is concerned with the interaction of broad economic aggregates (such as general price inflation, unemployment of resources in the economy and the growth of national output). It is also concerned with the interaction between different sectors of the economy ('macro' implies large scale). You will learn more about macroeconomics in Chapter 2.

Positive and normative economics

Positive economics refers to economic statements that describe how things *are*. Such statements can be universally true, true in some circumstances or universally false. This can be established through empirical research.

Normative economics refers to economic statements that prescribe how things *should be*. Such statements can be informed by positive economics but can never be shown to be true or false since they depend on value judgements. For example, the following statement is positive:

> The presence of patents for drugs has led to greater expenditure on research and development in the pharmaceutical industry.

In principle the presence of drug patents can be observed and so can the level of expenditure on research. With the appropriate statistical techniques we may or may not find that this is the case or it might be the case only in some countries or under certain circumstances. The following statement is normative:

> Patenting should be implemented in the pharmaceutical industry.

To be useful to policy-makers, economists make use of both positive and normative economics. Positive statements can describe what will happen (or not happen) if a particular policy is carried out, but in order to make a recommendation we need to evaluate the policy according to one or more criteria. Two such criteria that you've already encountered are efficiency and equity. Other criteria often encountered in economics are economic growth and macroeconomic stability (which you will read about in Chapter 2). Be aware that studies often contain both positive and normative statements; in everything you read you should try to spot statements that go beyond description (like this one!).

Economists have a reputation for disagreeing with each other. This is understandable when one considers that:

- economists are keen to influence policy;
- policy recommendations are normative and are underpinned by value judgements;
- value judgements vary between individuals.

On this basis one should expect a great deal of disagreement among economists, reflecting disagreement in the wider world. Reassuringly, surveys, such as those reported by Alston *et al.* (1993) or Fuller and Geide-Stevenson (2003) seem to confirm that there is more agreement among economists on positive issues than there is on normative ones. Economists are slow at reaching a consensus on particular ideas because, due to the nature of the topics under study, it is either impossible or difficult to conduct experiments that can monitor changes in the variables of interest and at the same time hold all other potential influencing factors constant.

Can economics be applied to the health sector?

Anyone who has worked in the health sector will be well aware of the scarcity of resources. There are various reasons why the demand for health services continues to exceed supply:

- an *ageing population* in which the elderly potentially require more health services than younger adults;
- *new health technologies* which mean more conditions have become treatable;
- increased *expectations* from people.

Choices are inevitably made about what treatments are provided and about who receives treatment; that is, there is some form of rationing. Economists advocate making such rationing decisions explicit. Most importantly in the context of limited resources, the provision of one service, X, necessarily means that a second service, Y, is displaced. The health gain that we would have got from service Y is the opportunity cost of our decision to provide service X. Economists try to ensure that the opportunity cost of providing X (i.e. health gain from Y) does not exceed the health gain from X.

As economics is the study of scarcity and choice it follows that if economics is relevant anywhere then it should be relevant in the health sector. However, health services have some interesting characteristics that mean crude economic models should be used cautiously (Arrow 1963). None of these characteristics is unique to the health sector but the combination of characteristics together with their sheer number has contributed to health economics becoming a distinct sub-discipline of economics. One characteristic of many health economists that has moved them away somewhat from mainstream economics is their focus on health or health-related utility as the *maximand* or objective of health services. This approach is often referred to as 'extra-welfarism' and is distinct from 'welfarism' which focuses on the objective of maximizing utility or welfare. In the context of evaluating health services, 'welfarism' is potentially a much broader objective in so far as it can include a wide range of non-health benefits such as reassurance and choice.

The aim of health economists is often to inform decision-makers so that the choices they make maximize health benefits to the population. Health economics is not

concerned with 'saving money' but with improving the level and distribution of population health with the resources available. Over the course of this book you will be able
to decide for yourself the extent to which the specific methods of health economics
provide useful insights for health policy.

Summary

In this chapter you have read about some of the fundamental concepts of economics,
not least of which are scarcity and opportunity cost. The premise of economic analyses
is that there are never enough resources to do everything that we might like (scarcity)
and thus once we make a choice as to how a resource is to be used, something else
must be given up (opportunity cost). Economics provides us with a framework for
rationally addressing this problem. You have also gained an understanding of the types
of questions economists can help to address in the health sector and the different
perspectives they take. For example, economics may adopt a micro or macro perspective, and be positive or normative. Health economics is a sub-discipline of economics,
which applies the theories and methods of economics to all aspects of health and
health care.

References

Alston RM, Kearl JR and Vaughan MB (1993) Is there a consensus among economists in the 1990s? *American Economic Review* 82:203–9.

Arrow KJ (1963) Uncertainty and the welfare economics of medical care. *American Economic Review* 53:941–73.

Fuller D and Geide-Stevenson D (2003) Consensus among economists: revisited. *Journal of Economic Education* 34: 369–87.

Mooney G (1994) *Key Issues in health economics*. Exeter: Harvester Wheatsheaf.

Mooney G and Shiell A (1996) *A workbook in core health economics*. Sydney: Department of Public Health and Community Medicine, University of Sydney.

Neuhauser D and Lewicki AM (1976) National health insurance and the sixth stool guaiac. *Policy Analysis* 24:175–96.

Shepard DS and Thompson MS (1979) First principles of cost-effectiveness analysis in health. *Public Health Report* 94(6): 535–43.

WHO (World Health Organization) (1998) *Health promotion glossary*, WHO/HPR/HEP/98.1, http://www.who.int/hpr/NPH/docs/hp_glossary_en.pdf.

Further reading

Fuchs, VR (2000) The future of health economics, *Journal of Health Economics* 19(2):141–57.

McPake B, Kumaranayake L and Normand C (2002) *Health economics – an international perspective*. London: Routledge, Chapter 1.

Morris S, Devlin N and Parkin D (2007) *Economic analysis in health care*. Chichester: Wiley, Chapter 1, Sections 1.1, 1.3, 1.8, 1.9.

Olsen JA (2010) *Principles of health economics and policy*. Oxford: Oxford University Press, Chapters 1 and 2.

Witter S, Ensor T, Jowett M and Thompson R (2000) *Health economics for developing countries*. London: Macmillan Education, Part 1.

Macroeconomics, globalization and health

Richard Smith

Overview

The aim of this chapter is to introduce you to the macroeconomics of health and health care, focusing on the features of health systems. This is in contrast to the rest of the book, and health economics more generally, which tends to be 'micro' focused – with the unit of analysis being individuals, households or 'firms' such as hospitals. This chapter will outline the core features of what macroeconomics means, and then give an insight into the relationship between the macro economy and health. Key issues facing health and health systems from trade will also be discussed.

Learning objectives

After working through this chapter, you will be able to:

- define macroeconomics and distinguish it from microeconomics
- explain key macroeconomic terms, including gross domestic product (GDP), gross national product (GNP), national income, inflation, economic growth, trade, currency depreciation, balance of payments (BOP)
- identify links between macroeconomic activity and health and health care
- describe the relationship between health care expenditure and GDP, population and health
- describe the routes through which greater macroeconomic integration at the global level may impact on health and health care via international trade

Key terms

Appreciate. When a currency is rising relative to other currencies, it is appreciating in value.

Balance of payments (BOP). Measures currency flows between countries.

Constant dollars. Correspond to values that have been adjusted for inflation, and so reflect the 'real' or actual purchasing power.

Current dollars. Actual dollars spent, without adjustment for inflation.

Depreciate. When a currency is falling relative to other currencies, it is depreciating in value.

Depression. Sustained, long-term downturn in economic activity – more severe than a recession.

Gross domestic product (GDP). An indicator used to measure the output of an economy. It is the total value of goods and services produced within one year in a country. GDP is concerned with the output produced in a specific geographic location, regardless of the nationality of who produces it (e.g. a foreign-owned company).

Gross national income (GNI). Measures the economic activities undertaken by citizens and firms of that country, regardless of where it takes place. GNI is GDP plus income earned by citizens abroad, minus income earned in that country by foreign citizens.

Inflation. General rise in prices over time. This means that money loses its value through time.

Purchasing power parity (PPP). Exchange rate that equates the price of a basket of identical traded goods and services in different countries.

What is macroeconomics?

Simply speaking, macroeconomics looks at the performance and functioning of the economy as a whole – the relationships between economic growth, output, employment and inflation. These are terms we are used to seeing every day, but what do they mean?

Economic growth

Put simply, *economic growth* is a positive change in the level of production of goods and services by a country over a certain period of time. GDP is the main indicator that is used to measure the size or output of an economy. GDP is the total value of goods and services produced within one year in a country.

In contrast, GNI, formerly called 'gross national product' (GNP) also measures output. GNI is concerned with measuring the output of economic activities undertaken by citizens and firms of that country, regardless of where that activity takes place (i.e. home or abroad).

Per capita GNI is used internationally to classify countries into stages of development. Each year, the World Bank revises the per capita GNI benchmarks that are used to classify countries. Table 2.1 displays the World Bank's 2011 classification of countries, based on annual 2009 GNI data.

One problem with comparing GDP across countries is that prices vary in different countries. This affects the total amount of the GDP. For example, the GDP for India and the USA is calculated by using prices in their own countries, even though the average cost of the same good might be much lower in India. Thus, in 2006, US GDP per capita was $37,767. India's per capita GDP was INR27,251. The exchange rate in 2006 was $1 = INR45.31. Using this exchange rate to convert rupees into US dollars, you find that India's per capita GDP was $601. This can give a misleading picture of the

Table 2.1 World Bank country classification

	2009 GNI per capita	Number of countries
Low-income countries	$995 or less	40
Lower middle-income countries	$996–3,945	56
Upper middle-income countries	$3,946–12,195	48
High-income countries	$12,196 or more	69

Source: World Bank (2011)

relative wealth of the two countries. Goods in India tend to cost less than they do in the USA and therefore a dollar in India is worth more than a dollar in the USA. So if you replace Indian prices with American prices in order to value goods and services produced in India, you get a more valid comparison of GDP. This adjustment of prices is called *purchasing power parity* (PPP). Using PPP data, the International Monetary Fund estimated that per capita GDP for India was $4,183 in 2006. International comparisons of GDP often use PPP-adjusted values to obtain more valid results.

Inflation

Inflation is another common macroeconomic concept. It refers to the general rise in prices through time, which results in a decrease in the value of money. For example, if prices increased by 5 per cent over a year, what you could buy with $1.00 last year would cost $1.05 this year. So a dollar today is worth less than a dollar last year, in terms of its purchasing power. Economists measure inflation using a *price index*.

A price index is created by defining which goods are frequently purchased by households, such as food items. These goods are placed in a (virtual!) basket and their price is monitored. The overall price change of the goods in the basket measures inflation. The price index is set at 100 for a particular year (the *base* year), and subsequent changes in prices are talked about *relative* to this base year. Thus, if the price index was set at 100 for the year 2000, and the price index was 112.4 in 2001, the inflation for 2001 would be 12.4 per cent.

Often we refer to 'current dollars' and 'constant dollars' when discussing inflation. Current dollars or currency refers to the actual dollars spent. Constant dollars or currency refers to values that have been adjusted for inflation, and therefore reflects the 'real' or actual purchasing power. In economic analysis, it is common to use constant values, so that real trends can be analysed over time after taking out the effect of inflation.

Exchange rates and balance of payments

Exchange rates tell you how much one country's money is worth in another country's currency. If the value of a currency is going down relative to another, it is *depreciating*. If it is rising relative to other currencies, it is said to *appreciate* in value. Fluctuations in exchange rates are very important as every country imports and exports goods and services. There are also flows of money between countries. The *balance of payments* (BOP) is used to measure these flows between countries. Usually, payments are measured in the currency of the country that is paying. Payments made to other countries are seen as debits (e.g. imports), and payments received from other countries are seen as credits (e.g. exports). So an important indicator of a country's performance in international trade and investment is the level of *surplus* or *deficit* in their balance of payments.

International trade

Another important element of macroeconomics is *international trade*. According to the 'law of comparative advantage', free trade between countries is justified because it encourages countries to export goods that they are best at producing – i.e. specialization. The reason why one country might be better at producing a certain type of good than another is simply that it is endowed with the combination of resources that are most suitable for producing that good. For instance, a country with lots of sunshine and wide-open spaces of land could be seen to have a comparative advantage in agriculture. Each trader engages in the production of a good that best suits their endowment of skills and resources such that they can specialize in its production and then trade their good for other goods from others who are similarly relatively more efficient at producing those other goods. Thus, through specialization, free trade increases global production, which increases product variety and reduces the cost of goods generally such that overall wealth is increased. Those countries that engage in trade will therefore see increasing GDP, a wider selection of available goods and services, higher employment and higher government revenues (due to higher income). The problem of course is that, in practice, many countries create barriers to trade to 'protect' domestic industries – barriers such as tariffs, import restrictions and bans. The effect of such protection is that it enables countries to continue to produce goods in which they have no comparative advantage, but at the same time discourages those countries who do actually hold the comparative advantage in such products. Why would a country do this? Usually it is to protect a specific interest group (e.g. a farm lobby, unions, industry groups, etc.).

What are the key areas where macroeconomics affects health?

There is a range of proximal and distal determinants and linkages between events at the macro level (that is, beyond health care) and health. The main ones are illustrated in Figure 2.1. The lower half of the figure represents the individual country under consideration, and the upper half shows the aspects of the international system, which has expanded considerably in influence in recent decades through globalization. The arrows between the various components indicate the major linkages. This is a deliberately simplified picture to provide a concise and understandable frame of reference.

So, let's think a little more about these major elements and linkages. 'Health' is highlighted as the major element at the bottom of the figure, with the assumption that this is the primary focus of those reading this chapter. A range of influences are seen to impact upon health (including the health sector of course). Taking the lower half of the figure first, what we may term as the 'standard' influences on health are illustrated. These include *risk factors*, representing genetic predisposition to disease, environmental influences and infectious disease. Next is what is termed the *'household economy'*, which represents factors associated with how people behave and, crucially, invest (or disinvest) in their health by what they consume and in the activities they undertake. We then have the *health sector*, which, as we learned in Chapter 1, comprises those goods

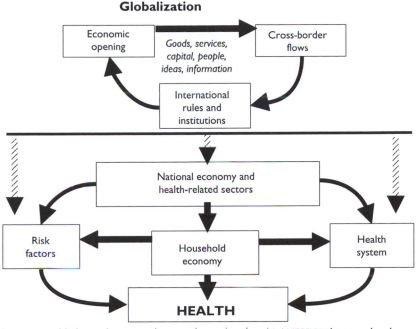

Figure 2.1 Major elements and linkages between them at the national and international macro level
Source: Smith (2006)

and services consumed principally to improve health status. Finally, encompassing all these, we find the *national economy*, representing the meta-influences of government structures, markets and their influence on economic well-being.

In the upper half of the figure, the influences of factors that are usually outside national government jurisdictions are illustrated. For example, there are a wide variety of international influences directly upon risk factors for health, including: an increased exposure to infectious disease through cross-border transmission of communicable diseases; marketing of unhealthy products and behaviours; and environmental degradation, the effects of which are often not contained within country borders. Increased interaction in the global economic system will also affect health through influences upon the national economy and wealth (Sachs 2001; Blouin *et al.* 2009). It is well established for instance that economic prosperity is generally positively associated with increased life expectancy, although increased wealth often brings with it an increase in many chronic illnesses. Finally, health care will be affected through the direct provision and distribution of health-related goods, services and people, such as access to pharmaceutical products, health-related knowledge and technology (e.g. new genomic developments) and the movement of patients and professionals (Smith *et al.* 2009). Also note that in the upper half of the figure we see the importance of international legal and political frameworks that underpin much of these activities, such as bilateral, regional and multilateral trade agreements.

In terms of linkages between these influences, the black arrows indicate those between elements at the global or national level, and the striped arrows indicate specific forms of linkages between the global and the domestic circumstance. The first striped arrow shows how increased macroeconomic trade will bring associated changes in risk factors for disease. These will include both communicable diseases, as trade encourages people and goods to cross borders; and non-communicable diseases, as changes in the patterns of food consumption, for example, are influenced by changes in income and industry advertising. Second, increased macro-level interaction will impact upon the domestic economy through changes in income and the distribution of that income, as well as influencing tax receipts. This will influence the household economy and also the abilities of government to be engaged in public finance and/or provision of health care. Finally, the third striped arrow indicates that there will be direct interactions in terms of health-related goods and services, such as pharmaceuticals and associated technologies, health care workers and patients.

It is important to note that this chapter focuses on the influence of macroeconomics on health. For discussion of the influence of health on the macro economy we recommend the papers that contributed to the WHO Commission on Macroeconomics and Health including Sachs (2001) and a paper by the International Monetary Fund (Hsiao and Heller 2007).

Macroeconomics and the household

Much macroeconomic policy is concerned with economic growth – increasing levels of GDP. This is because higher GDP leads to greater opportunities to consume which, in the specific context here, will result, all else being equal, in better health. In this respect, engaging in global macroeconomic integration – or international trade – is a key factor leading to economic growth through specialization, or the 'law of comparative advantage'.

Wealth and health

In general, analyses suggest that 'wealthier countries are healthier countries' (Pritchett and Summers 1996). The relevant factors in this relationship are improved nutrition, sanitation, water and education (Smith 1999). In terms of economic growth, while some evidence suggests that trade liberalization will be poverty-alleviating in the long run, it is not always seen in such a positive light. At least in the short term, it is often the adverse consequences, particularly to the most poor, that are observed (e.g. increased cost of living, development of urban slums, chronic disease, pollution and exploitative and unsafe working conditions).

Distributional impacts

One of the criticisms of conventional macroeconomic approaches is the inadequate attention paid to *distributional impacts* – most are generally based on the aggregate indicators such as 'total' income, trade volume, employment, etc. This reflects a focus on growth and efficiency over equity. Thus, although trade liberalization may be advantageous, the crucial factor in how advantageous and to whom depends on 'how countries manage the process of integrating into the global economies' (Lall 2004: 79). For example, mass employment creation through industrialization and economic growth is often accompanied by job destruction as labour moves from one sector or industry to another (Ghose 2003). In the absence of social safety nets, not only does such economic insecurity potentially push people into poverty, it can also impact indirectly on health through the stress caused by economic and social dislocation (Wilkinson and Marmot 2003).

Economic stability

Another important aspect of macroeconomic growth and health is that of the *stability* of the growth. Economic instability results in volatile markets, increased frequency of external shocks and increased impact of such shocks. These translate into economic insecurity for an individual, which is closely linked to increased stress-related illness (Wilkinson and Marmot 2003). It will also affect the adequacy of financial planning for ill health by the household and the (public and private) health sector, and generate investor reluctance (including within the health sector itself).

Economic stability is affected, amongst other things, by the proportion of income/ growth dependent on trade, with the general view that trade liberalization, especially in financial services and in the movement of capital, results in volatile markets. Of course, being an open economy does not automatically lead to economic instability/ shocks − a critical caveat relates to the size of the economy. Thus, although absolute levels of trade may be high, the trade share of GDP in large, developed, countries tends to be small (~10%) and thus they tend to have the capacity to absorb the shocks imposed by external markets. For smaller, often developing countries, trade contributes a much higher share of GDP as they rely more on imports and exports to secure factor inputs and economies of scale. Thus, an economy more reliant on trade will be inherently more 'unstable' − unable to absorb external economic 'shocks', such as an oil shortage, exchange rate fluctuations and international competition.

Macroeconomics and risk factors for disease

It is well documented that there are a variety of 'social determinants of health', which refer to the general conditions in which people live and work and which influence their ability to lead healthy lives or not. These include factors such as employment, nutrition, environmental conditions and education (Sachs 2001). These 'social determinants' contribute to the risk of different diseases and are often seen to differ in their role in influencing communicable and non-communicable diseases.

Communicable diseases

The contribution of macroeconomics to the spread of communicable diseases takes place in two ways. First, the overall environment in which people live (concerned with pollution, sanitation, etc.) is determined − in large part − by their income and wealth. Second, the increased international movement of people, animals and goods associated with increased trade will affect the movement of disease. This is illustrated well by the example of SARS.

The case of SARS
Severe acute respiratory syndrome (SARS) is an infectious disease that can be spread between humans. It emerged in late 2002 and was transmitted in a similar way to the cold virus. Having started in the Guandong province of China, the disease was transmitted with great rapidity to Australia, Brazil, Canada, China, Hong Kong, South Africa, Spain and the USA. This led to serious public health concerns. The

SARS outbreak peaked during the second quarter of 2003 and was declared over by July 2003. Although approximately 10,000 individuals were infected, of whom 10 per cent died, the overall impact on health was far less devastating than initially feared. However, the possible economic impact of SARS was also a focus of concern. During the outbreak, there was a noticeable downturn in travel and tourism income for many infected countries. It was also anticipated that fear of disease would impact upon those industries which gather people in public places such as restaurants, cinemas and retail establishments. The overall estimate of the global macroeconomic burden was between US$ 30–100 billion (around $3–10 million per case). *Source:* Keogh-Brown and Smith (2008)

Non-communicable diseases

Perhaps less obvious is the relationship between macroeconomic activity and non-communicable diseases. Although macroeconomic growth can be beneficial when it leads to an expansion in the consumption of the goods that *improve* health, such as clean water, safe food and education, it also facilitates the increased consumption of goods which may be harmful or hazardous to health, which may be termed 'bads'. Trade liberalization will reduce the price of imported 'bads', through reduced tariff and non-tariff barriers, and increase the marketing of 'bads', such as tobacco, alcohol and 'fast food'. In the case of alcohol and tobacco, the development of regional trade agreements (RTAs) has helped to significantly reduce barriers to trade in these products, by breaking up the hitherto protected markets that contribute to enhanced consumption (Onzivu 2002; OECD 2003).

In terms of food-related products, increased macroeconomic integration will affect the entire food supply chain (levels of food imports and exports, foreign direct investment in the agro-food industry and the harmonization of regulations that affect food), which subsequently affects what is available at what price, with what level of safety, and how it is marketed. For example, in what is termed the 'nutrition transition', populations in developing countries are shifting away from diets high in cereals and complex carbohydrates, to high-calorie, nutrient-poor diets high in fats, sweeteners and processed foods (Popkin 1998). Increased trade liberalization is one driver of the nutrition transition because it has had the effect of increasing the availability and lowering the prices of foods associated with the growth of diet-related chronic diseases, as well as increasing the amount of advertising of high-calorie foods worldwide (Hawkes 2006). Furthermore, trade and economic development encourages the use of labour-replacing technologies such as cars and creates greater leisure time, both of which in turn can be seen to encourage more sedentary lifestyles.

Macroeconomics and the health sector

Health care spending

Perhaps the most visible link between macroeconomics and health is at the overall level of health care spending. We learnt in Chapter 1 that most nations, rich or poor, face the problem of rising health care costs and confront two basic questions: how to finance this rising burden and how to contain the pressures for health expenditure growth.

Most countries spend less than 10 per cent of GDP, and this is seen as perhaps the stable upper limit. Of course, for low-income countries (LICs), and some middle-income countries (MICs), GDP levels are so low that this level produces very little actual health care, and so aid assistance is required. Government income, and hence the ability to finance and/or provide public services, is generated primarily through taxes. Tax income is broadly divided into taxes that are 'easy to collect' (such as import tariffs) and those that are 'hard to collect' (such as consumption taxes, income tax and VAT) (Aizenman and Jinjarak 2009). Tariff revenues are a very important source of public revenue in many developing countries, ranging from less than 1 per cent within OECD member countries to around 80 per cent in Guinea, with typical examples of Cameroon at 28 per cent and India at 18 per cent (De Cordoba *et al.* 2006).

Trade liberalization, by definition, reduces the proportion of government income from 'easy to collect' sources. Although theoretically governments should be able to shift tax bases from tariffs to domestic taxes, such as sales or income taxes, in practice developing countries, especially LICs, find this difficult, largely because of the informal nature of their economies with large subsistence sectors. LICs are usually able to recover only around 30 per cent of lost tariff revenue compared to high income countries (HICs) that recover closer to 100 per cent (Baunsgaard and Keen 2005), resulting in a decline of government income available to pursue public policies, be they through health care, education, water, sanitation or a social safety net.

Exchange rates

You learnt earlier that the exchange rate is a key determinant of the relative prices of imported and domestically produced goods and services. For many countries, products such as pharmaceuticals, but also various elements of other technologies, such as computer equipment, surgical tools and even light bulbs, used to provide health care, are imported. Changes in the exchange rate brought about by macroeconomic developments may therefore see the price, and hence cost, of health care increase or decrease. Conversely, changes in demand for domestically produced goods from overseas importers may see the price of those goods change domestically in response (e.g. increased foreign demand may push up local prices). Increased linkage between economies at the macro level thus generates greater levels of exogenous influences (i.e. those beyond the control of the domestic health sector) over prices, and hence increases the cost of health care. Activity 2.1 shows how exchange rates and inflation can impact upon a drugs budget.

Activity 2.1 Where did your drug budget go?

You are responsible for procuring drugs in your country. The Ministry of Health has made a major effort to improve drug supplies and almost doubled the drug budget over the past five years. However, the extra effort did not have any effect. What went wrong? There are two parts to this question.

Part A: conversion to foreign exchange

Row 1 in Table 2.2 shows the drugs budget in kwacha (Kw), your local currency. Since drugs have to be imported, foreign exchange is required. You need to convert the kwacha budget to US dollars using the exchange rates provided in row 2.

1 Calculate the total amount available in your drugs budget in US dollars for the years 2002–2005. Write your answer for each year in the empty spaces in row 3 of Table 2.2.

2 What has happened to the purchasing power of the kwacha in US$ terms?

For example, in 2000, Kw1 was worth $1.23. So Kw3,265,793 is equivalent to 3,265,793 × 1.23 = $4,016,925.

Table 2.2 National drugs budget

Year	2000	2001	2002	2003	2004	2005
1 Drugs budget (kwacha)	3,265,793	4,021,997	3,355,807	3,453,768	5,731,221	7,500,000
2 Exchange rate 1 kwacha = US$	1.23	1.12	0.91	0.83	0.67	0.59
3 Total in current US$	4,016,925	4,504,637				

Feedback

1 See the results in Table 2.3.

2 Note the trend of the kwacha's value against the dollar. While the drugs budget has more than doubled in kwacha terms, you can see that in dollars the budget has only slightly increased (row 3 of Table 2.3). This is because the kwacha is worth less in US dollars each year. The kwacha has *depreciated* in terms of the US dollar, which means that the value of the *kwacha* has gone down relative to the dollar.

Table 2.3 Effect of depreciation of exchange rate on national drugs budget

Year	2000	2001	2002	2003	2004	2005
1 Drugs budget (kwacha)	3,265,793	4,021,997	3,355,807	3,453,768	5,731,221	7,500,000
2 Exchange rate 1 kwacha = US$	1.23	1.12	0.91	0.83	0.67	0.59
3 Total in current US$	4,016,925	4,504,637	**3,053,784**	**2,866,627**	**3,839,918**	**4,425,000**

Part B: adjusting for price increases

Most of your drugs are imported from a neighbouring country and paid for in US dollars. However, each year prices are rising in your neighbouring country, so that $1 in 2000 buys less than $1 in 2005. You want to calculate the actual purchasing power of your drugs budget, taking into account price increases in your neighbouring country. An economist has given you data on price levels in your neighbouring country in the form of a price index (row 4 in Table 2.4). For example, between 2000 and 2001

Table 2.4 National drugs budget and inflation

Year	2000	2001	2002	2003	2004	2005
1 Drugs budget (kwacha)	3,265,793	4,021,997	3,355,807	3,453,768	5,731,221	7,500,000
2 Exchange rate 1 kwacha = US$	1.23	1.12	0.91	0.83	0.67	0.59
3 Total in current US$	4,016,925	4,504,637	**3,053,784**	**2,866,627**	**3,839,918**	**4,425,000**
4 Price index of country where drugs are imported from (2000 = 100)	100	112.4	126.3	142.0	159.6	179.4
5 Deflator (100/price index)	1.0	0.89				
6 Total in real US$ (constant dollars)	4,016,925	4,009,127				

prices rose by 12.4 per cent in your neighbouring country, so the price index went from 100 to 112.4.

You want to calculate the actual purchasing power of your drugs budget, taking into account price increases in your neighbouring country. The economist has told you that you can calculate the 'real' purchasing power by following the steps below.

1 Calculate the deflator – the amount by which your purchasing price has been reduced due to rising prices.
2 Calculate the real purchasing power of your budget.
3 What happens to the drug budget once you take into account overall price changes?

Feedback

1 To compare the difference in your purchasing power between 2000 and 2001, you need to divide the price index for 2000 by the price index for 2001. As the price index for 2000 is 100, the deflator is equal to 100 divided by the price index for 2001: 100/112.4 = 0.89 (row 5). So $1 in 2001 is only worth $0.89, and cannot buy as much as in 2000.
2 Calculate the 'real' purchasing value of your US dollar drugs budget by multiplying the current US dollar amounts (row 3) by the deflator. So for example in 2001, the real purchasing value is 4,504,637 × 0.89 = 4,009,127, shown in row 6. Complete the rest of row 6 by entering your answers in the empty spaces. You can check them against Table 2.5.
3 Once price increases (inflation) are considered, the value of your drugs budget in 2005 is only about 60 per cent of the budget in 2000. So despite the fact that the government doubled the drugs budget in kwacha, the budget was eaten away by inflation and the depreciation of the currency.

Table 2.5 Effect of depreciation and inflation on national drugs budget

Year	2000	2001	2002	2003	2004	2005
1 Drugs budget (kwacha)	3,265,793	4,021,997	3,355,807	3,453,768	5,731,221	7,500,000
2 Exchange rate 1 kwacha = US$	1.23	1.12	0.91	0.83	0.67	0.59
3 Total in current US$	4,016,925	4,504,637	**3,053,784**	**2,866,627**	**3,839,918**	**4,425,000**
4 Price index of country where drugs are imported from (2000 = 100)	100	112.4	126.3	142.0	159.6	179.4
5 Deflator (100/ price index)	1.0	0.89	**0.792**	**0.704**	**0.627**	**0.557**
6 Total in real US$ (constant dollars)	4,016,925	4,009,127	**2,418,597**	**2,018,105**	**2,407,629**	**2,464,725**

Trade of health-related goods and services

Finally, the health sector is increasingly involved in the direct trade of health-related goods and services. For instance, spending on pharmaceuticals represents a significant portion of health expenditure in all countries. They are also the single most important health-related product traded, comprising some 55 per cent of all health-related trade by value (the share of the next most significant health-related goods traded, small devices and equipment, is 19 per cent). The market is highly concentrated, with North America, Europe and Japan accounting for around 75 per cent of sales (by value) (Smith *et al.* 2009).

Overall, HICs produce and export high value patented pharmaceuticals and LICs and MICs import these products, although some produce and export low-value generic products. This leads to many developing countries experiencing a trade deficit in modern medicines, which often fuels an overall health sector deficit. Interestingly, however, even among most HICs there are considerable trade deficits in pharmaceuticals, given their overall levels of consumption. Trade in health services has also expanded greatly in the last decade due to the push by the World Trade Organization (WTO) for trade in services more generally under the General Agreements on Tariffs and Trade (GATTs).

Globalization has in part been made possible due to improvements in information and communication technology (Yach 1998). These improvements have also contributed to the remote provision of health services from one country to another, known as 'e-health'. Examples of services provided include diagnostics, radiology, laboratory testing, remote surgery and tele-consultation.

Another type of trade in health services arises from the consumption of health services abroad. This is also known as 'health tourism' and entails people choosing to go to another country to obtain health care treatment. This attracts approximately 4 million patients each year, with the global market being estimated to be $US40–60 billion (Datta and Krishnan 2003).

Health and medical tourism: the case of Jordan

Due to the high quality of medical services provided, Arab patients started visiting Jordan for medical treatment as early as the 1970s. In the 1990s Jordan began to consciously promote its health services exports. In 1998, the Ministry of Health established an office at the Queen Alia Airport to facilitate the entry of foreign patients. While Jordan has invested in upgrading and modernizing its public hospitals and medical schools, it is private sector hospitals that dominate the market for medical tourism. The private sector accounts for 54 per cent of the hospitals in the country and 46 per cent of available beds. Jordan's private hospitals are state-of-the-art and many have links with renowned hospitals and medical centres in Europe and North America.

Revenue from medical tourism was estimated to have crossed the $US1 billion mark in 2003. The vast majority of medical tourists in Jordan come from the Arab world, mainly from Yemen, Sudan, Bahrain, Syria, Libya, Palestine, Saudi Arabia and others. Most patients seek treatment in cardiology, neurology, bone and other internal diseases.

As liberalization increases and migration becomes easier, the movement of people across borders also increases. As a result, many health professionals choose to leave their home countries for richer, more developed ones. This is the case for doctors, nurses, pharmacists, physician assistants, dentists and clinical laboratory technicians. It is estimated that in the UK the total number of foreign doctors increased from 20,923 in 1970 to 69,813 in 2003 (Connell *et al.* 2007). These figures may not seem that significant, but they often represent a large share of a country's total doctors. In Ghana, for example, the number of doctors leaving accounts for 30 per cent of the total number of doctors (Connell et al., 2007).

Summary

Macroeconomics is increasingly important for health and health sectors, especially as economies become more integrated in international trade and financial systems. This chapter described the key concepts within macroeconomics, and their application with respect to health and health care. Health is essential not only for human development, but for economic development as well. You have seen that external and macroeconomic impacts on health can be profound and adverse. The growing interconnectedness between countries means that health sectors are more vulnerable to shocks from events that are happening around the world.

References

Aizenman J and Jinjarak Y (2009) Globalization and Developing Countries: A Shrinking Tax Base? *Journal of Development Studies* 45(5):653–71.

Baunsgaard T and Keen M (2005) *Tax revenue and (or?) trade liberalization.* IMF Working Paper No. 05/112.

Blouin C, Chopra M and van der Hoeven R (2009) Trade and social determinants of health. *Lancet* 7:373(9662):502–7.

Connell J *et al.* (2007) Sub-Saharan Africa: beyond the health worker migration crisis? *Social Science & Medicine* 64:1876–91.

Datta P and Krishnan GS (2003) The health travellers. *Business World*, 22 December, www.businessworldindia.com/issue/pharma.asp.

De Cordoba SF, Laird S and Vanzetti D (2006) *Smoke and mirrors: making sense of the WTO industrial tariff negotiations.* United Nations Conference on Trade and Development Policy Issues in International Trade and Commodities Study Series No. 30, Trade Analysis Branch, Division on International Trade in Goods and Services and Commodities. New York and Geneva: UNCTAD, United Nations.

Ghose AK (2003) *Jobs and incomes in a globalizing world.* Geneva: International Labour Office.

Hawkes C (2006) Uneven dietary development: linking the policies and processes of globalization with the nutrition transition, obesity and diet-related chronic diseases. *Global Health* 28:2(1):4.

Hsiao W and Heller PS (2007) What should macroeconomists know about health care policy? IMF Working Paper WP/07/13, www.imf.org/external/pubs/cat/longres.cfm?sk=20103.0.

Keogh-Brown M and Smith RD (2008) The economic impact of SARS: how does the reality match the predictions. *Health Policy* 88:110–20.

Lall S (2004) The employment impact of globalization in developing countries, in Lee E and Vivarelli M (eds) *Understanding globalization, employment and poverty reduction.* Houndmills: Palgrave Macmillan for the ILO, pp. 73–101.

Onzivu W (2002) The public health implications of the Association of South East Asian Nations (ASEAN) legal regime on tobacco control. *Australian Journal of Asian Law* 4(2):160–87.

Organization for Economic Cooperation and Development (OECD) (2003) Regionalism and multilateral Trading System. Paris: OECD ISBN: 9264101373. http://www.oecd.org/dataoecd/23/12/8895922.pdf

Popkin BM (1998) The nutrition transition and its health implications in lower income countries. *Public Health Nutrition* 1:5–21.

Pritchett L and Summers LH (1996) Wealthier is healthier. *The Journal of Human Resources* XXXI: 841–68.

Sachs J (2001) *Macroeconomics and health: investing in health for economic development,* report of the Commission on Macroeconomics and Health. Geneva: World Health Organization.

Smith J (1999) Healthy bodies and thick wallets: the dual relationship between health and economic status. *Journal of Economic Perspective* 13(2):143–66.

Smith RD (2006) Trade in health services: current challenges and future prospects of globalisation, in Jones AM (ed) *Elgar companion to health economics* (2nd edn). Cheltenham: Edward Elgar.

Smith RD, Correa C and Oh C (2009) Trade, TRIPS, and pharmaceuticals. *Lancet* 373:684–91.

Wilkinson RG and Marmot MG (eds) (2003) *Social determinants of health: the solid facts.* Geneva: World Health Organization.

World Bank (2011) *Country and lending groups,* http://data.worldbank.org/about/country-classifications/country-and-lending-groups#Low_income.

Yach D (1998) Telecommunications for health – new opportunities for action. *Health Promotion International* 13:339–47.

Further reading

Bloom D and Canning D (2000) The health and wealth of nations. *Science* 287(5456): 1207–9.

Pritchett L and Summers LH (1996) Wealthier is healthier. *The Journal of Human Resources* XXXI:841–68.

Sachs J (2001) *Macroeconomics and health: investing in health for economic development,* report of the Commission on Macroeconomics and Health. Geneva: World Health Organization.

Smith RD (2006) Trade in health services: current challenges and future prospects of globalisation, in: Jones AM (ed) *Elgar companion to health economics* (2nd edn). Cheltenham: Edward Elgar.

Smith RD and Lee K (2009) Trade and health: an agenda for action. *Lancet* 373:768–73.

SECTION 2

Demand and supply

A simple model of demand

Virginia Wiseman and Stephen Jan

Overview

In this and the next three chapters, you will be looking at supply and demand and how they affect the price and quantity of goods provided through markets. In particular you will be thinking about how they influence activity and price in health care. You will start off in this chapter by looking at a simple model of demand and identifying the key variables that determine demand. Later in the chapter you will move on to analyse why demand for health care is more complicated and what distinguishes it from the demand for other products. You will see how information about demand can be used as an aid to planning in the health sector.

Learning objectives

After working through this chapter, you will be able to:

- define the term 'demand'
- show graphically the relationship between demand and price through a demand curve
- list the factors which influence the demand for health care
- define consumer surplus and explain why it can be used as a measure of benefit
- describe how demand theory can be used in health sector planning

Key terms

Complement. A good that is often needed when consuming another good. For instance, sugar can be seen to be a complement to tea.

Consumer surplus. The difference between what a consumer actually pays for a good and the maximum they would have been willing to pay for it. In a sense it represents the 'profit' to a consumer. By definition, if a consumer is rational, then they *only* purchase goods that they feel are worth more than what they have to pay for them.

Demand. Reflects the choices made by consumers over the consumption of specific goods. In almost all cases we would expect that if price goes up, all else being equal, the quantity demanded for a good goes down.

Demand curve. A graph showing the relationship between the quantity demanded of a good and its price when all other variables are unchanged.

Inferior goods.   Goods for which demand decreases as income increases.

Law of diminishing marginal utility.   A hypothesis that states that as consumption of a good increases so the marginal utility (extra benefit gained) decreases.

Market demand.   Summation of all individual demand for a particular good within a market.

Normal goods.   Goods for which demand increases as income increases.

Substitutes.   Goods that can be used in place of other goods (e.g. tea and coffee may be seen as substitutes).

Utility.   Satisfaction a person gets from consuming a good.

The concept of demand

The term 'demand' is used to describe the relationship between the amount of a good that consumers are willing and able to buy at various prices. There are two broad reasons why we might want to analyse demand. First, it can be used to help predict likely reactions and consumer behaviour. For example, if a charge is introduced for a drug or a test, what will be the effect on the number of people using that drug or test? Second, knowing something about people's demand for health care may say something about how much they value a good. This can in turn inform policy decisions such as how much a particular good should be subsidized. Here we will begin by examining a simple model of demand and identifying which variables influence the demand for goods.

Wants and demand

As consumers we all have various 'wants' for goods from which we gain some satisfaction. As shown in Chapter 1, given our limited income we cannot consume all we would like to and as a result we have to make choices.

Note that for demand to exist it is not necessary to actually purchase something. For example, my willingness to pay for a packet of paracetamol at a particular moment in time might be that I am prepared to spend £5. If paracetamol is currently selling at £7 then despite the fact that I have a demand for paracetamol, no transaction will take place. If however paracetamol is available at £5 (or less) then a transaction will take place. Therefore the *quantity demanded* is the amount that households are willing and able to buy and this is not necessarily the same as how much they *do* buy.

Determinants of demand

The quantity demanded is conventionally represented by the following function:

Demand = f (P, Y, Pc, Ps, T)

where

f (...) is standard mathematical notation and means 'is a function of'
P = price of the good
Y = income
Pc = price of complementary goods
Ps = price of substitute goods
T = tastes or preferences

Each of these symbols will now be explained.

The amount of a particular good that a household will want to buy is a function of the *price* (P) of the good. If paracetamol is priced at £1 per pack, you might be prepared to buy more per year than if it were priced at £10 per pack. For most goods, the higher the price, the less of that good people will want to buy; the lower the price, the more quantity is demanded.

The amount demanded is also related to the size of a consumer's *income* (Y). The higher your income, the more likely it is that more of a good will be demanded at any given price. Therefore if your income falls, you might consume less paracetamol per year.

The demand for a particular good is also influenced by the *relative prices of other goods* (Pc and Ps). For example, if the price of paracetamol remains fixed at £5 per pack, but the price of a substitute good, say aspirin, falls, you may now purchase less paracetamol per year than before as it is now relatively less attractive.

It is important to make a distinction between *complementary* and *substitute* goods. Complementary goods are those bought in conjunction with your product (e.g. a syringe and a needle). Substitute goods are goods which you can use instead of your good (e.g. if you are buying paracetamol for a headache then a substitute might be aspirin). If the price of a complementary good rises then demand for your good may fall. If the price of a substitute good increases, demand for your good may increase.

The price you are willing to pay for paracetamol is also a function of your *tastes or preferences*. If your tastes change (you experience an allergic reaction to paracetamol) then your demand for it will change and you will be prepared to pay less (or possibly nothing at all) for paracetamol. Note that your demand for paracetamol is not just a function of your taste for that particular medicine but also your taste for other goods.

The determinants of demand can be complex, as the next excerpt from a paper by Wiseman *et al.* (2007) illustrates:

> The provision of insecticide-treated nets (ITNs) in malarious regions is widely accepted as an essential public health service. One of the key reasons cited for this is that when used properly, intact ITNs provide almost complete protection from mosquito bites. While both the efficacy and cost-effectiveness of ITNs has been widely reported in the literature, little is known about the range, strength or interaction between the different factors influencing their demand at the household level. This study modelled the determinants of bed net ownership in the Farafenni region of The Gambia.

Results showed that household size, expenditure on other malaria prevention products and practices, age, education, ethnicity, occupation of household head, whether the road to a community was impassable at certain times of the year were all significant determinants of bed net ownership. Specifically, the likelihood of net ownership decreases with a rise in the number of household members in the 20 to 29 age bracket and increases with the number aged between 5 and 9. The more a household spends on other forms of malaria prevention (e.g. coils and repellents) then the less likely they are to own a bed net. The older the household head and the more education he or she has had, then the greater the likelihood of bed net ownership. Households where the head is a business person are also more likely to own a net. The more people in a household that are immediately related to the household head also increase the chances of bed net ownership (at the 10% level). Wollof and Fula households are less likely to own a bed net compared with the reference household headed by a Mandinka farmer.* Lastly, households located in communities that are cut off from main roads at different times of the year due to flooding and other causes are less likely to own a net.

*Wollof, Fula and Mandinka are different tribal groups living in the Farafenni region of The Gambia.

Demand curve

Let us begin by looking at the relationship between price and the quantity demanded and from there we will derive a demand curve. As a potential consumer of paracetamol, if paracetamol is priced at £20 per pack I may not be prepared to buy any per year. If the price is £15 I may buy one pack per year and so on until at £5 I would be prepared to buy five packs. Even if packs of paracetamol were being given away free of charge, I would not take more than seven packs. Table 3.1 describes this relationship.

Table 3.1 Relationship between price and quantity demanded

Price of paracetamol (per pack)	Quantity demanded in one year
£20	0
£15	1
£10	3
£5	5
0	7

From this information we can derive a 'demand curve' (also known as a demand schedule), as presented in Figure 3.1. The demand curve is a graphical representation of the relationship between price and quantity demanded, holding all other things constant. Remember, the 'law of demand' states that as the price of a good increases demand falls, other things remaining the same. Each point on the curve relates to the quantity demanded at a different price. Demand curves normally slope downwards. This is because for *normal goods*, consumers tend to buy more as the price falls. Although it is referred to as a 'curve' it is usually presented as a straight line for illustrative purposes. Its actual shape of course is an empirical question.

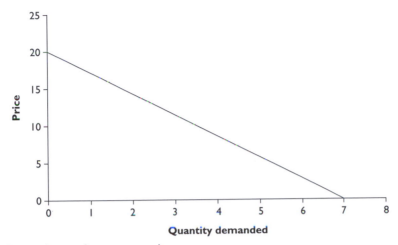

Figure 3.1 Demand curve for paracetamol

From this demand curve we can calculate how many packs of paracetamol will be demanded at a given price or, alternatively, what the price has to be to ensure a given quantity is demanded.

Slope of the demand curve

We said above that the demand curve usually slopes downwards – but why? There are two important effects that help explain why the demand curve slopes downwards from left to right (i.e. why the quantity demanded of a good falls as price rises). If for instance the price of coffee rises, consumption of coffee falls and the consumption of other drinks like hot chocolate or tea tends to rise. There is no reason to believe that the satisfaction consumers gain from a cup of coffee or a cup of tea has changed. However, the switch in demand occurs because the satisfaction obtained *per pound (£) spent* on coffee falls in relation to *a pound spent* on tea. Economists call this the *substitution-effect* – it is an attempt on the part of consumers to adjust consumption in response to a price change. This partly explains why the demand curve slopes downwards.

The other important effect is the *income effect*. The two most important determinants of the total amount of goods you consume are your income and prices. When the price of a good rises (such as petrol), if you continue to buy the same amount as before, you will have less income available to buy other goods. So the rise in the price of petrol is similar to a fall in real income. This income effect means that you will buy less of a good when its price rises in order to have enough income available to buy other goods.

Together, the income effect (a limited budget means you can only purchase lower quantities of the good) and the substitution effect (you swap with alternative goods that are cheaper) give a downward sloping demand curve.

Market demand

Up to this point we have been focusing on the individual consumer. You may be wondering what the implications are of measuring demand when there is more than one consumer. This is known as *market demand* and is simply the sum of the quantities demanded by each consumer or household at different prices. For example, assuming that there are only two consumers then the market demand is derived from the individuals' demand as shown in Table 3.2.

Table 3.2 Market demand for paracetamol

Price of paracetamol	Quantity demanded by consumer A per year	Quantity demanded by consumer B per year	Quantity demanded by both A and B per year
£20	0	2	2
£15	1	5	6
£10	3	6	9
£5	5	8	13
0	7	9	16

So far we have kept things rather simplistic, using examples such as paracetamol. However, we will see in the following two examples that there are many pertinent health care financing questions that involve the analysis of demand.

The RAND Experiment in the USA (Manning et *al.* 1987)

The RAND Health Insurance Experiment (HIE) in the USA was a landmark study in health economics. The HIE randomized people to various health insurance plans, each imposing a different dollar charge on the use of medical services. Covered expenses included most medical services. The results clearly showed that utilization responds to amounts paid out-of-pocket. Plans with the higher charges resulted in fewer face-to-face visits, suggesting a negative relationship between price and the quantity of medical services demanded in a year. This suggests the use of health services is sensitive to price as predicted by demand theory.

Removal of users' fees in Zambia (Masiye et *al.* 2010)

The introduction of cost-sharing policies, with a specific focus on user fee payments, became a dominant feature of health financing reform in many African and other low- and middle-income countries (LICs and MICs) in the 1980s and 1990s. However, research soon highlighted the dramatic negative impact of user fees on service utilization. On 13 January 2006, the President of Zambia announced a policy to abolish user fees at primary health care facilities in designated rural districts. This was a major policy shift from targeted exemptions to free primary health care across the board. This study reviewed the performance of free health care in Zambia, following 15 months of implementation. Using a comprehensive national facility-based data set, it was found that utilization increased among the rural population aged at least 5 years by 55 per cent. Importantly, utilization increases were greatest in the districts with the highest levels of poverty and material deprivation.

We will return to the topic of user fees in Chapters 8 and 13 and their implications for equity in Chapter 17.

A change in demand

When we talk about a change in demand, this is typically demonstrated as a shift or a movement along the demand curve.

A *movement* along the demand curve is caused by a change in the price of the good, as was illustrated when a pack of paracetamol fell from £15 to £10 and the corresponding quantity demanded rose from one to three packs per year.

A *shift* in the curve results from a change in other variables (e.g. tastes and preferences, incomes, prices of other goods, etc.). For example, consider what will happen to demand if income rises. If no other changes occur, for most goods the quantity demanded will rise with income.

Activity 3.1

1 Suppose that there is a health education campaign to highlight to the general public the benefits of regular dental check-ups (for which people must pay directly). What do you think would be the effect on the quantity demanded of dental services? Mark this effect on Figure 3.2, labelling it clearly.

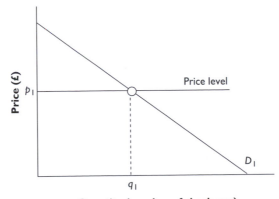

Figure 3.2 The demand for dental health checks

2 Suppose that the dental clinic relocates to an area outside the city such that it is far from the majority of the population, thus deterring people from using the service. Mark this effect on Figure 3.2, labelling it clearly.

Feedback

1 The health promotion programme, if effective, will result in an increased preference for dental check-ups. This means that quantity demanded increases at each price level – that is, the demand curve shifts to the right (from D_1 to D_2 in Figure 3.3).
2 If the clinic becomes more distant from the people then this means that travel to the clinic becomes more expensive in terms of time and transport costs. Travel to the clinic can be considered a *complement* to the check-up. The increasing cost of travel will result in a decrease in quantity demanded for the check-up at all prices. The demand curve shifts to the left (from D_1 to D_3 in Figure 3.3).

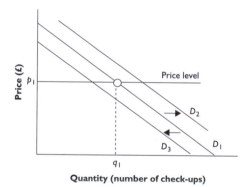

Figure 3.3 Changes in the demand for dental health checks

Activity 3.2

1 Suppose that the price charged for a dental check-up falls, from P_1 to P_2. Mark the effect on Figure 3.4.

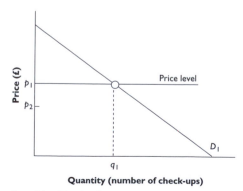

Figure 3.4 The demand for dental health checks

2 If people's income falls, what would be the effect on demand for dental check-ups? Again mark the change on Figure 3.4.

Feedback

1 This fall in price can be represented by a movement along the demand curve. As the demand curve slopes downwards, quantity demanded increases (from q_1 to q_2 in Figure 3.5).

2 If a dental check-up is a normal good (and you have no reason to believe it is not) then the fall in income will result in a decrease in quantity demanded at all prices. Hence the demand curve shifts to the left (from D_1 to D_2 in Figure 3.5).

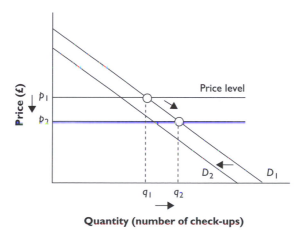

Figure 3.5 Changes in the demand for dental health checks

Demand and utility

Now let's drill down a bit deeper into the relationship between people's preferences and their demand. In this model of individual consumption, choices are constrained by income and by the prices of goods. We will assume that each individual has a given amount of income to spend, that everyone consumes all the goods they purchase within the relevant time period, and that individuals cannot influence the prices of the goods they buy.

The way in which an individual allocates their income across goods will depend on their likes and dislikes (i.e. their preferences). According to economists, the way we allocate our incomes across a wide range of goods available indicates some attempt to maximize our utility so that it reflects our preferences.

Total utility is the total satisfaction that a person gets from the consumption of goods. Total utility depends on the person's level of consumption – more consumption generally gives more total utility. *Marginal utility* is the change in total utility resulting from a one-unit increase in the quantity of a good consumed. You will recall from Chapter 1 that *diminishing marginal utility* means that as we consume more and more of a particular good the utility obtained from each extra unit of consumption will tend to fall.

Things become more complicated when prices and several goods are introduced. In order to maximize utility what you want to ensure is that the last pound (or any other monetary unit) spent on each good yields the same utility to you as the first. According to utility theory, when deciding how to allocate your income across different goods, utility is maximized when:

$$\frac{\text{Marginal utility of good A}}{\text{Price of good A}} = \frac{\text{Marginal utility of good B}}{\text{Price of good B}} = \frac{\text{Marginal utility of good C}}{\text{Price of good C}}$$

A consumer therefore maximizes their utility when the ratio of marginal utility to price is equal for all goods. At this point you are probably thinking, 'I don't allocate my income like this'. This is a *theory*, but nevertheless a powerful one in economics. For a number of markets, it has been shown to fairly accurately describe how people (albeit subconsciously) allocate their spending, but perhaps its value is more as a *normative* assumption rather than a *positive* observation – i.e. if we believe that maximizing utility is a desirable policy outcome, then this model provides a basis for how it can be achieved.

Read the following excerpt from Parkin *et al.* (2008) where they explain the theory of marginal utility in more detail and provide some justification for its use.

Water is essential to life itself while diamonds are just inessential luxuries. So water is much more valuable than diamonds. Yet the price of water is a tiny fraction of the price of a diamond. Why? This question is the paradox of value that has puzzled philosophers for centuries. Adam Smith tried but failed to solve this paradox. Not until the theory of marginal utility had been developed could anyone give a satisfactory answer.

You can solve Adam Smith's puzzle by distinguishing between *total* utility and *marginal* utility. The total utility that we get from water is enormous. But remember, the more we consume of something, the smaller is its marginal utility. We use so much water that the marginal utility – the benefit we get from one more glass of water – diminishes to a tiny value. Diamonds, on the other hand, have a small total utility relative to water, but because we buy few diamonds, they have a high marginal utility.

When an individual has maximized total utility, he or she has allocated his or her budget in the way that makes the marginal utility per pound spent equal for all goods. That is, the marginal utility from a good divided by the price of the good is equal for all goods. This equality of marginal utilities per pound spent holds true for diamonds and water. Diamonds have a high price and a high marginal utility. Water has a low price and a low marginal utility. When the high marginal utility of diamonds is divided by the high price of diamonds, the result is a number that equals the low marginal utility of water divided by the low price of water. The marginal utility per pound spent is the same for diamonds as for water.

Another way to think about the paradox of value is through the concept of *consumer surplus*.

Consumer surplus

So far we have learned that the demand curve shows a consumer's willingness to pay. It tells us his or her marginal benefit – the maximum price that a consumer is willing to pay for an extra unit of a good when utility is maximized. Now that you have an understanding of the concept of marginal utility, it is important to be able to distinguish between value (determined by the consumer) and price (determined by the market).

Consumer surplus is the difference between the total amount that consumers are *willing and able to pay* for a good (indicated by the demand curve) and the total amount that they *actually do pay* (i.e. the market price for the product). Using our earlier demand curve for dental checks, we see that the area under the demand curve represents the value placed on the good by consumers. The area under the price line represents the cost to consumers. Hence the consumer surplus is the area between the demand curve and the price line. In a sense it is the 'profit' a consumer makes when they makes a decision to purchase something and is measured by the difference between the price paid and the maximum the consumer would have been willing to pay. The shaded area in Figure 3.6 indicates the consumer surplus.

Quantity (number of check-ups)

Figure 3.6 The demand for dental health checks showing consumer surplus

Continuing with our earlier example in Activity 3.1, the gain in consumer surplus *after* the health education campaign is indicated in Figure 3.7(overleaf) by the shaded area to the right of D_1, the original demand curve.

Activity 3.4

Go back to Figures 3.3 and 3.5 and shade in the areas that represent the *changes* in consumer surplus as a result of the following.

1 The relocation of the dental clinic to an area outside the city (mark this on Figure 3.3).
2 The fall in the price charged for a dental check-up, *ceteris paribus*, from p_1 to p_2 (mark this effect on Figure 3.5).
3 Again on Figure 3.5, mark the change in consumer surplus if people's income falls.

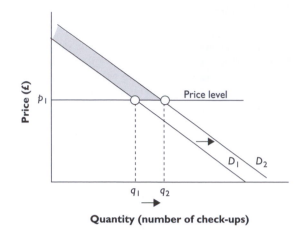

Figure 3.7 The demand for dental health checks after health education campaign

Feedback

1 The loss of consumer surplus associated with the change of location (Figure 3.3) is indicated by the tinted area in Figure 3.8.

2 & 3. The *gain* in consumer surplus associated with the drop in price shown in Figure 3.5 is indicated by the dark tinted area in Figure 3.9, while the light tinted area indicates the *loss* of consumer surplus associated with the fall in income.

We will return to the concept of consumer surplus in the next chapter when we look at price elasticity of demand and in Chapter 8 when we compare different types of market structure. The concept of consumer surplus is also fundamental in cost–benefit analysis where benefits are defined as net increases in consumer surplus (Fox-Rushby and Cairns 2005).

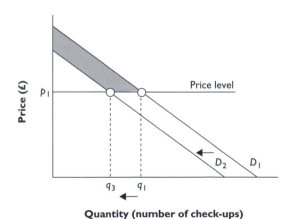

Figure 3.8 Changes in consumer surplus resulting from a change in demand

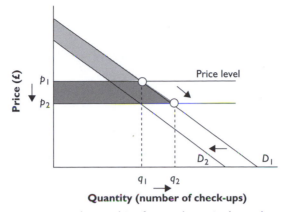

Figure 3.9 Changes in consumer surplus resulting from a change in demand

Demand for health care

Economists assume that individuals allocate their limited budget to try and maximize their utility and that when individuals do this they are using their resources efficiently (i.e. individuals are acting 'rationally'). A demand curve illustrates this phenomenon – it is a description of the planned quantity demanded at each price when utility is maximized.

When we translate this thinking to health care, problems arise. For example, unlike most other goods, health care does not yield utility directly. Few people enjoy the experience of consuming health care. Its value comes from the positive effect one hopes it has on health and, in turn, the satisfaction we derive from the activities we can do when we are healthy (that is, working and leisure activities). Demand for health services is therefore a *derived demand*.

The appropriateness and applicability of the concept of demand to health care has been debated at length. Some time ago now, Pauly (1988) surmised that about three quarters of medical markets do not fit well with the conventional economic model.

Activity 3.5

Can you think of other ways in which the demand for health care is different from the demand for other goods?

Feedback

Here are some ways in which the demand for health care is more complicated than the simple model of demand presented in this chapter.

1 The demand for health care is often for a single one-off intervention rather than multiple or repeated requests as often occurs with the consumption of DVDs or soap.
2 It is generally assumed in economics that consumers are able to make informed decisions about their consumption patterns. Consumers are said to be 'sovereign'.

However, in the case of health care, consumers often delegate this decision-making power to health professionals who are much better informed.

3 Patients' perceptions of their need and of their capacity to benefit, both of which shape their demand, may be strongly influenced by their doctor – the supplier of health care.

4 Another complication relates to the fact that health care is extremely *heterogeneous*. Every patient has a slightly different combination of ailments and symptoms, and therefore every patient needs to buy a slightly different package of care. Furthermore, individuals will vary in how they respond to treatments.

5 A major difference is that payment for many health services comes, partly or wholly, from a third party (either an insurance company or a government) which means individual users of services may not be sensitive to the price of these services.

Some aspects of health care may fit the simple demand model better than others. For example, our earlier example of the market for paracetamol – a person with a head-ache knows with a relatively high degree of certainty the effects of consuming this medi-cine. They can buy paracetamol according to their preferences and without going through a third party. In the next chapter you will explore some more complicated models of demand.

Advanced reading box: Indifference curve analysis

One reason our earlier model is sometimes called a 'simple model of consumer demand' is that we treat the consumer's decision about the purchase of each good as an isolated event. We have side-lined the problem that every purchase of a good involves a trade-off. If we spend more money on good Y then we have less money to spend on good X. This is where indifference curve analysis comes in. This type of analysis can be used to examine how a consumer would change the combination of two goods if there was a change in their income or a change in price. Indifference curve analysis combines two concepts: indifference curves and budget lines.

Indifference curve

An indifference curve is a line that shows all possible combinations of two goods between which a person is indifferent. So for each point on the indifference curve, the utility a person receives from consuming different combinations of two goods is the same. For example, in Figure 3.10 the indifference curve is ID1. A person would derive the same utility from consuming 3 units of X and 5 units of Y as they would from consuming 6 units of X and 2 units of Y.

The shape of the indifference curve

Figure 3.10 shows that the indifference curve is not a straight line. It curves inward because of the concept of the diminishing marginal rate of substitution between the two goods.

The marginal rate of substitution is the amount of one good (e.g. X) that has to be given up if a person is to obtain one extra unit of the other good (e.g. Y).

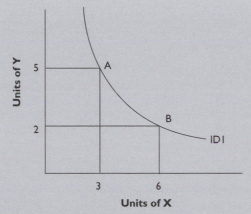

Figure 3.10 The indifference curve

The marginal rate of substitution (MRS) =

change in good X/change in good Y =

slope of the indifference curve

Using Figure 3.10, the marginal rate of substitution between point A and Point B is:

MRS = −3/3 = −1 = 1 (the convention is to ignore the sign, making the answer 1, not −1).

The reason why the marginal rate of substitution diminishes is due to the principle of *diminishing marginal utility*. You will recall that this principle states that the more units of a good consumed the less additional satisfaction will be gained from extra units consumed. It is possible to draw more than one indifference curve on the same diagram – this is called an *indifference curve map*. The general rule is that indifference curves further to the right show combinations of the two goods that yield a higher utility and vice versa.

The budget line
The budget line is important to the analysis of consumer behaviour. The budget line illustrates all the possible combinations of two goods that can be purchased at given prices with a set budget. Remember that the amount of a good that a person can buy will depend upon their income and the price of the good. Figure 3.11 constructs a budget line for a given budget of £40, £4 per unit of X and £2 per unit of Y. With a limited budget the consumer can only consume a limited combination of X and Y (the maximum combinations are on the actual budget line). A change in income will cause a shift in the budget line but its slope will remain the same. A rise in income will cause the budget line to shift outward while a fall in income will result in an inward shift.

Combining indifference curves and budget lines
By bringing together the indifference curve and the budget line, it is possible to identify the consumption point between two goods that a rational consumer with a given budget would buy. A rational, maximising consumer would prefer to be on the highest possible indifference curve given their budget constraint. This point occurs where the

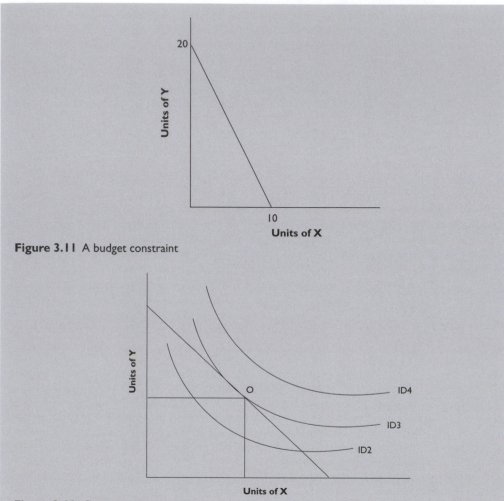

Figure 3.11 A budget constraint

Figure 3.12 Optimum consumption

indifference curve touches the budget line. In Figure 3.12, the optimum consumption point is at point O on indifference curve ID3 (i.e. where MRS equals the ratio of prices).

Deriving the demand curve

For a change in price, a demand curve can be derived using indifference curve analysis. Our original budget constraint (where X costs £4 and Y costs £2 and income is £40) is shown by the black unbroken line. If the price of X falls to £2 the new budget line is shown by the dotted line. The consumer can now buy twice as much of X as before. The points A and B represent the best the consumer can do at prices £4 and £2 respectively. So at price £4 we can see that about 6 units are demanded and at price £2 about 10 units are demanded. These represent the points of tangency in Figure 3.13(a). These points can be used to begin deriving the consumer's demand curve for X shown in Figure 3.13(b).

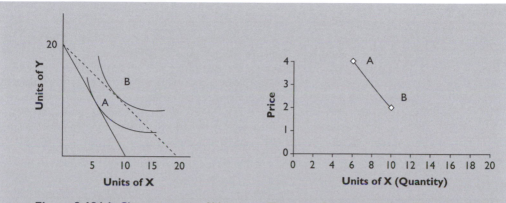

Figure 3.13(a) Change in price of X   **Figure 3.13(b)** Demand curve for X

Changes in income can also lead to a change in demand. As we have already seen, if income increases the budget line shifts outward (i.e. to the right) and will be tangent to a new, higher indifference curve. This in turn will lead to a shift in the demand curve because more units of the good are demanded at each price. A decrease in income will cause an inward shift of the demand curve.

Income and substitution effects revisited

It was noted earlier that economists decompose the effect of a change in price on the quantity demanded into an income and a substitution effect. For example, when the price of a good falls, the quantity demanded rises for two reasons. First, real income is higher because the same money income buys more at the lower prices (i.e. income effect). For normal goods (i.e. demand increases as income increases), the income effect of a price fall is positive. Second, consumers substitute the now cheaper good for ones whose price has not fallen, real income held constant. This increase in demand is called the substitution effect of a price decline.

The total effect of a price change is therefore the substitution effect **and** the income effect working at the same time. For normal goods, the income and substitution effects reinforce each other (i.e. cause a change in the same direction). For inferior goods (i.e. demand decreases as income increases), the two effects work in opposite directions as Figure 3.14 shows. Note that, the substitution effect tends to dominate thereby confirming the law of demand.

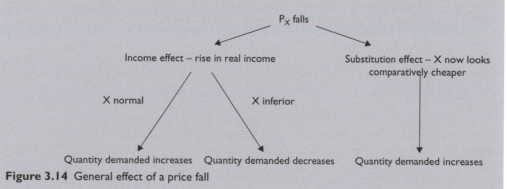

Figure 3.14 General effect of a price fall

Summary

In this chapter you have learned that demand describes the relationship between the amount of a good consumers are *willing* to buy at different prices (all other things remaining the same). Consumers purchase those goods which, subject to their income constraint, maximize their utility. Quantity demanded is determined by many different variables including price, income, preferences (or tastes) and the relative price of other goods. The relationship between price and quantity demanded is illustrated by a demand curve which typically slopes downward from left to right. The next chapter presents specific tools for measuring demand.

References

Fox-Rushby J and Cairns J (2005) *Economic evaluation*. Maidenhead: Open University Press.

Manning WG *et al.* (1987) Health insurance and the demand for medical care: evidence from a randomized experiment. *American Economic Review* 77(3):251–77.

Masiye F, Chitah B and McIntyre D (2010) From targeted exemptions to user fee abolition in health care: experience from rural Zambia. *Social Science & Medicine* 72(4):743–50.

Parkin M, Powell M and Mathews K (2008) *Economics* (7th edn). Harlow: Addison-Wesley.

Pauly M (1988) Is medical care different? in Greenberg W (ed) *Competition in the health care sector: ten years later*. Durham, NC: Duke University Press.

Wiseman V *et al.* (2007) Determinants of bed net use in The Gambia: implications for malaria control. *American Journal of Tropical Medicine and Hygiene* 76:830–6.

Further reading

Jan S *et al.* (2005) *Economic analysis for management and policy*. Maidenhead: Open University Press: 30–41.

Manning WG *et al.* (1987) Health insurance and the demand for medical care: evidence from a randomized experiment. *American Economic Review* 77(3):251–77.

Masiye F, Chitah B and McIntyre D (2010) From targeted exemptions to user fee abolition in health care: experience from rural Zambia. *Social Science & Medicine* 72(4):743–50.

Tamblyn R *et al.* (2001) Adverse effects associated with prescription drug cost-sharing among poor and elderly persons. *Journal of the American Medical Association* 285:2328–9.

Measuring demand

Virginia Wiseman

Overview

In Chapter 3 we looked at the concept of demand and its determinants. You also gained an understanding of how changes in demand can be graphically represented. In this chapter we take a more in-depth look at demand. First, you will find out how to measure the responsiveness of demand to changes in price. Then you will look at how such measurements can be used in practice.

Learning objectives

After working through this chapter, you will be able to:

- describe how to measure demand in practice
- define price elasticity of demand (PED)
- calculate PED over a portion of the demand curve
- describe the relationship between PED and revenue
- discuss issues concerning imposing (or increasing) taxes or health service charges
- describe how demand theory can be used in health service planning

Key terms

Cross price-elasticity of demand. The percentage change in quantity demanded of a good divided by the percentage change in the price of another related good.

Income elasticity of demand. The percentage change in quantity demanded of a good divided by the percentage change in population income.

Price elastic. Change in price produces a more than proportionate change in quantity demanded.

Price elasticity of demand. The percentage change in quantity demanded divided by the associated percentage change in price.

Price elasticity of supply. The percentage change in quantity supplied of a good divided by the percentage change in the good's own price.

Price inelastic. Change in price produces less than proportionate change in quantity demanded.

Elasticity and the responsiveness of demand

It is important to know about the responsiveness of demand to changes in certain variables so that appropriate policies can be designed to alter it if required. Responsiveness is measured by economists and referred to as the *elasticity of demand*; it is reflected in the shape and slope of the demand curve.

The responsiveness of quantity demanded to a change in price is called *price elasticity*. You may also be aware that elasticity can be measured for changes in income (income elasticity) and for changes in the price of other goods (cross-price elasticity).

Many studies estimate demand elasticity. It can be useful for policy-makers and planners to know what will happen if prices rise or fall. Will there be a big change or a little change in the quantity demanded in response to price changes? The amount of health care demanded is sometimes measured by the quantity of services used, such as inpatient days or outpatient visits. More often, it is measured by the total cost of the services. Either of these measures can be used to estimate demand elasticity.

Inelastic and elastic demand

Elasticity provides a way of measuring how sensitive demand (or supply) is to factors such as a change in price. For many goods and services a price increase means that people buy less, but in some cases the price rise has very little impact on quantities consumed. Price elasticity of demand allows us to calculate *how much* demand changes as a result of a change in price.

Figure 4.1 shows three demand curves that cover the entire range of possible elasticities of demand. In Figure 4.1(a), the quantity demanded is constant regardless of the price. If the quantity demanded remains constant when the price changes, then the elasticity of demand is zero and demand is said to be *perfectly inelastic*. One good that has a low elasticity of demand is insulin. Insulin is of such importance to some diabetics that a price change is unlikely to have much effect on the amount patients will purchase.

If the percentage change in the quantity demanded equals the percentage change in price, the elasticity of demand is 1 and demand is said to be *unit elastic*. The demand curve in Figure 4.1(b) is an example of unit elastic demand.

Between the examples shown in parts (a) and (b) of Figure 4.1 are the more general cases when the percentage change in the quantity demanded is less than the percentage change in price. In these cases, the price elasticity of demand is less than 1 and demand is said to be inelastic. Petrol and tobacco are examples of goods that are typically inelastic in demand.

For the sake of illustration, if the quantity demanded is infinitely responsive to a price change, then price elasticity of demand is infinity and demand is said to be *perfectly elastic*. The demand curve in Figure 4.1(c) is an example of perfectly elastic demand.

Between the examples shown in parts (b) and (c) of Figure 4.1 are the general cases when the percentage change in the quantity demanded *exceeds* the percentage change in price. In these cases, price elasticity of demand is greater than 1 and demand is said to be elastic. Cereal and shampoo are examples of goods typically with elastic demand. In health care, the demand for some forms of cosmetic surgery is elastic.

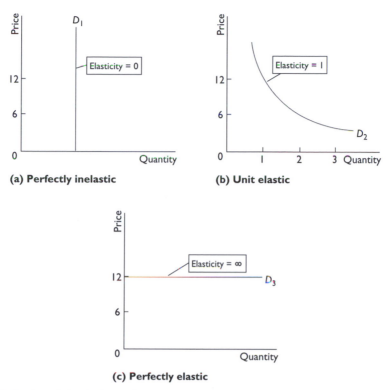

Figure 4.1 Inelastic and elastic demand
Source: Parkin *et al.* (2008)

Calculating price elasticity

There are three points to note before we calculate price elasticity.

First, price elasticity of demand is calculated by dividing the proportionate change in quantity demanded by the proportionate change in price. Note that *elasticity* is different to the *slope* of a demand curve. 'Slope' measures the *absolute* change in one variable given an *absolute* change in another variable (e.g. change in quantity demanded divided by an initial change in price). Elasticities do not depend on the types of measures used and are most useful when you want to compare the responsiveness of demand in different markets. 'Slopes' on the other hand are dependent on the unit in which the good is measured. Consider a demand curve for paracetamol that has quantity measured in terms of number of grams of paracetamol. This will be much steeper than a similar demand curve that has quantity measured in tonnes of paracetamol. However, for each price level the elasticity will be the same for both curves.

Second, price elasticity of demand will always be negative. This indicates that as the price of a good increases, all other factors held constant, consumers will demand less of that good. When we analyse price elasticities we are concerned with their absolute value, so we ignore the negative value.

Third, the magnitude of the elasticity estimate provides a measure of how *responsive* demand is. If the value of the price elasticity estimate is *greater than 1* in absolute value, then demand is said to be elastic. When demand is elastic, consumers are very responsive to changes in price. As such, a small price change will lead to a relatively large change in quantity demanded. In contrast, if the value of the elasticity of demand estimate is *less than 1* in absolute value, then demand is said to be inelastic and consumers are not very responsive to price changes. This is summarized below (where PED represents price elasticity of demand):

If PED > 1 then demand is price elastic (demand is sensitive to price changes)
If PED = 1 then demand is unit elastic
If PED < 1 then demand is price inelastic (demand is not sensitive to price changes)

With these key points in mind, let us now undertake some calculations. The following formula is used to estimate the price elasticity of demand:

$$\text{Price elasticity of demand} = \frac{\text{Percentage change in quantity demanded}}{\text{Percentage change in price}}$$

To use this formula we need to know the quantities demanded at different prices. This information is embodied in Figure 4.2, which illustrates the demand for paracetamol sold by one pharmacy.

Figure 4.2 shows one section on the demand curve for paracetamol and how the quantity demanded responds to a small change in price. Initially the price is £5 per pack and 17 packs are sold per week. This is shown as the point A in the diagram. The price increases to £6 per pack and the quantity demanded decreases to 15 pack per week (point B in figure 4.2). When the price increases by £1 per pack, the quantity demanded decreases by two packs per week.

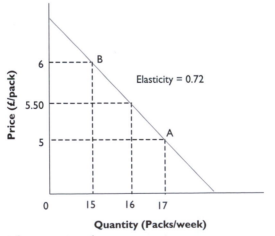

Figure 4.2 Demand curve for paracetamol

To estimate the elasticity of demand, we express the changes in price and quantity demanded as percentages of the average price and the average quantity. By using the average price and quantity we are able to calculate elasticity at a point on the demand curve midway between the original point and the new point. The original price is £5 and the new price is £6 so the average price is £5.50.

$\Delta P/P_{ave} = (£1/£5.50) = 18\%$ (where Δ denotes 'change in')
This tells us that the £1 price increase is 18 per cent of the average price

The original quantity demanded is 17 packs per week and the new quantity demanded is 15 packs per week. So the average quantity demanded is 16 packs per week. The 2 pack per week decrease in the quantity demanded is approximately 13 per cent of the average quantity. This is shown by:

$\Delta Q/Q_{ave} = (£2/£16) = -13\%$

So the price elasticity of demand, which is the percentage change in the quantity demanded (13 per cent) divided by the percentage change in price (18 per cent) is −0.72. That is shown by:

Price elasticity of demand = $\%\Delta Q/\%\Delta P$

$$= -13\%/18\%$$

$$= -0.72$$

Now that we have calculated the value of price elasticity of demand, we need to understand what it represents. First, remember that we are concerned with absolute values and therefore ignore the negative sign. We calculated the price elasticity of demand to be 0.72, so our good is price inelastic (PED < 1) and thus demand is not very sensitive to price changes. Moreover, the value of 0.72 for the price elasticity of paracetamol tells us that a 1 per cent rise in the price of paracetamol will lead to a 0.72 per cent fall in the quantity demanded. Alternatively, a 1 per cent fall in price will lead to a 0.72 per cent rise in quantity demanded.

A number of factors can affect the elasticity of demand for a good. Here are some examples, but you will undoubtedly be able to think of others:

- *Availability of substitute goods*: the more and closer the substitutes available, the higher elasticity is likely to be, as people can easily switch from one good to another if an even minor price change is made. Note that the number of substitutes depends on how broadly a good is defined.
- *Percentage of income*: goods that take a large portion of a consumer's income tend to have greater elasticity.
- *Time period*: elasticity tends to be greater over the long run as consumers have more time to adjust their behaviour and to search for substitutes.
- *Necessity*: the more necessary a good is, the lower the elasticity, as people will attempt to buy it no matter the price, such as in the case of insulin for those that need it.
- *Who pays*: where the purchaser does not directly pay for the good they consume, such as in the case of employer-sponsored health insurance, demand is likely to be more inelastic.
- *Brand loyalty*: an attachment to a certain brand can often make consumers insensitive to price changes, resulting in more inelastic demand.

The overall demand for health care services is expected to be relatively inelastic, in large part because there are few close substitutes for medical services. If you are sick, you will not be very price sensitive. However, as noted earlier, there are exceptions to this rule (e.g. elective surgery such as plastic surgery, purchases of glasses) but most studies find that patients are fairly insensitive to changes in health care prices.

Revenue and elasticity

Price elasticities are also useful because of their relationship with revenue. Figure 4.3 shows how the revenue to providers can be represented diagrammatically. Total

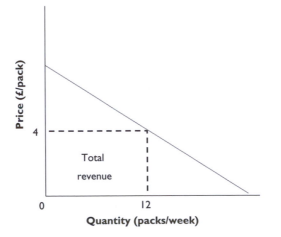

Figure 4.3 Revenue

revenue is the number of units of a good sold (horizontal axis) multiplied by the price per unit (vertical axis). The quantity sold here is 12 packs and the market price is £4. Therefore total revenue is 12 × 4 = £48. This is shown by the area of the rectangular box.

As the price rises some revenue will be gained on each unit sold but some will be lost because fewer units will be sold. We can now put these two concepts of revenue and elasticity together. If demand is price elastic then revenue will decrease if the price is increased. If demand is price inelastic then revenue will increase if price goes up.

Let's flesh this out a little more. We said before that total revenue is equal to price multiplied by quantity demanded. So if price increases then total revenue can only fall if there is a proportionally larger decrease in the quantity demanded. This is what happens when the price elasticity of demand is elastic. The increase in revenue on each unit sold is more than offset by the decrease in revenue due to a reduction in the quantity sold.

The flip side to this is that if price elasticity of demand is inelastic then an increase in price will lead to a proportionately smaller decrease in quantity demanded. So the increase in revenue on each unit sold is not fully offset by the decrease in revenue associated with the fall in units sold.

The relationship between revenue and elasticity may take a little time to digest but it can be summarized as follows:

• the change in total revenue depends on the elasticity of demand;

- if demand is elastic, a 1 per cent price rise decreases the quantity sold by more than 1 per cent and total revenue decreases;
- if demand is unit elastic, a 1 per cent price rise decreases the quantity sold by 1 per cent and so total revenue does not change;
- if demand is inelastic, a 1 per cent price rise decreases the quantity sold by less than 1 per cent and total revenue increases.

Activity 4.1

Based on what you have read on elasticity, try answering the following questions.

1 Without referring to the text, see if you can define price elasticity of demand.
2 As the manager of a vaccination clinic, you want to increase the influenza vaccine price. Figure 4.4 shows the demand curve for influenza vaccine. The current demand (q*) and price (p*) are marked at point A on the demand curve. Point B shows the new demand (q) and price (p). Is price elasticity of demand elastic, inelastic or unit elastic? Can you explain why?
3 What would be the impact on the total revenue considering this price increase?

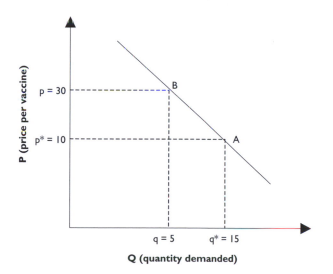

Figure 4.4 The demand curve for influenza vaccine

Feedback

1 Price elasticity of demand is a measure of the responsiveness of quantity demand to a change in price:

$$PED = \frac{\text{Percentage change in quantity demanded}}{\text{Percentage change in price}}$$

2 Calculate the PED as follows:

(ΔQ/Qave)/(ΔP/Pave) = ((5–15)/10)/((30–10/20) = (–10/10)/(20/20)) = –1; absolute

PED is therefore unit elastic (i.e. % change in quantity=% change in price)

3 There is no impact on total revenue because demand is unit elastic: the change in quantity demanded is in the same proportion as the change in price. A change in price in either direction therefore would result in no change in revenue.

Some other elasticities

Elasticities are not just used to measure the responsiveness of quantity demanded to price. They can be used to measure the responsiveness of any variable to any other variable. In addition to price elasticity of demand the following elasticities are often calculated:

- *Cross-price elasticity of demand* is the percentage change in quantity demanded of the good divided by the percentage change in the price of another related good. If the related good is a complement then the cross-elasticity of demand is less than zero because a positive change in price brings about a negative change in quantity demanded. If the related good is a substitute then the cross-elasticity of demand is more than zero because a positive change in price brings about a positive change in quantity demanded. The closer the substitute, the higher the cross-price elasticity of demand.
- *Income elasticity of demand* is the percentage change in quantity demanded of the good divided by the percentage change in population income. If an increase in income brings about an increase in quantity demanded then income elasticity of demand is positive and the good is described as a 'normal good'. If an increase in income brings a decrease in quantity demanded then income elasticity of demand is negative and the good is described as an 'inferior good'.
- *Price elasticity of supply* is the percentage change in quantity supplied of a good divided by the percentage change in the good's price. Supply is generally more responsive to price in the long term than it is in the short term. For example, over short periods of time, firms cannot easily change the sizes of their factories (or in the case of health care, new facilities cannot be built) to produce more or less of a good or service.

Case study 1: user fees

Where user fees are to be introduced or raised by a project or health service, the impact of such changes on demand can be analysed using estimates of price elasticity. The following example is adapted from *A Handbook for the Economic Analysis of Health Sector Projects* by the Asian Development Bank produced in 2000 which uses data from Gertler and Molyneaux (1996).

 'The study uses one of the most rigorous ways of estimating price elasticity and that is to use data from randomised controlled tests which allow user charges to be experimentally varied while holding other influences on demand constant.

Such data were made available in Indonesia for the provinces of Kalimantan Timur and Nusa Tengarra Barat. The study design was integrated into the local decision-making body and rather than raising fees everywhere. Fee changes were staggered to generate price variation based on an experimental design. User fees were increased in health centres in some districts but not in others.' The study assesses, among other things, the impact of higher fees on demand for public health centres in Indonesia. The price elasticity estimates for public health centres are shown in Table 4.1.

Table 4.1 Price elasticity of demand for public health centre visits

	Children		Adults	
	Urban	*Rural*	*Urban*	*Rural*
Visits to health centres	−1.07	−0.63	−1.04	−0.01

Source: Asian Development Bank (2000)

Activity 4.2

1 What do the figures of −1.07 and −0.01 imply about a 10 per cent change in user fees?

2 As we have already learned, an elasticity of above unity implies that raising fees will not bring in extra revenue since quantity will also decline proportionately. In which areas (rural or urban) would you expect raising fees to bring in extra revenue? Why?

Feedback

1 A figure of −1.07 implies that a 10 per cent change in user fees is almost matched by a 10.7 per cent decline in use of health facilities by children in urban areas (unit elastic). Alternatively, a figure of −0.01 means that a 10 per cent rise in fees leads to only a 0.1 per cent decline in use by adults in rural areas (inelastic).

2 Raising fees at health centres will only bring in extra revenue in rural areas. This is because demand is price inelastic. Hence, the increase in revenue achieved from the higher price charged is greater than the loss of revenue caused by the loss in quantity demanded. It is interesting to note however that the study found (although not shown here) that the reductions in utilization of health centres were not merely for minor conditions, since after the fee increases there was evidence of higher incidence of infectious disease and longer duration of illness.

Case study 2: cigarette taxation

Levying of taxes on cigarettes is sometimes used to reduce cigarette consumption, thus improving health and raising government revenue. Here we will examine some of the other consequences of imposing cigarette taxation, in particular the way taxation can impact on different social groups. A particular concern is to avoid regressive taxation – that is, a tax that takes a decreasing proportion of income as income rises.

In an article by Borren and Sutton (1992) the authors estimated a cigarette demand function for each of five different social classes in the UK. They wanted to compare the responsiveness of these different classes to rises in cigarette taxation and then to see where the burden of taxation was at greatest. They wanted to find out whether or not the policy of increasing taxation on cigarettes is *regressive*. The social class system referred to in the text is defined as:

Class I – professionals (non-manual)
Class II – managers (non-manual)
Class III – skilled workers (non-manual and manual)
Class IV – semi-skilled workers (manual)
Class V – unskilled workers (manual)

These authors then built a model of demand using time series data from a number of UK sources including data on the quantity demanded, price (relative to other prices in the economy) and income. They estimated separate demand curves for each population and their associated price elasticities. The burden of taxation was calculated for each group.

Activity 4.3

Now look at the results Borren and Sutton obtained (Table 4.2 and Figure 4.5) and consider their implications for policy. Try to answer the following questions.

1 What do the numbers in Table 4.2 mean?
2 What groups are likely to reduce their smoking the most?
3 Who is likely to bear the burden of higher levels of taxation?

Feedback

1 These are the price elasticities of demand for each class/sex group. For each group, PED is constant across the demand curve because this is the functional form

Table 4.2 Price elasticities of demand for men (1961–85) and for women (1958–87)

	Class I	Class II	Class III	Class IV	Class V
Men	−0.69	−0.48	−0.84	−0.89	−0.31
Women	−1.04	−0.93	−0.65	−0.85	−0.45

Source: Borren and Sutton (1992)

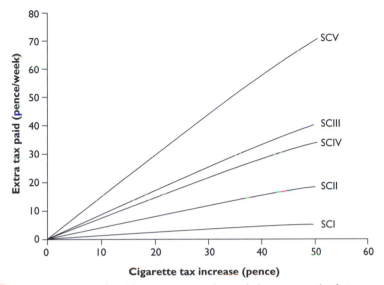

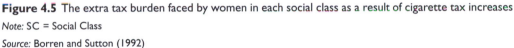

Figure 4.5 The extra tax burden faced by women in each social class as a result of cigarette tax increases

Note: SC = Social Class

Source: Borren and Sutton (1992)

the investigators have assumed. All the elasticities have a minus sign in front of them. This is perfectly normal – it reflects the fact that the change in quantity demanded is in the opposite direction to the change in price (that is, the demand curve slopes downwards). However, remember that since PED is always negative economists have developed the convention of omitting the sign. For other types of elasticity, signs should always be indicated appropriately to show the direction of change (as well as the magnitude of change).

2 You get this answer directly from the price elasticities. The elasticities with the largest magnitude indicate large percentage reductions in cigarette consumption relative to the price change. They indicate that men in Classes III and IV and women in Classes I, II and IV will be most responsive in relative terms. However, these groups have different starting points in terms of initial smoking consumption. A large percentage change in a low smoking group might represent a smaller absolute change in consumption than a small percentage change in a high smoking group.

3 The model was used to predict the increased tax burden associated with various tax levels for each group. Figure 4.5 presents these predictions graphically for women. It seems that increasing tax levels on cigarettes will increase the tax burden of social Class V more than social Class I. The authors concluded that the policy of imposing taxation on cigarettes is regressive.

Case study 3: taxes and tariffs on insecticide-treated bed nets (ITNs)

The following edited extract from Simon *et al.* (2002) illustrates how price elasticity of demand can be used to estimate the impact of tax and tariff reduction on ITN purchases. Note that due to a lack of evidence on price elasticities of demand for ITNs, the authors have modelled at two situations, one in which demand responds modestly to price changes (i.e. price elasticity of demand = 0.5) and one where it is more responsive (i.e. price elasticity of demand =1.5).

One of the steps called for in the fight against malaria is the removal of tariffs and taxes on insecticide treated bednets (ITNs), netting materials, and insecticides, with a view to reducing the retail prices of ITNs and thus increasing utilization. In this paper, we develop an approach for analyzing the extent to which reform of tariff and tax policy can be expected to increase ITN purchases...

In 2001, tariffs and taxes on netting materials were reduced from 40% to 5%. Tariffs and taxes on insecticides for public health use, which had been 42%, were eliminated completely. Using a combination of actual cost data provided by colleagues in Nigeria and inferred costs based on known retail prices and margins, we estimate that the reduction in tariffs and taxes on netting materials and insecticides would lead to an 18% decline in retail prices, from US$ 5.61 to US$ 4.61 per ITN (Table 5). At a price elasticity of demand of −0.5 there would be a 9% increase in retail purchases. If, on the other hand, the price elasticity of demand were −1.5, retail purchases would rise by 27%...

We conclude that the elimination of tariffs and taxes should lead to some reduction in retail prices and that the price changes should induce a modest increase in ITN purchases in developing countries in the short run. However, the percentage increase in demand is likely to be comparatively smaller than the percentage of tariffs and taxes removed...

The policy change discussed in this paper has implications for public finance as well as for public health. Removing or reducing tariffs and taxes decreases government revenues. Eliminating a 25% tariff on a US$ 5.00 imported net, for example, costs the government in question US$ 1.25 in tax revenues for each net imported. However, this loss may be offset directly by a reduction in the cost of malaria case management at public health facilities resulting from ITN use, and indirectly by the higher tax revenues paid by healthier, more productive citizens (26). A country considering such a policy change should evaluate the public finance trade-off involved.

Note that although the reduction of tariffs and taxes can contribute to the expansion of ITN use, it is clear from the Nigerian example that barriers to ITN use are varied. As we learned in the previous chapter, price is just one determinant of demand. Other factors that are likely to influence the short term response of households to lower prices for ITNs include cultural beliefs, time of year, travel time to suppliers and so on.

Table 4.3 Example of models 1 and 2 showing the effect of tariff and tax policy reform on ITN purchases in Nigeria

Retail price for an ITN (US$)		
Costs per ITN	Old rate	New rate
Supply price per ITN (net + treatment kit packaged together)	4.74	3.74
Domestic shipping cost	0.10	0.10
Distributor's mark-up	0.24	0.24
Wholesaler's mark-up	0.25	0.25
Retailer's mark-up	0.27	0.27
Retail price	**5.61**	**4.61**
Results		
Change in retail price attributable to tariff and tax reform	−17.9%	
Change in retail purchases attributable to tariff and tax reform if E = −0.5[c]	8.9%	
Change in retail purchases attributable to tariff and tax reform if E = −1.5	26.9%	

[a] Cost, insurance, freight.
[b] Value-added tax.
[c] E = price elasticity of demand.
Source: Adapted from Table 5 in Simon et al. (2002)

Summary

In this chapter you have learned what is meant by price elasticity of demand (PED) and how to calculate it. You also learned about the relationship between elasticity and total revenue and the factors that influence elasticity of demand – closeness of substitutes, the price of complements and the proportion of income spent on the good. Finally, you looked at some practical applications of the concept of elasticity and its usefulness in decision-making.

References

Asian Development Bank (2000) *A Handbook for the economic analysis of health sector projects*. Manila: Asian Development Bank.
Borren P and Sutton M (1992) Are increases in cigarette taxation regressive? *Health Economics* 1:245–53.
Gertler P and Molyneaux J (1996) *Financing public health sector expenditures through user fees: theory and evidence from an explicit social experiment in Indonesia*. Santa Monica: RAND.
Parkin M, Powell M and Mathews K (2008) *Economics* (7th edn). Harlow: Addison-Wesley.
Simon JL, Larson BA, Zusman A and Rosen A. (2002) How will the reduction of tariffs and taxes on insecticide-treated bednets affect household purchases? *Bulletin of the World Health Organization* 80(11):892–9.

Further reading

Borren P and Sutton M (1992) Are increases in cigarette taxation regressive? *Health Economics* 1:245–53.
Donaldson C *et al.* (2005) *Economics of health care financing: the visible hand.* Basingstoke: Palgrave Macmillan: 98–02.
Parkin M, Powell M and Mathews K (2008) *Economics* (7th edn). Harlow: Addison-Wesley: 81–7.
Simon JL, Larson BA, Zusman A and Rosen A (2002) How will the reduction of tariffs and taxes on insecticide-treated bednets affect household purchases? *Bulletin of the World Health Organization* 80(11):892–9.

Supply: production in the long and short run

Lorna Guinness (ed.)

Overview

You have now learned about the economic theory of demand and the demand for health care. In this and the next chapter you will go on to learn about the economic theory of supply and applying that theory to the supply of health care. This chapter focuses on the constraints which producers are under and the relationship between inputs and outputs. You will then use this theory to look at issues of scale in primary health care provision.

Learning objectives

After working through this chapter, you will be able to:

- define the term 'quantity supplied'
- explain when it might be better to substitute between production inputs
- define efficient and inefficient production

Key terms

Diminishing returns to scale. A situation when a proportionate increase in all inputs yields a less than proportionate increase in output.

Fixed input. An input to production that does not vary in the short run. The time for which at least one input cannot be changed actually defines the short run.

Long run. A decision-making time frame over which quantities of *all* inputs to production can be varied.

Output. The good or service that is the result of the production process (in the case of health services, the service that is delivered).

Outcome. A change in health status as a result of the system processes (in the health services context, the change in health status as a result of care).

Production function. The functional relationship that indicates how inputs are transformed into outputs in the most efficient way.

Production possibilities frontier. The boundary between the combinations of goods that can be produced and those that cannot with the resources available.

Returns to a factor. This measures the addition to output as one factor to production is increased.

Returns to scale. This measures the addition to output as the scale of operations increases in the long run so that all inputs can be varied.

Short run. A decision-making time frame within which at least one input (the fixed input – see above) cannot be varied.

Technical (operational) efficiency. A point at which a producer cannot produce more output without using more of at least one input.

Variable input. An input to production that varies directly with the level of output.

Supply analysis

The analysis of supply examines the behaviour of firms (or producers) ranging from large corporations to the sole provider in either the public or private sectors. Supply is the willingness and ability to sell a good at each and every price over a given period of time. It depends on a number of factors influencing the relationship between inputs and outputs (the production function) and cost of producing those outputs.

The production possibilities frontier

Outputs are defined as the goods produced in a production process. Whereas the ultimate goal of health care might be good health, this is difficult to define and measure. The mix of *outputs* and *outcomes* expected from health care means the relationship between inputs and outcome is complex. Traditionally, intermediate outputs have been used to explore production and supply in health care (e.g. vaccinations carried out, hips replaced or kidney transplants performed). Although these measures do not provide health outcomes, nor can they capture outputs such as support provided by the medical staff, they are still important in helping understand the issue of efficiency in relation to the provision of health services.

In Chapter 1 you learned about the fundamental economic concepts of choice, opportunity cost and scarcity. These concepts are important in decisions about allocation of resources and when producers or health care providers are making decisions about supply. The production possibilities frontier (PPF) is a tool that economists use to illustrate the different combinations of outputs that are achievable with a limited set of resources.

Consider a clinic that provides ambulatory care for patients with tuberculosis (TB) or angina. Let's suppose that:

- the only input is nurse time;
- TB and angina consultations are of the same duration;
- given current staffing the maximum number of consultations per day is 200.

Figure 5.1 shows what the PPF might look like for our clinic. In this example, a straight line represents the PPF – we can produce a maximum of 200 consultations per day regardless of how we prioritize the two conditions. The straight line relationship implies that transferring a nurse from one disease to another has no impact on the overall number of consultations. At the extremes, the graph shows that either 200 TB cases can be cared for, or 200 cases of angina.

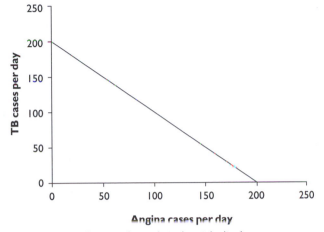

Figure 5.1 Production possibilities frontier for a clinic (straight line)

Suppose instead that some nurses have skills that mean they are better at TB consultations (they can achieve more with a given amount of time) and others are better at treating angina. In these circumstances transferring a nurse who is a specialist in angina treatment from TB to angina could actually increase output. The PPF in this case is illustrated in Figure 5.2. The frontier is now concave to the origin, rather than straight. It is the form that we typically expect PPFs to take, as long as it is the case that resources are not equally productive in all activities. As we gradually increase a

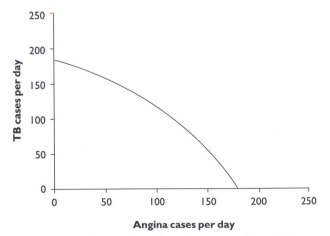

Figure 5.2 Production possibilities frontier for a clinic (concave to the origin)

particular output level, with each additional increment we have to use resources that are less and less suitable (less productive). In terms of Figure 5.2, this means that if nurses are allocated to their specialities they would be able to produce more than 200 consultations. For example, at around 100 angina consultations, 120 TB consultations could be produced, giving 220 consultations per day. However, putting all nurses on TB means some of the angina nurses would not be as efficient in producing TB consultations and would therefore produce fewer consultations in a day. This leads to less than 200 consultations per day.

Figure 5.3 shows a PPF for a hypothetical economy. The graph shows the production of health care relative to everything else in the economy. Technical efficiency (where, as you read in Chapter 1, a given output is produced with the least inputs) requires that we are at a point where we cannot increase one output without reducing another – hence the PPF represents technically efficient points by definition. As in Figure 5.2, every point on the PPF in Figure 5.3 represents a technically efficient level of production. Rather than showing the trade-off between TB and angina consultations, as in Figure 5.2, Figure 5.3 looks at the trade-off between producing health care versus everything else in the economy (i.e. the opportunity cost of health care). So, in terms of Figure 5.3, the opportunity cost of increasing health care from 0 to 500 units is the benefit from the 600 units (3,600 – 3,000) of other commodities (food, education, transport) that we have to go without in order to achieve it. Notice from Figure 5.3 that as we continue to increase the amount of health care, the opportunity cost of each 500-unit increase becomes greater and greater.

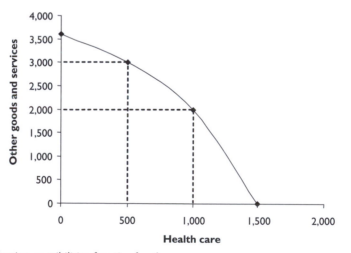

Figure 5.3 Production possibilities frontier for the economy

Activity 5.1

To extend your understanding of the concepts just described, try the following questions:

1 Which of the points in Figure 5.4 (A, B, C and D) are:
   a) Technically efficient?
   b) Technically inefficient?
   c) Not feasible?

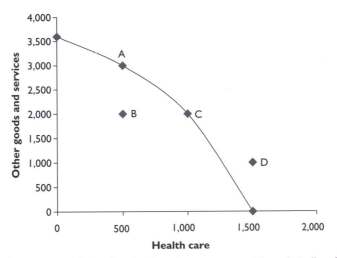

Figure 5.4 A production possibilities frontier for the economy with technically efficient, technically inefficient and not feasible points of production

2 What is the opportunity cost of increasing health care from 500 to 1,000 units?
a) Starting from point A?
b) Starting from point B? (This is not such an easy question!)
3 Show on Figure 5.4, other things remaining the same, what you think would happen to the PPF if:
a) there is a decrease in the size of the population or
b) there is an improvement in health technology.

Feedback

1 a) Points A and C are technically efficient as they lie exactly on the PPF so that you cannot increase one output without reducing other outputs.
b) Point B is technically inefficient as it lies within the PPF. This means there is excess capacity. If the health care output was increased, there does not need to be a reduction in the output of other goods and services.
c) Point D is not feasible given current technology – it lies outside the PPF.
2 The opportunity cost of an increase in health care of 500 units from point A is the benefit associated with the 1,000 units of other commodities that have to be given up to achieve it. If there is a move from point B to point C the cost is effectively zero since the production of other commodities does not need to be reduced. However, the opportunity cost is in fact still 1,000 units of other commodities. This is because, by moving from B to C, the society misses out on the benefits that they could have gained by moving from B to A instead (assuming that point A is the best alternative to point C).
3 Labour is a vital input in the production of all commodities, especially health. A fall in population size will result in a reduction in the amount of production that is feasible. Hence the PPF shifts towards the origin (PPF2 in Figure 5.5). An improvement in health technology, by definition means that more can be produced with a given set of resources. Hence this would shift the PPF outwards (PPF3 in Figure 5.5). Note that as the technology improvement applies only to health care, the maximum level of non-health production does not change so that PPF3 crosses the y axis at the same point as PPF1.

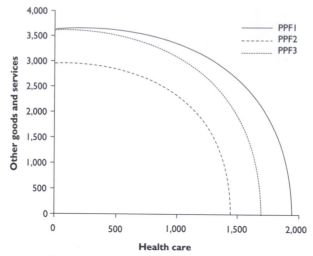

Figure 5.5 Production possibilities frontier for the economy – shifts of the PPF

The important implications of this analysis are:

- If a system is technically inefficient then it is possible to produce more commodities and therefore more welfare with current resources.
- If a system is already operating at a technically efficient level, then to increase the quantity produced of one commodity you have to reduce the quantity produced of some other commodity. There is a trade-off, an opportunity cost.
- The only other way that more of every product can be produced is if there is technological improvement such that more output can be produced with the same amount of resources or if there is an increase in the amount of resources available (such as an increase in population size).

Now let's look at the production process in health care in more detail. You will look at this over two different decision-making time frames, distinguished by the variability of inputs to production. In the *long run*, all inputs to production can be varied. In the *short run* there are limits to this as some inputs are fixed. Examples of *fixed inputs* include investments such as hospital buildings or X-ray machines. These fixed inputs do not vary with the level of output. *Variable inputs*, in contrast, vary with the level of output (e.g. X-ray film, syringes and needles, personnel time). In the short run, it is only these variable inputs that can be altered.

Production in the short run

Suppose you are the manager of a community nursing service in a rural area. You carry out a survey to find out how output varies according to the number of nurses hired. With this you calculate the output associated with each nursing level and plot it in a graph (Figure 5.6). This graph, plotting inputs against outputs, is known as the *production function*.

Nurses are not the only input in this production function. As a manager you also have two cross-country vehicles at your disposal. At the end of the year, the Ministry of Health may provide more vehicles or else it may reallocate the ones you have already.

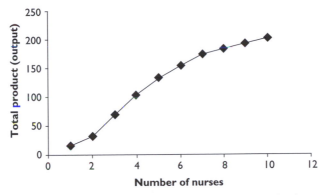

Figure 5.6 A production function for the community nursing service (problem)

For now you can only influence the number of patients treated by varying the amount of nurse time. Hence, vehicles represent a fixed cost and nurses a variable cost. Table 5.1 shows the full short-run production function of your service. It shows the total product (in terms of patient contacts per day – column 2) achievable with two vehicles (total fixed cost – column 5) for different numbers of nurses (column 1). It also shows the marginal product (column 3), that is, the extra output achieved for each additional input (i.e. each additional nurse).

Table 5.1 Short-run production function for community nursing service

Number of nurses	Total product	Marginal product	Total variable cost	Total fixed cost (i.e. vehicle cost)	Total cost	Average (total) cost
1	15	15	30	50	80	5.33
2	30	15	60	50	110	3.67
3	70	40	90	50	140	2
4	100	30	120	50	170	1.7
5	130	30	150	50	200	1.54
6	150					
7	170					
8	180					
9	190					
10	200					

Activity 5.2

1 Complete the marginal product column of Table 5.1. This has been started for you. Are there diminishing returns associated with increasing the number of nurses (i.e. does the marginal number of patient contacts per day for each nurse decrease as the number of nurses increases)? What might explain this relationship?

2 Suppose that a nurse is paid £30 per day and vehicles cost £25 per vehicle per day and assume that there are no other costs. Calculate the total variable cost (number of nurses × cost per nurse), total fixed cost (number of vehicles × cost per vehicle) and the total cost (total variable cost + total fixed cost) columns in the table. These calculations have also been started for you.

3 Finish calculating average total cost (total cost/total product). Plot average cost against total product in Figure 5.7.

4 Explain the shape of the short-run average cost curve.

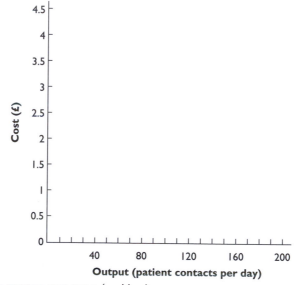

Figure 5.7 Short-run average cost curve (problem)

Feedback

1 Marginal product is the total product associated with x number of nurses minus the total product with one less nurse. For the third nurse this is $70 - 30 = 40$. The rest are shown in Table 5.2.

Marginal product starts at 15, increases to 40 and then decreases gradually down to 10 extra visits per day. From this you can say that there are increasing marginal returns as the number of nurses increases up to three. With an increase in the number of nurses beyond three there are diminishing marginal returns thereafter. This tells us about the productivity of each extra nurse employed in terms of patient contacts per day, but it does not say anything about the number of nurses that should be employed. This depends on the relationship between average and marginal product as well as other factors including cost. The increasing returns might be explained by specialization of the nurses. Perhaps, with three nurses, each can visit a separate village or perhaps each nurse can specialize in a particular disease area. The decreasing returns might be explained by geographical spread. Each time an extra nurse is added they have to travel further and further away to treat more patients. They have to spend more time travelling and have less time to meet patients. Hence the marginal product diminishes.

Table 5.2 Short-run production function for the community nursing service (solution)

Number of nurses	Total product	Marginal product	Total variable cost	Total fixed cost (i.e. vehicle cost)	Total cost	Average (total) cost
1	15	15	30	50	80	5.33
2	30	15	60	50	110	3.67
3	70	40	90	50	140	2
4	100	30	120	50	170	1.7
5	130	30	150	50	200	1.54
6	150	20	180	50	230	1.53
7	170	20	210	50	260	1.53
8	180	10	240	50	290	1.61
9	190	10	270	50	320	1.68
10	200	10	300	50	350	1.75

2 The variable cost is the number of nurses multiplied by £30. For two nurses this is 2 × £30 = £60. The fixed cost is the number of vehicles, 2 × £25 = £50. Total cost is fixed cost + variable cost. For two nurses total cost is £60 + £50 = £110. The rest of the costs are shown in Table 5.2.

3 Average cost is total cost divided by total product. For two nurses the average cost is £110 ÷ 30 = £3.67. The other results are shown in Table 5.2 and the curve is plotted in Figure 5.8.

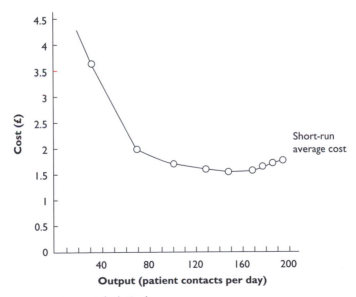

Figure 5.8 Short-run average cost (solution)

4 The short-term average cost curve is U-shaped (it falls at first, then gradually levels out before beginning to rise). The falling average costs at the start of the curve are explained by two factors:

- increasing returns to nurses (this implies decreasing average variable costs as output rises);
- the spreading of fixed costs over a larger output – for example, average fixed costs are £1.67 when output is 30, but only £0.50 when output is 100.

Average fixed costs are continually diminishing as output rises. However, the increasing returns to nurses eventually give way to diminishing returns. This implies increasing average variable costs. Eventually the increase in variable cost exceeds the decrease in average fixed cost and at this point the average cost curve starts rising.

Production in the long run

You will now consider production in the long run. Imagine it is the end of the financial year. As the manager of the community nursing service you are required to assess your potential for increasing total product. This is so that the Ministry can make an assessment of capital requirements for the forthcoming year. Together with your nursing staff you estimate your potential production to be as shown in Table 5.3.

Table 5.3 Total product (patient contacts per day) (problem)

Vehicles	Nurses									
	1	2	3	4	5	6	7	8	9	10
0	5	10	15	20	22	24	26	28	29	30
1	15	20	25	30	35	45	60	75	90	100
2	15	30	70	100	130	150	170	180	190	200
3	15	30	100	150	180	200	200	200	200	200
4	15	30	100	180	195	200	200	200	200	200
5	15	30	100	180	200	200	200	200	200	200

The table shows the maximum output achievable for a given combination of inputs. You will see, for example, that the third row (two vehicles) shows the same information as the second column in Table 5.1. Your concern is to ensure the service is *technically efficient* which means that no input can be decreased without also decreasing output.

Activity 5.3

Shade the items in Table 5.3 that are technically inefficient.

Feedback

There are several combinations of vehicles and nurses that are technically inefficient. For example, seven nurses and three vehicles is technically inefficient because you can decrease the number of nurses to six and still have a total product of 200 contacts per day. Similarly, the combination of six nurses and four vehicles is technically inefficient because you can decrease the number of vehicles to three and still have a total product of 200 contacts per day. The technically inefficient combinations are shaded in Table 5.4.

Table 5.4 Total product (patient contacts per day) (solution)

Vehicles	Nurses									
	1	2	3	4	5	6	7	8	9	10
0	5	10	15	20	22	24	26	28	29	30
1	15	20	25	30	35	45	60	75	90	100
2	15	30	70	100	130	150	170	180	190	200
3	15	30	100	150	180	200	200	200	200	200
4	15	30	100	180	195	200	200	200	200	200
5	15	30	100	180	200	200	200	200	200	200

Another concern you will have as a manager is what output you gain for each successive increase in input. Is the impact (or return) constant or does it vary with the overall size of the service?

Returns to a factor indicates the addition to output by increasing only *one factor*. *Returns to scale*, on the other hand, indicates the addition to output attained by increasing *all factors* by the same proportion. People talk about returns to a factor in the short term because at least one factor is fixed. Returns to scale is a long-run phenomenon because only in the long term can all factors be increased proportionally.

Increasing returns to scale are explained in the same way as increasing returns to a factor – by improved division of labour and increased specialization. In the long term there is less constraint on specialization because the quantity of all factors is variable. Hence there may be increasing returns to scale over ranges where there were decreasing returns to a factor.

Decreasing returns to scale are usually explained by the difficulties involved with managing and coordinating all the decisions that need to be made to run a large organization.

Activity 5.4

Table 5.5 compares the total product associated with one vehicle and one nurse with that for two vehicles and two nurses and so on. Are there constant returns to scale? What might explain the pattern you observe?

Table 5.5 Returns to scale

Input combinations	Total product	Extra product
1, 1	15	15
2, 2	30	15
3, 3	100	70
4, 4	180	80
5, 5	200	20

Feedback

The output added by one nurse and one vehicle is 15 visits (see Table 5.5). If you add another nurse and another vehicle then you get 15 more visits. Over this range you can say that there are constant returns to scale. As you add another nurse and another vehicle you get an additional 70 visits. The increase in output is more than proportionate to the increase in inputs. This means there are increasing returns to scale. If you do so again you get even more (80 visits), but afterwards the extra product from one nurse and one vehicle is only 20 visits. Therefore there are decreasing returns to scale. This may be explained by the geographical spread of the population and the fact that the population and therefore output is limited.

Advanced reading box: Input substitution and isoquants
As you have seen, the production possibilities frontier can be used to identify efficient allocation between outputs. But how can firms choose among the most efficient combination of inputs? Firms (health care providers) have a number of options from which to choose the combination of inputs that maximizes output. In theory, when making these decisions they consider the marginal product of each input (i.e. the change in output for each unit increase in input). The relationship between the marginal products for different inputs can be shown using an *isoquant*. Each isoquant represents the same level of output produced through different combinations of inputs.

Let's say we are looking at changing the doctor:nurse ratios in a clinic for delivering day surgery. Point A in Figure 5.9 shows current practice with two nurses and one doctor. An alternative way to achieve the same level of output would be at point B with three doctors and one nurse. Because of diminishing marginal product of each input the isoquants are convex: as you move from left to right the quantity of doctors used increases (and quantity of nurses decreases) and each additional doctor (unit of input) results in a smaller increase in total output.

The slope of an isoquant is called the *marginal rate of technical substitution* (MRTS) and tells us the rate at which one input can be given for another while maintaining the same output. It is equal to the marginal product of nurses ÷ the marginal product of doctors. For example, if four nurses and two doctors produce the same output as two nurses and three doctors then the marginal product from one doctor is two nurses. Thus the MRTS is 2 (along this part of the isoquant, the output from one doctor is twice that of one nurse). You will read more about the application of isoquants in the advanced reading box in chapter 6.

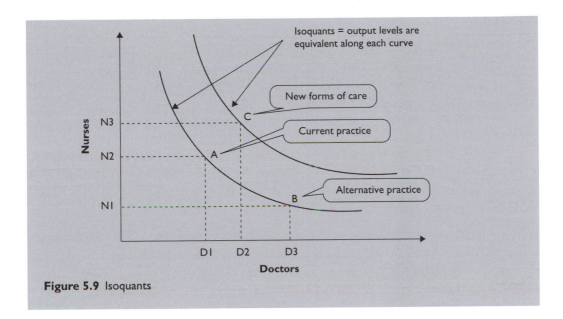

Figure 5.9 Isoquants

Activity 5.5

Now look at the graph in Figure 5.10 taken from Wensing *et al.* (2006). Inputs (GP hours per patient) are plotted against practice size (number of patients registered). What does the graph tell us about returns to scale of GP practices?

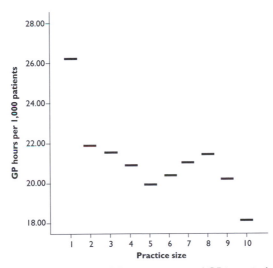

Figure 5.10 The relationship between GP practice size and GP input in 1,188 practices in the Netherlands
Practice sizes (number of patients registered): Class 1: 1,400–2,292; Class 2: 2,300–2,480; Class 3: 2,500–2,630; Class 4: 2,635–2,740; Class 5: 2,750–2,899; Class 6: 2,990–3,170; Class 7: 3,200–4,169; Class 8: 4,200–5,340; Class 9: 5,400–7,200; Class 10: 7,206–15,365.
Source: Wensing *et al.* (2006)

Feedback

Wensing reports that physician workload per 1,000 patients differs across levels of practice size. In class 1 (smallest practices), physicians worked on average 26.2 hours per 1,000 patients and in class 10 (largest practices) physicians worked on average 18.1 hours. As practice size increases from class 1 to class 5, there are increasing returns to the factor of GP time. Up to GP practice size 8, there is a suggestion of a U-shaped curve indicating decreasing returns to the factor beyond size 5, however the average physician input is lowest in the largest practice size 10.

The figure implies that practice size has an important effect on the technical efficiency of GP practices. Although there may be some other factors affecting efficiency, such as scope of services provided, bigger GP practices appear to be more efficient than smaller ones in this setting.

Summary

This chapter has presented the key tools that economists use for understanding the production process. You learned how the production function describes the relationship between inputs and output (or product) and the nature of this relationship. You went on to learn about marginal outputs and returns to scale. In the short run, returns to scale are because of increasing returns to factor (due to increased specialization) and the spreading of fixed costs. In the long run they are due to increasing returns to scale (due to increased specialization). As these relationships shed light on the efficiency of different production processes or services, these concepts are critical in decisions about the introduction of new technological processes, scale of activity and allocation of human resources.

Reference

Wensing, MP et al. (2006) Physician workload in primary care: what is the optimal size of practices? A cross-sectional study. Health Policy 77:260–7.

Further reading

Adang E and Wensing M (2008) Economic barriers to implementation of innovations in health care: is the long run–short run efficiency discrepancy a paradox? Health Policy 88:236–42.
Folland S. et al. (eds) (2010) The economics of health and health care. Harlow: Pearson, Chapter 6.
Morris S et al. (2007) Economic analysis in health care. Chichester: Wiley, Chapter 3.

Supply: costs, economies of scale and the supply curve

Lorna Guinness

Overview

In the previous chapter you began to explore the theory behind supply and the supply curve. Until now you have been looking at the production function. You may well be asking, 'How do costs fit into this?' This chapter looks at the relationship between output and cost. You will then use this theory to discuss the advantages and disadvantages of large-scale production of health care and, finally, to construct a supply curve.

Learning objectives

After working through this chapter, you will be able to:

- estimate and graph simple cost functions
- describe the relationship between scale of production and cost
- diagnose economies and diseconomies of scale
- discuss the advantages and disadvantage of large-scale health services
- describe how supply curves are derived
- list the factors which influence the supply of a good

Key terms

Economic (productive) efficiency. A situation in which a producer cannot produce more without increasing cost.

Economic profit. Total revenue minus total cost and distinct from normal profit.

Economies of scale. The conditions under which long-run average cost decreases as output increases.

Fixed cost. A cost of production that does not vary with the level of output.

Normal profit. The return a firm receives from inputs such as a director's role in organizing and running the business. This is part of the firm's opportunity cost.

Producer surplus. The difference between the amount that a producer receives from the sale of a good and the lowest amount that producer is willing to accept for that good.

> **Scale efficiency.** A situation where the provider is producing at an output level such that average cost is minimized.
>
> **Variable cost.** A cost of production that varies directly with the level of output.

Cost functions

Let's start your study of costs by looking at the cost function. Cost functions show the relationship between total costs and output. In the short run, *fixed costs* remain constant and are incurred even when output is zero. *Variable costs* increase with the level of output. Think about the emergency department of a hospital over a 24-hour period. The output (patients seen) varies considerably and at certain points there may be no patients at all (output is zero). Costs such as personnel, beds and other furnishings, equipment and even insurance do not change. These are the fixed costs and are still incurred at the same level whether output is zero or at its peak. On the other hand, costs associated with each patient such as the cost of needles and syringes, dressings and medication vary with the level of patient numbers. These are the variable costs. Total costs are the sum of the fixed and variable costs. The relationship between total, fixed and variable costs is shown in Figure 6.1.

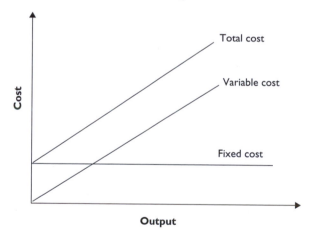

Figure 6.1 Short-run total, fixed and variable cost functions

Now we will continue with your analysis from Chapter 5 of the long-term options for the community nursing service.

Activity 6.1

1 In Table 6.1 finish filling in the total cost associated with each input combination using the factor prices mentioned in Activity 5.2 – ignoring the operationally inefficient combinations. Also calculate the average cost for each combination and enter it between the parentheses.

2 What is the lowest cost for the following output levels: 20, 30, 100, 180, 200?

Table 6.1 Total cost (average cost) in £ per day

Vehicles	Nurses									
	1	2	3	4	5	6	7	8	9	10
0	30	60	90	120	150	180	210			300
	(6)	(6)	(6)	(6)	(6.82)	(7.5)	(8.08)	( )	( )	(10)
1	55	85	115	145	175	205	235			325
	(3.67)	(4.25)	(4.6)	(4.83)	(5)	(4.56)	(3.92)	( )	( )	(3.25)
2		110	140	170	200	230	260	290	320	350
		(3.67)	(2)	(1.7)	(1.54)	(1.53)	(1.53)	(1.61)	(1.68)	(1.75)
3			165	195	225	255				
			(1.65)	(1.3)	(1.25)	(1.28)				
4				220	250					
				(1.22)	(1.28)					
5					275					
					(1.38)					

Feedback

1 Total cost is equal to the number of nurses multiplied by £30 plus the number of vehicles multiplied by £25. For two nurses and two vehicles that is (2 × 30) + (2 × 25) = £110. Average cost is total cost divided by output (output is given in Table 5.3). For two nurses and two vehicles this is 110 ÷ 30 = £3.67. The full set of total and average costs is shown in Table 6.2.

Table 6.2 Total cost (average cost) in £ per day (solution)

Vehicles	Nurses									
	1	2	3	4	5	6	7	8	9	10
0	30	60	90	120	150	180	210	240	270	300
	(6)	(6)	(6)	(6)	(6.82)	(7.5)	(8.18)	(8.57)	(9.31)	(10)
1	55	85	115	145	175	205	235	265	295	325
	(3.67)	(4.25)	(4.6)	(4.83)	(5)	(4.56)	(3.92)	(3.53)	(3.28)	(3.25)
2		110	140	170	200	230	260	290	320	350
		(3.67)	(2)	(1.7)	(1.54)	(1.53)	(1.53)	(1.61)	(1.68)	(1.75)
3			165	195	225	255				
			(1.65)	(1.3)	(1.25)	(1.28)				
4				220	250					
				(1.22)	(1.28)					
5					275					
					(1.38)					

2 There are three input combinations that give an output of 30: 2N2V, 4N1V and 10N. These have costs of £110, £145 and £300 respectively. Therefore the lowest cost method of producing 30 visits is two nurses and two vehicles. The other minimum cost points are given in Table 6.3. Every point in this table is *economically efficient* because

at these points output cannot be increased without incurring extra cost. Or, put another way, they are situations where cost cannot be reduced without reducing the total product.

Table 6.3 Long-run costs

Total product	Input combination	Total cost (£)	Average cost (£)
20	2 nurses, 1 vehicle	85	4.25
30	2 nurses, 2 vehicles	110	3.67
100	3 nurses, 3 vehicles	165	1.65
180	4 nurses, 4 vehicles	220	1.22
200	6 nurses, 3 vehicles	255	1.28

Another concern you will have as a manager is how the average cost of a nurse visit varies with the size of the service. In other words, are there *economies* (or *diseconomies*) *of scale*? Generally, economies of scale (i.e. average costs falling as output increases) are explained by three factors:

• increasing returns to scale (which you learned about in Chapter 5);
• falling factor prices with increased scale (usually associated with ability to bulk buy);
• spreading of fixed costs over a larger output.

Likewise, diseconomies of scale (i.e. increasing average costs with respect to output) are explained by:

• decreasing returns to scale;
• increasing factor prices with increased scale (this may result from a scarcity of a factor to production, for example recruiting doctors to work in isolated areas often requires an increased financial incentive).

Table 6.4 summarises the relationship between cost and output in the long run compared to the short run. Figure 6.2 also shows this relationship, however, in this case, factor prices are assumed to be stable and the relationship between cost and output is caused by returns to scale alone.

Table 6.4 Causes of trends in average cost with respect to total product

	Short run	Long run
Average cost falls as output rises (economies of scale)	1. Increasing returns to *factor* (i.e. specialization)	1 Increasing returns to *scale* (i.e. specialization)
	2. Spreading of fixed costs	2 Decreasing factor prices
		3 Spreading of fixed costs
Average cost rises as output rises (diseconomies of scale)	1. Decreasing returns to *factor*	1 Decreasing returns to *scale* (i.e. bureaucracy)
		2 Increasing factor prices

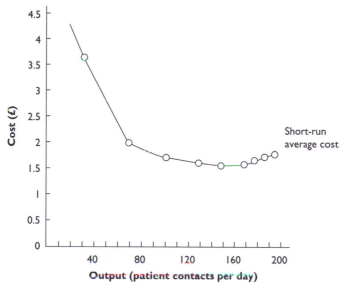

Figure 6.2 Short-run average cost

Activity 6.2

1 For which input/output combination in Table 6.3 are average costs at their lowest?
2 In Figure 6.2, plot the long-run average cost curve from Activity 5.2 alongside the short-term curve. Does it display economies of scale? Why?
3 Consider what would happen if factor prices, such as the price of vehicles or of nurses, were to change.

Feedback

1 The output level with the lowest average cost (from Table 6.3) is 180 visits per day using four vehicles and four nurses. This is described as *scale-efficient* because at this output level the cost per visit is minimized. Therefore the size of the operation is optimal.
2 Figure 6.3 shows the long-run average cost plotted next to the short-run average cost curve that was plotted in Activity 5.2. The long-run curve has the same shape as the short-run curve – U-shaped. At higher levels of output the long-run cost curve is below the short-run curve. This is because the use of two vehicles is an inefficient technique for producing this level of output. The U-shaped long-run cost curve implies economies of scale initially followed by diseconomies of scale for higher levels of output.
3 If the vehicle costs were higher, say £35 per day, then all input combinations with one or more vehicles would be more costly. The greater the number of vehicles the more would be the additional cost. A rise in the cost of vehicles, if the rise is large enough, will cause a cost-efficient provider to substitute from vehicles to nurses. For example, Table 6.5 shows the cost of producing 180 visits a day using different input

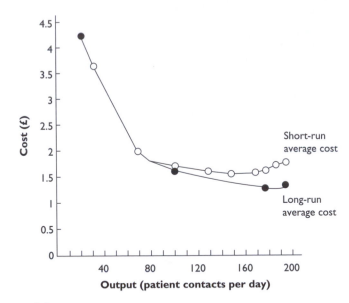

Figure 6.3 Long-run and short-run average cost

Table 6.5 Total cost of 180 visits

Input combination	Cost if vehicle price is £25	Cost if vehicle price is £35
4 nurses, 4 vehicles	220	260
5 nurses, 3 vehicles	225	255
10 nurses	300	300

combinations. It shows the effect of an increase in the price of vehicles from £25 to £35. At £25, four nurses and four vehicles will be the least-cost method of producing 180 visits. However, at £35 five nurses and three vehicles will be the least-cost method of producing 180 visits. Hence the increase in vehicle price causes a substitution from vehicles to nurses. The change from £25 to £35 shifts the long-run average cost curve upwards. The substitution means that costs do not increase as much as they would have if the input levels had remained unchanged.

A rise in the price of *nurses*, on the other hand, will cause a cost-efficient provider to substitute nurses with vehicles. A country where the price of labour is high relative to the price of capital is likely to have more capital-intensive production. A country where the price of labour is low relative to the price of capital is likely to have more labour-intensive production.

What do you think are the implications of the above cost analysis for community nursing service resource allocation? You can look at this question from two perspectives: first, the perspective of the producer (or provider), and second, the perspective of the service as a whole.

As far as the producer goes, the analysis does not tell us very much about the appropriate output level, although it does tell us which input combinations are *economically efficient* for each output level – i.e. where the producer is not able to produce more without increasing cost. The actual output level has to depend on the budget as well as the cost. If the budget of the community nursing service is £110 a day then they will be able to make 30 visits a day – see Table 6.3. Alternatively, if the budget is £275 a day then they will be able to produce 200 patient visits each day.

Advanced reading box: Isocost lines and efficiency

To identify the least cost method of production, information about the marginal product and marginal rate of substitution needs to be combined with information regarding the costs of the different inputs. An isocost line shows the different combinations of inputs that can be obtained for a given cost. In Figure 6.4 the point A (current practice) lies on the isocost line XY; let's say this represents a cost of £1,000. All combinations of inputs along this line will result in the same total cost of £1,000. There is another isocost line VW representing all combinations of inputs with a total cost of £1,500. The slope of the isocost line is dependent on the relative prices of each input. Therefore if the price of one input changes relative to another the slope of the isocost line will change. For example, if the wages for doctors then falls, the isocost line XY would become less steep (XZ); similarly if the wages for nurses falls then the isocost line will become more steep.

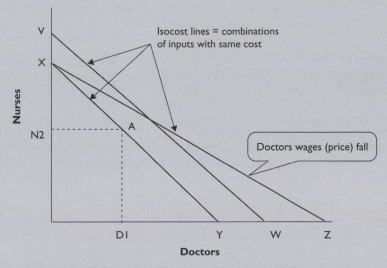

Figure 6.4 Isocost lines

The least cost technique is the combination of inputs that minimizes the total cost of producing a certain output. This will occur where the isocost curve is at a tangent to the isoquant curve. If production occurs at any other point on the isoquant the total cost will be higher (e.g. at points B and C in Figure 6.5 output levels are equal to those at point A but the total cost will be higher than at point A. Point A lies on the isocost line XY (£1,000) whereas points B and C lie on the isocost line VW (£1,500).

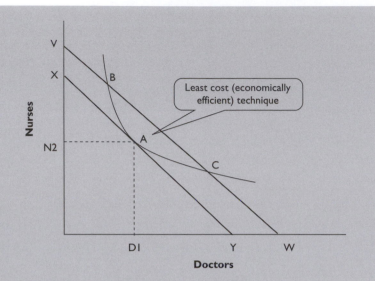

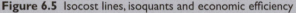

Figure 6.5 Isocost lines, isoquants and economic efficiency

The isoquant and isocost lines provide us with another way of looking at efficiency. Technical efficiency has already been defined as when no input can be decreased without also decreasing output. This is also a point on an isoquant. The point at which there is tangency between the isoquant and isocost (i.e. where their slopes are equal) is known as a point of economic efficiency – i.e. a producer is not able to produce more without increasing cost. It is the minimum cost of producing a given output or the maximum output for an attainable budget.

Diagnosing economies of scale

Economists use cost functions to explore the relationship between costs and outputs – i.e. the efficiency of health services – and understand better what might influence this relationship. They estimate cost functions by applying a combination of statistical analysis and economic theory to health service data, known as *econometric analysis* (Guinness *et al.* 2007). This type of analysis is important in diagnosing economies of scale.

You have learned about average cost curves (Figure 6.3) and the point of *scale efficiency* where average cost is minimized. Similarly you can plot a marginal cost curve. A marginal cost curve always intersects the average cost curve at its minimum. An example is shown in Figure 6.6. If the marginal cost is lower than average cost, then average cost must be falling (i.e. there are economies of scale). Conversely, if marginal cost is greater than average cost then average cost must be rising (i.e. there are diseconomies of scale). If you add one unit of output and the cost of this extra unit is more than the average cost of all the other units, then of course it must increase the average cost. Conversely, if you add one unit of output and the cost of this extra unit is less than the average cost of all the other units then it must pull down the average cost.

The implication of all this is that by using a cost function, marginal cost can be estimated for different output levels. Comparing these estimates of marginal costs with

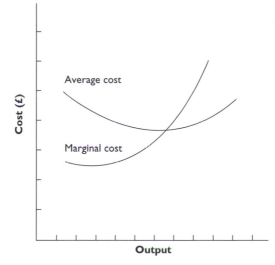

Figure 6.6 Marginal and average cost

average cost estimates from the same data set allows the diagnosis of economies or diseconomies of scale.

Activity 6.3

Now, let's continue with the analysis of community nursing services. Suppose you are the regional director of community nursing services. You have 50 nursing centres spread across the region and each one has produced a cost analysis for the end of year financial report. You have to decide whether to redistribute vehicles between the different units. You also have the power to create additional units or merge current units. The situation at present is that every patient who needs treatment is being treated – if a patient is not being visited by one unit then they are being visited by a neighbouring unit instead. This amounts to 5,000 patient visits per day. However, the government is cutting the budget and therefore cost savings are imperative. You want to cut costs without rationing care.

There are two possibilities for making the cost savings:

* encourage providers to be efficient by reviewing their choice of inputs and substituting between factors where necessary;
* change the scale of provider units in order to exploit economies of scale.

You carry out the first strategy but you still need to make more cost savings, so now you have to carry out the second strategy. Suppose that every provider has the cost function outlined in Table 6.3 and each is producing 100 visits at least cost. You can work out how much cost can be saved by changing the scale of providers as follows.

There is a demand of 5,000 patient visits a day across the region being produced at a total cost of £8,250 a day (i.e. 5,000 × £1.65). But if every unit was scale-efficient and produced 180 visits a day then only 28 units would be needed to supply the 5,000 visits. The total cost of these 28 units would be £6,100 (5,000 × £1.22). The cost saving would therefore be £8,250 − £6,100 = £2,150 each day.

Now see if you can estimate the cost savings if the scenario is slightly different.

1 Suppose again that each provider has the same cost function but instead of there being 50 units each producing 100 visits per day, there are 25 units each producing 200 visits a day. What cost savings can be made?
2 Suppose this time that there are 10 units producing 200 visits a day and 30 producing 100 a day. Again, what cost savings can be made?

Feedback

1 The cost of current production is 5,000 × £1.28 = £6,400. The cost of the revised scale-efficient output is £6,100. Therefore there is a potential cost saving of £300 per day (£6,400 − £6,100).
2 The cost of the 10 units is 10 × 200 × £1.28 = £2,560. The cost of the 30 units is 30 × 100 × £1.65 = £4,950. Therefore the total cost of current production of £2,560 + £4,950 = £7,510 per day. The potential cost saving is £7,510 − £6,100 = £1,410.

Diagnosing economies of scale appears simple but in reality it can be quite difficult. When inefficiency is exhibited it may not be a result of the size of the hospital but due to technical or operational inefficiency in the system. For example, bed days could be reduced and output maintained. This highlights one of the difficulties encountered when trying to assess the efficiency of hospitals – to assess whether a hospital is scale-efficient you have to assume that it is technically and economically efficient, which need not be the case. There are several ways in which health services might seek to improve the efficiency of their operations (see Chapter 1). Another reason why it is difficult to assess the relative efficiency of different providers is that you need to adjust for differences in the types of patient they are treating and, even more importantly, take into account the health outcomes being achieved. You may also want to consider if there are *economies of scope* which imply that average costs fall as the range of services expands.

Furthermore, when comparing the efficiency of different services, you should make sure that output is measured consistently across providers. It is difficult to quantify hospital output in a single measure. For example, should outpatient visits receive the same weighting as inpatient visits? Inputs should be measured consistently across providers as well. This is not always the case in practice because hospitals may have different methods of calculating capital costs and because a hospital may not be responsible for (and therefore may not record) all of its costs.

Do mergers achieve greater efficiency: is bigger better?

As you saw in Activity 6.3, when provider units are producing below the scale-efficient output there are potential cost savings from merging. On the other hand, when provider units are producing above the scale-efficient output there are potential cost savings from decentralizing production. If some provider units are above and some are below, then there will be cost savings from transferring production between provider units. Does the size of a hospital or GP practice affect its efficiency? The issue of mergers to improve the efficiency of health services has received increasing emphasis worldwide in the search for ways to increase the efficiency of health services. However, the evidence suggests that only for small hospitals are there economies of scale, that larger hospitals may actually have diseconomies of scale and that the optimal size is less than 200 beds (Posnett 1999). This suggests that, purely on grounds of cost, large hospitals should not be constructed. Of course, other relevant considerations, such as feasibility of staffing, might outweigh concerns about efficiency.

Similar steps could be taken in other health care services, although implementation might be difficult. To encourage efficient use of resources, health services should collect financial data and managers should be trained to carry out cost analyses. There is also a need for staff to be aware of the financial constraints of the service if implementation is to be effective.

A good illustration of the issue of economies of scale in practice is the movement to create hospital mergers in the USA and mergers of primary care trusts in the UK in the 1990s, along with similar measures adopted by other countries such as Norway. The explicit motives behind this move were: to take advantage of economies of scale and scope (particularly in terms of management costs), reducing excess capacity; to improve quality including the quality of training; to improve human resources management; and to increase negotiating power in relation to purchasers. Unfortunately these positive outcomes have largely not been realized. In the USA, hospital consolidation has *increased* costs by at least 2 per cent; in Norway, cost efficiency was found to deteriorate; and in the UK management cost savings were considerably less than expected. This is largely put down to the difficulties in organizing the newly-consolidated entity and the problems encountered in trying to bring together former 'rivals' (Fulop *et al.* 2002; Weil 2010).

Activity 6.4

'The NHS white paper *The New NHS* (1997) suggested that primary care groups would typically serve populations of about 100 000, reflecting a policy of devolving responsibility and decision making to local communities ... It has rapidly become apparent, however, that many health authorities and primary care groups consider a population of 100 000 to be too small, particularly for transition to trust status. Two thirds of trusts were considering mergers within their first six months, seemingly reflecting a widely held view that the optimum size was probably closer to 200 000 than 100 000.'

(Bojke *et al.* 2001)

In their paper Bojke and his colleagues explored whether this increase in scale was a good thing for health services as a whole. They found that bigger was *not* necessarily better in terms of performance and economies of scale. Can you think of any reasons for this?

Feedback

In their review of the evidence, these authors found a number of reasons why mergers did not result in economies of scale:

• There is no evidence to suggest that there are economies of scale beyond population levels of 100,000. Evidence from US-managed care organizations suggests that the per capita cost of providing care is minimized at population levels that are no larger, and possibly smaller, than the average size of primary care groups and trusts.

- The predicted managerial economies of scale achieved through the reduction of senior executive staff is not being realized to the extent predicted. The numbers are not being reduced as expected and those that stay are receiving higher remuneration because of the increased responsibility.
- The effect of size on bargaining power with providers is not necessarily realized. In particular, larger primary care groups and trusts may not be permitted to move their business to another provider.
- The optimal population size for commissioning depends on the services being commissioned. For more specialist services, commissioning on behalf of larger populations may be more appropriate. For more general services this may not be the case due to the high volume of demand.
- There is some evidence of economies of scale in pooling risks (you will read more about risk pooling in Chapters 11 and 12), but the marginal gains from pooling diminish rapidly with increasing population size. The average size of primary care groups and trusts, and their funding, is already sufficient such that they do not face substantial risks of bankruptcy.
- There is no evidence that clinical governance activity benefits from economies of scale: larger organizations encounter increased problems in sustaining professional commitment and involvement in quality improvement activity.

It is clear that mergers were going ahead under the assumption that economies of scale would be realized. However, there is only limited evidence to support this and a better understanding of the true nature of economies of scale is important in planning mergers or increasing the scale of activity. As you have also seen, cost functions help producers determine the optimal level of production. Now you will explore how they form one of the building blocks in the construction of the supply curve.

The supply curve

In Chapter 4 you came across the demand curve: the relationship between quantity demanded and price of a good. Similarly, a *supply curve* is used to show the relationship between quantity supplied and price. The supply curve reflects a producer's willingness to sell at each price and therefore the cost of production. In fact the marginal cost is the minimum price that a producer would receive to persuade them to sell an additional unit of the good produced. In this way you can see that the supply curve is the marginal cost curve. Just as the demand curve shows the relationship between demand and the price level, the supply curve illustrates the relationship between what a producer is willing to produce and the price level. When the good is being sold at a low price, only a few suppliers would be willing to sell it, thus the quantity supplied will be low. When the price exceeds the marginal cost there is a *producer surplus* (see Figure 6.7). In this case more suppliers would be willing to sell the good, thus supply will be high. Firms will only find it profitable to raise output if they can sell the good at a price high enough to cover their costs. This translates into *economic profit* – i.e. total revenue minus total cost is greater than zero.

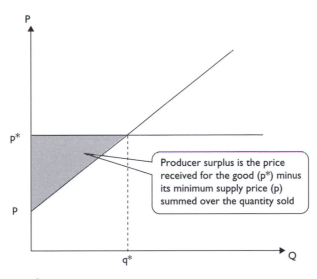

Figure 6.7 Producer surplus

In Chapter 3, we learned that quantity demanded has a number of factors influencing it, in addition to price. Supply has its own influences as well. The main determinants of supply include:

- the price of the good;
- the prices of inputs used to produce the good (e.g. raw food, people's time);
- the prices of related goods;
- expected future prices;
- the number of other suppliers;
- technology.

The supply curve illustrates that there is positive relationship between the price of a good and quantity supplied (everything else remaining the same). Figure 6.8 shows

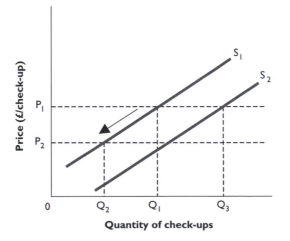

Figure 6.8 Supply for dental health checks

the supply of dental health checks. S_1 is the original supply curve for dental check-ups. At price P_1 dentists are prepared to provide Q_1 check-ups.

A *movement* along the supply curve is associated with a change in price. That is, if the price of a good changes from P_1 to P_2 then the quantity supplied will decrease from Q_1 to Q_2. If the price of the good stays the same but another factor influencing the behaviour of a supplier changes, then the supply curve will *shift*. For example, if there is an increase in the number of qualified dentists then, other factors remaining constant, the quantity supplied is expected to increase at each price level. This is reflected in a rightward shift in the supply curve from S_1 to S_2 and, at constant prices (P_1), the increase in quantity supplied from Q_1 to Q_3.

Activity 6.5

Are there ways in which the supply of health services in your country seems more complicated than the model given in this chapter?

Feedback

The supply of health services in practice is more complicated than the basic model of supply in the following respects.

1 The model of supply you have been reading about assumes that producers' sole aim is to maximize profits. However, producers of health care around the world include government agencies and non-profit organizations as well as profit-making firms.
2 Even where producers are largely private there is a lot of government intervention – subsidies, price regulation, public finance, etc.
3 To talk of *a supply* of health care assumes that health care has an output that can be objectively measured. In fact, almost every individual patient receives a unique 'bundle' of services that makes up their treatment – health care is not a homogeneous product. It is very difficult to measure the inputs and the outputs of health care (especially quality of care).
4 Unlike manufactured goods, health care is provided by groups of professionals who provide training, regulations and ethical codes which will all affect the provision of health care.

Summary

In this chapter you have learned about the theory behind the supply curve. You have learned how the cost function describes the relationship between output and cost and the supply curve describes the relationship between quantity supplied and price. You have also learned about the average and marginal cost curves and their importance in diagnosing economies of scale, and examined the issue of economies of scale in health services. The marginal cost curve was also shown to be the basis for the supply curve and you went on to explore other factors, aside from cost, that influence supply. In the next chapter you will use your knowledge of the demand and supply curves to see how they interact and help in the analysis of markets.

References

Bojke C, Gravelle H and Wilkin D (2001) Is bigger better for primary care groups and trusts? *British Medical Journal* 322(10 March):599–602.

Fulop N *et al.* (2002) Process and impact of mergers of NHS trusts: multicentre case study and management cost analysis. *British Medical Journal* 325(7358):246.

Guinness L, Kumaranayake L and Hanson K (2007) A cost function for HIV prevention services: is there a 'u'-shape? *Cost Effective Resource Allocation* 5(1):13.

Posnett J (1999) Is bigger better? Concentration in the provision of secondary care. *British Medical Journal* 319:1063–5.

Weil T (2010) Hospital mergers: a panacea? *Journal of Health Services Research and Policy* 15(4):251–3.

Further reading

Bojke C, Gravelle H and Wilkin D (2001) Is bigger better for primary care groups and trusts? *British Medical Journal* 322(10 March):599–602.

Brooker S, Kabatereine N, Fleming F and Devlin N (2008) Cost and cost-effectiveness of nationwide school-based helminth control in Uganda: intra-country variation and effects of scaling-up. *Health Policy and Planning* 23:24–35.

Johns B and Torres TT (2005) Costs of scaling up health interventions: a systematic review. *Health Policy Plan* 20(1):1–13

SECTION 3

Markets

A simple market model

Virginia Wiseman and Lorna Guinness

Overview

In Chapters 3 and 4 you learned about demand, how it is defined, how it can be measured and its determinants. Then in Chapters 5 and 6 you explored the theory behind the supply curve. In this chapter we will see how these two 'basic ingredients' of a market – demand and supply – interact. We will first look at markets in general, and then as they apply to health care.

Learning objectives

After working through this chapter, you will be able to:

- explain how price is determined by the forces of supply and demand
- list and describe the assumptions of a perfectly competitive market
- give examples of markets which are highly competitive and those less so
- give examples of health care markets and make predictions about how policy changes will affect demand and supply
- explain why perfectly competitive markets are efficient

Key terms

Allocative efficiency. A situation in which the factors of production have been allocated so as to reflect what people demand (i.e. demand matches supply). Social welfare is maximized as MB = MC in all markets and there can be no substitution between markets to increase welfare beyond its current level.

Market equilibrium. A situation where the price in a given market is such that the quantity demanded is equal to the quantity supplied.

Pareto efficiency. A situation in which there is no way of making any person better off without making someone else worse off (a point on the production possibilities frontier).

Perfect competition. A market in which there are many suppliers, each selling an identical product and many buyers who are completely informed about the price of each supplier's product, and there are no restrictions on entry into the market.

Price taker. A supplier that cannot influence the price of the good or service they supply.

Why is it important to learn about markets?

Understanding the different types of health care markets and the way suppliers and consumers interact is important for a number of reasons. Many health services wish to weigh up the pros and cons of introducing a degree of competition into the health care market. Others may be considering the introduction (or extension) of user fees or of a health insurance scheme. Some providers seek to analyse the effect of government regulation on the private market. These different policy initiatives all constitute changes to the health care market. Analysing their impact is often done using the tools of supply and demand.

It is also important to learn about markets in order to be aware of their limitations, especially in the context of health care. In this chapter and subsequent ones we will see that markets in health care operate very differently from other markets and so call into question the basis for these reforms.

The basic ingredients of a market

There are many types of markets. A *perfectly competitive market* (sometimes termed a 'free market') is a market in which there is no intervention or regulation by the state, except to enforce private contracts and the ownership of property. A perfectly competitive market is the opposite of a *controlled market*, in which the state directly regulates how goods, services and labour may be used, priced or distributed. In this chapter we are going to look at how perfectly competitive markets might work. The reason for this is twofold. First, the interaction of supply and demand in a perfectly competitive market forms the theoretical building blocks of market analysis. Second, many health systems around the world are currently implementing or reviewing 'market-oriented' reforms within the health sector. These reforms are based on the idea that markets work well (or are efficient), which is in turn based on this perfectly competitive model.

Analysing the impact on markets (including health care) of different policy initiatives is often done using the tools of supply and demand. We have already explored the demand and supply functions. In this chapter we are going to merge these two concepts to illustrate what might happen in markets when different events happen.

Market equilibrium

Economists, like physicists and engineers, use the term *equilibrium* to describe a system that is balanced, stable and in a state of harmony. When that system is a market, equilibrium occurs when all participants are satisfied. They have no reason to change their behaviour and therefore there is a tendency for production or prices in that market to remain unchanged. At any other price, either consumers or producers are dissatisfied and will seek to change their behaviour (demand or supply more or less), which will alter the price until equilibrium is found and no more change occurs.

For example, if there is excess demand, consumers bid up the price, while if there is excess supply producers cut the price. These two processes continue until equilibrium is restored. So the free interaction of consumers and producers in the market automatically leads to a situation where the quantity supplied matches the quantity demanded (i.e. allocative efficiency).

Continuing your analysis of the market for dental check-ups, from Chapter 6, Figure 7.1 describes what the hypothetical market would look like in equilibrium.

a) Equilibrium

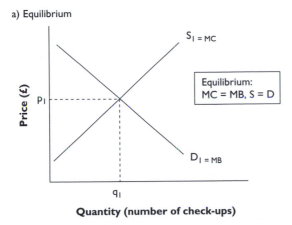

b) Excess demand

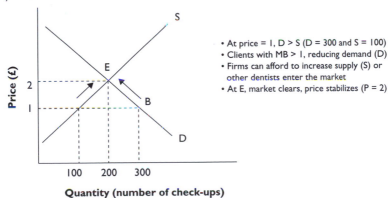

- At price = 1, D > S (D = 300 and S = 100)
- Clients with MB > 1, reducing demand (D)
- Firms can afford to increase supply (S) or other dentists enter the market
- At E, market clears, price stabilizes (P = 2)

c) Excess supply

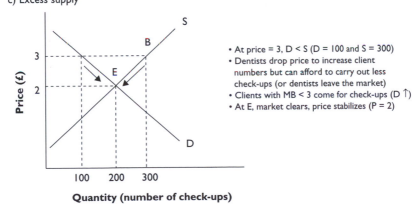

- At price = 3, D < S (D = 100 and S = 300)
- Dentists drop price to increase client numbers but can afford to carry out less check-ups (or dentists leave the market)
- Clients with MB < 3 come for check-ups (D ↑)
- At E, market clears, price stabilizes (P = 2)

Figure 7.1 Market for dental check-ups

You will remember that the supply curve reflects the seller's marginal costs (the cost of producing one extra unit) (MC) and that the demand curve reflects the marginal utility (extra benefit) (MB) that consumers receive from consuming each unit. Figure 7.1 shows that there is only one price at which the quantity of check-ups people wish to purchase is the same as the quantity dentists wish to sell. This is called the equilibrium price (P_1). As noted above, at any other price either consumers or producers would be dissatisfied and seek to change the price. For example, if there is excess demand consumers bid up the price while if there is excess supply producers cut the price. As we said earlier, these two processes continue until equilibrium is restored.

Now, suppose the market for dental check-ups is currently in equilibrium. What would happen if the city's dental clinics were to relocate outside the city? On the supply side it is conceivable that building and land costs are lower beyond the city limits. These reduced costs may result in an increase in the quantity of check-ups supplied at all prices. In this case the supply curve will shift to the right. Note that this example has been simplified. It may actually cost more to attract dentists to work outside a city, for instance.

Demand will also be influenced. For example, if the clinic becomes more distant and people have to travel further then they may incur higher transport and time costs. The increasing costs may result in a decrease in the quantity of check-ups demanded at all prices. The demand curve shifts to the left. The effect of an increase in supply will be a fall in the equilibrium price, as will the effect of a fall in demand. Therefore the overall result of relocation will be a fall in price. The overall effect on quantity traded, however, is less clear. An increase in supply will (all things constant) increase the quantity traded, whereas a fall in demand will decrease the quantity traded. One effect will partially offset the other.

Two different results are conceivable. Firstly, the overall result might be an increase in the quantity traded as shown in Figure 7.2.

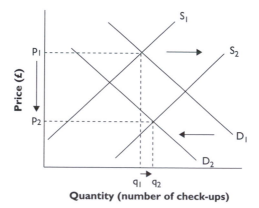

Figure 7.2 Effect of relocating dental clinics (1)

Alternatively, you could experience a decrease in quantity traded as shown in the Figure 7.3.

Another possibility is that there is no change in quantity demanded. The final result will depend on the responsiveness of demand to the increase in travel costs and on the responsiveness of supply to the fall in costs.

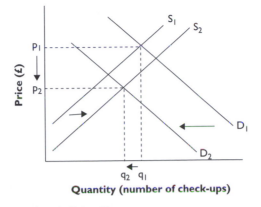

Figure 7.3 Effect of relocating dental clinics (2)

We have just demonstrated that free markets will automatically produce an equilibrium price and quantity. This was first postulated by Adam Smith in his seminal work, *The Wealth of Nations* in 1776. Here is an extract from that book.

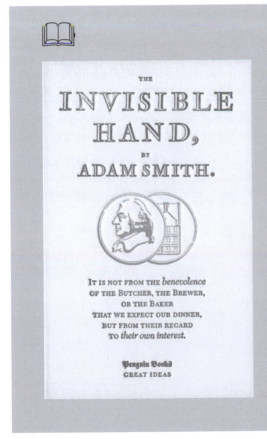

THE

INVISIBLE HAND,

BY

ADAM SMITH.

IT IS NOT FROM THE *benevolence* OF THE BUTCHER, THE BREWER, OR THE BAKER THAT WE EXPECT OUR DINNER, BUT FROM THEIR REGARD TO *their own interest*.

Penguin Books
GREAT IDEAS

...every individual necessarily labours to render the annual revenue of the society as great as he can. He generally, indeed, neither intends to promote the public interest, nor knows how much he is promoting it. By preferring the support of domestic to that of foreign industry, he intends only his own security; and by directing that industry in such a manner as its produce may be of the greatest value, he intends only his own gain, and he is in this, as in many other cases, led by an invisible hand to promote an end which was no part of his intention. Nor is it always the worse for the society that it was no part of it. By pursuing his own interest he frequently promotes that of the society more effectually than when he really intends to promote it. I have never known much good done by those who affected to trade for the public good.

(Smith 1776)

According to Adam Smith, the system in which the 'invisible hand' is assumed to work is the 'free' market. We will learn more about the conditions necessary for the operation of free markets in the next two sections.

Perfectly competitive markets and efficiency

You will no doubt have already realized that the term 'efficiency' can have many different meanings. Some of these were touched upon in Chapter 1. The different meanings relate to different levels of decision-making and refer to how well scarce resources are allocated. So how exactly does this occur in a perfectly competitive market? *Allocative efficiency* describes a situation where resources are allocated and commodities distributed in a way that maximizes social welfare. Social welfare is total social benefit minus total social cost. For a particular market, social welfare is represented by the area below the marginal social benefit curve and above the marginal social cost curve. Social welfare is maximized at the point where marginal social benefit (MSB) equals marginal social cost (MSC), the point P*Q* shown in Figure 7.4.

If MSB is greater than MSC then you can increase social welfare by increasing quantity because the extra benefit is greater than the extra cost and vice versa: if MSB is less than MSC then you can increase social welfare by decreasing quantity because the benefit lost is less than the cost saved. A free market will be *allocatively* efficient if demand is equal to MSB and supply is equal to MSC.

On the supply side, you have already encountered the efficiency conditions that allow supply to be equal to MSC in Chapters 5 and 6: producers need to be both *technically* and *economically* (productively) *efficient*. Without these conditions in place there will always be a way of improving the allocation of resources without making anyone worse off. In Chapter 8 you will explore situations where demand does not necessarily reflect MSB.

Read the following extract from Palmer and Torgerson (1999) who provide an overview of the different definitions of efficiency and how they are commonly used in decision-making in health services.

Economists argue that the achievement of (greater) efficiency from scarce resources should be a major criterion for priority-setting. This note, taken from Palmer and Torgerson (1999) examines three concepts of efficiency: technical, productive and allocative.

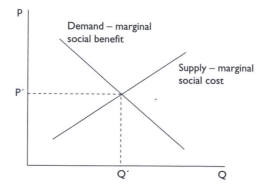

Figure 7.4 Allocative efficiency

Technical efficiency – refers to the physical relation between resources (capital and labour) and health outcome. A technically efficient position is achieved when the maximum possible improvement in outcome is obtained from a set of resource inputs. An intervention is technically inefficient if the same (or greater) outcome could be produced with less of one type of input. Consider treatment of osteoporosis using alendronate. A recent randomized trial showed that a 10mg daily dose was as effective as a 20mg dose. The lower dose is technically more efficient.

Productive efficiency [economic efficiency] – technical efficiency cannot, however, directly compare alternative interventions, where one intervention produces the same (or better) health outcome with less (or more) of one resource and more of another. Consider, for example, a policy of changing from maternal age screening to biochemical screening for Down's syndrome. Biochemical screening uses fewer amniocenteses but it requires the use of another resource – biochemical testing. Since different combinations of inputs are being used, the choice between interventions is based on the relative costs of these different inputs. The concept of productive efficiency refers to the maximisation of health outcome for a given cost, or the minimisation of cost for a given outcome. If the sum of the costs of the new biochemical screening programme is smaller than or the same as the maternal age programme and outcomes are equal or better, then the biochemical programme is productively efficient in relation to the maternal age programme. In health care, productive efficiency enables assessment of the relative value for money of interventions with directly comparable outcomes. It cannot address the impact of reallocating resources at a broader level – for example, from geriatric care to mental illness – because the health outcomes are incommensurate.

Allocative efficiency – to inform resource allocation decisions in this broader context a global measure of efficiency is required. The concept of allocative efficiency takes account not only of the productive efficiency with which healthcare resources are used to produce health outcomes but also the efficiency with which these outcomes are distributed among the community. Such a societal perspective is rooted in welfare economics and has implications for the definition of opportunity costs. In theory, the efficient pattern of resource use is such that any alternative pattern makes at least one person worse off. In practice, strict adherence to this criterion has proved impossible. Further, this criterion would eliminate as inefficient changes that resulted in many people becoming much better off at the expense of a few being made slightly worse off. Consequently, the following decision rule has been adapted: allocative efficiency is achieved when resources are allocated so as to maximise the welfare of the community.

Thus technical efficiency addresses the issue of using given resources to maximum advantage; productive efficiency of choosing different combinations of resources to achieve the maximum health benefit for a given cost; and allocative efficiency of achieving the right mixture of healthcare programmes to maximise the health of society. Although productive efficiency implies technical efficiency and allocative efficiency implies productive efficiency, none of the converse implications necessarily hold. Faced with limited resources, the concept of productive efficiency will eliminate as 'inefficient' some technically efficient resource input combinations, and the concept of allocative efficiency will eliminate some productively efficient resource allocations.

(Palmer and Torgerson 1999)

A word of warning: you will find in your further reading that the use of these terms does vary. For example, 'technical' efficiency is sometimes referred to as 'operational', 'technological', 'scale' or 'producer' efficiency. Productive efficiency is also referred to as economic efficiency. To complicate things further, allocative efficiency is sometimes used interchangeably with *Pareto efficiency*.

But what is Pareto efficiency? In Chapter 1 you learned that this is where no one can be made better off without making someone else worse off. So if resources are allocated inefficiently (in Pareto terms) it ought to be possible to make one person better off without making anyone else worse off. Where a policy or intervention does make others worse off there is a justification for compensation on efficiency grounds. In reality, Pareto efficiency is rarely possible as generally there are winners and losers from most transactions. It is only valid if the world can be seen to be the outcome of a perfectly competitive market where demand and supply curves are as described above and there is technical and economic efficiency. Importantly, when looking at Pareto efficiency, economists are only assessing the efficiency of resource distribution; it cannot tell us anything about how equitable that distribution is, as you will discover in the next activity.

Activity 7.1

1 What is the 'invisible hand' theory in economics?
2 Would you expect a Pareto efficient allocation to be equitable?

Feedback

1 This is an economic principle first postulated by Adam Smith in the eighteenth century. It describes a situation where perfectly competitive markets will automatically produce an equilibrium price and quantity. According to the invisible hand theory, each of us, acting in our own self-interests, generates a demand for goods and services that compels others to deliver those goods and services in the most efficient manner.

2 It is a good thing for a market to be Pareto efficient because it means that total benefit to society is maximized. This means that the sum of the utilities of every person is maximized. However, this might mean that some people have a very large amount of utility but others have a relatively small amount. An example might help you to understand this. Let's say you had a million oranges and everybody else had one each. This could still be Pareto efficient provided there is no way for you to obtain a million and one oranges without making anyone else worse off. This is why Pareto efficient allocation is not related to equity. In this case there is scope for government intervention even though there is efficiency – i.e. on equity grounds.

We have seen in this chapter that the market mechanism is quite effective at allocating resources in an efficient manner. However, perfectly competitive markets are not feasible in many situations and are an idealized view of the economic world. In reality economic transactions are much more complex. These complexities can lead to a reduction in efficiency and a subsequent loss of economic welfare. We will return to this in the next chapter and the subsequent chapters on health care financing. But first we will look at the conditions under which a competitive market might be realized.

Conditions for perfectly competitive markets

A free or perfectly competitive market can only operate efficiently if a number of important conditions are met, including these four:

* producers selling the same product (homogeneity);
* many sellers and buyers;
* no restrictions on potential sellers entering the market;
* buyers and sellers well informed about prices.

The health care system in the country where you live and work may exhibit these characteristics to varying degrees. For example, it is very common that for some services there is only one provider. In the next activity we will explore each of these characteristics in more detail.

Activity 7.2

1 We said above that under a perfectly competitive market, the product of that market must be *homogenous*. That is to say, the good or service must be standardized and mostly indistinguishable from one seller to the next. When we talked about dental check-ups in our previous example, we treated the check-ups as being the same, regardless of which dentist provided the service (i.e. we assumed homogeneity). Do you think dental check-ups in the state or city where you live are really homogenous? Can you think of examples of goods or products which are homogenous?

2 The second condition is that the market must be made up of *many sellers and buyers* and each of them must not make up a significant portion of the transactions. In this way, no one supplier has enough control over the market to influence prices; thus, all suppliers in this market are *price takers*. That is, they necessarily will sell their goods at the market price, which is a set amount beyond anyone's individual control. Can you think of a market where there are so many suppliers that no one seller can affect the market price?

3 The third condition is that there must be *no barriers to entering or exiting* the market. Potential suppliers must be able to enter a market if a profitable opportunity to do so exists. This means that the potential supplier will have the resources needed to enter the market at their disposal. On the other hand, existing suppliers must be able to leave the market if they wish as well. This means that the market is 'contestable', and as long as this holds then even if there are currently few sellers in the market they have to behave as if there were many since once they change their price then others may immediately enter to compete. Can you think of a market which is easy to enter? What about one which is hard to enter?

4 The final condition for perfect competition is that *information* must be readily available to both buyers and suppliers under perfectly competitive markets. Buyers and suppliers must know the prices set by all suppliers. Buyers should be able to know when a supplier is selling at a higher-than-market price and if the product being sold is counterfeit, defective or different in any way that would make the item in question unlike the specific homogenous good. Do you think that most real-world markets are perfectly competitive or not? Can you think of any examples of markets that satisfy these four conditions of perfect competition?

5 Do you think health services in your country are perfectly competitive? Explain why, or why not.

Feedback

1 Assuming a good is homogenous means that a buyer would be indifferent to purchasing from one supplier or the next and would seek out another supplier only if they could get a lower price. You may argue that dental check-ups are not very similar even within a relatively small geographic area. Some dentists may clean your teeth as part of a check-up while others do not. So treating dental check-ups as the same is a simplification when looking at demand. Most health care services are by nature *heterogeneous*. Individual patients typically receive a unique bundle of services that make up their treatment. In contrast, many health care products, like syringes or over the counter medicines, are more homogenous. Looking beyond health care, many agricultural goods, such as specific varieties of coffee beans, apples or tomatoes are examples of homogenous goods.

2 The hundreds of individual noodle stands that can be found in Bangkok, Thailand, are a good example of this condition. If an individual stand owner decided to raise prices above that of their competitors, buyers would not patronize their stand but could easily go to the next noodle stand. We know that in health care there are some services that are much more specialized than others and therefore the number of 'sellers' is relatively few. We also know that in some rural areas travel to other providers may be prohibitively expensive and in this case the local hospital in effect acts as a monopoly supplier to the local population.

3 The noodle stand market is one which is easy to enter, as you need very few items to set yourself up as a seller of noodles. The airline industry is an example of a market that is very difficult to enter. You would need to have funds to acquire the aeroplanes, but also negotiate landing rights at different airports, etc. In the case of health care, including dentistry, there are clear restrictions on entering the market, length and cost of training and practice licensing and registration being the most obvious.

4 Many real-world markets do not precisely follow this model. For example, the market for MP3 music players is very competitive with numerous suppliers and gadgets made by Apple, Microsoft, Sony, Samsung and Toshiba, among others. But because 73 per cent of people buying a new MP3 player choose an iPod, Apple has significant control over how much they are going to be sold for. If Apple decides to raise prices, some people may decide to buy Microsoft's or Sony's MP3 player instead, but most people will decide to pay the higher price for an iPod. This market doesn't fit the perfect competition model. However, selling tomatoes at the

Saturday market in Accra, Ghana, is a good example of a perfectly competitive market. Tomatoes are largely homogenous. Hundreds of sellers and thousands of buyers arrive every Saturday to buy and sell produce. There are no restrictions to enter the market and very little resources are required to do so. Information on prices is readily available. Perfectly competitive market conditions also state that suppliers are price takers. Indeed, if one woman decides to raise her prices above her competitors, buyers would simply buy from a different stall. Another example might be the market for the shares of a very large company. You can probably think of a few others.

In health care, most medical information is technically complex and so not easily understood by a layperson. This is compounded by the fact that many illnesses do not repeat themselves, so that the cost of gaining information about them is very high. You could argue that the only way a patient could become fully informed would be by training to be a doctor!

5 There are several ways that health services are not perfectly competitive.

a) For some areas of health care there may be many suppliers but for others not. Generally, primary care is provided by a large number of individual doctors and small group practices whereas specialist services often have few providers.

b) There are barriers to entry into the health care system. Doctors, nurses and other health professionals need qualifications and a licence before they can provide health care, and hospitals entail large start-up investments.

c) Different providers are not selling an identical product. The quality (or at least the reputation for quality) of care and service is known to vary between providers.

d) For a lot of health care, consumers are not fully informed about what services they need and cannot be sure about differences in quality between providers.

The health system in your country might feature these characteristics to a different extent but it will probably include most or all of them. For some services there might be only one provider.

While examples of perfectly competitive markets are hard to find in health care, this does not mean that market forces do not operate there, as we will see from the following examples.

Markets in health care

You now have an idea of how the forces of supply and demand operate in a perfectly competitive market setting and the stringent conditions necessary for their efficient operation. We will now consider some examples of markets in health care. But before doing this, take a moment to read the following quote which reminds us that efficiency is not the only reason given in support of markets in health care. Markets can yield other benefits too.

Value of markets in health care

Health care, due to its high upfront costs and centrality to humankind, is often considered 'different' and best left outside the domain of markets. But such blanket opposition ignores valid reasons for not dismissing the value markets could bring:

i.   **Efficiency.** In a market environment people can demonstrate their preferences for different goods and services by exercising choice. This both generates highly precise information about their preferences, so providers are motivated to supply the services people want (**allocative efficiency**), and provides the incentive for providers to be as efficient as possible in order to undercut competitors (**technical efficiency**).

ii. **Customer service and innovation.** In markets there is always the opportunity for people to come forward with new ideas to meet an unmet need: a powerful incentive to experiment, innovate and focus squarely on service users.

iii. **Resiliency.** A major criticism of government action in the field of public policy is that it has followed 'utopian social engineering', resulting in any wrong decision being felt hard and universally. In markets, where there are so many participants, it would be remarkable if all made the same mistakes.

iv. **Voluntary co-operation.** Markets form part of a sphere that is based on voluntary co-operation, in that the decisions of businesses, individuals and researchers are not forced on anyone else. This contrasts with monopoly where there are few alternative options.

v.   **Equity.** In centrally-planned systems, where there is no *formal* choice, middle and upper class people typically are better at *creating* choices and negotiating a better deal. With an appropriate redistribution of resources, markets give *everyone* this opportunity.

(CITIVAS 2009)

Free markets in health care?

Begin by reading the following extract from Green (2007).

How well does our theoretical model of a market explain what has been going on with cosmetic surgery? Look at this newspaper report on the growth of cosmetic dentistry.

Putting your money where your mouth is ...

Maggie Smith is a publisher in her late 40s who has just splashed out on a £1,400 'tooth lift'. '*I saw the treatment as an investment. Compared with the cost of a couple of outfits, it's not that expensive and it lasts much longer*'. Smith purchased her cosmetic dentistry from Dentics on London's Kings Road. Dentics opened its first 'tooth boutique' four years ago and now has three London branches. Customers can walk into the shop-fronted surgeries without an appointment and browse through albums of photos showing wayward canines tamed into piano keyboards by bleaching, filing down, building with resins or covering with porcelain veneers. Each treatment costs around £200.

Primary school teacher Elizabeth Eccose-Westley regarded the treatment as an affordable luxury. 'I'm not rich and I'm not vain, but at 42 I started to feel I was getting long in the tooth. I spent £1,000 on porcelain veneers, instead of a summer holiday, and it's really boosted my confidence. Give it another couple of years and people won't think twice about it. Everybody will be having it done'.

Emma Brooker in the Guardian, 16 September 1993

Clearly there is a demand for cosmetic dentistry – people are willing and able to pay for it. Both the women in the article viewed the cosmetic treatment as something which gave them 'utility', i.e. satisfaction, and they consciously compared the satisfaction gained with that from other purchases. The article also provides evidence that the market is growing.

Why is this happening?

Economic analysis
The initial supply and demand curves are shown in Figure 7.5 – the system is in equilibrium.

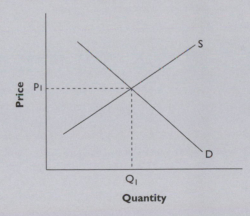

Figure 7.5 Market for cosmetic surgery

The first change is that technology has reduced the costs of such treatment – shifting the supply curve outwards. Demand also seems to be growing; why is this? According to a recent national survey, one in four people dislikes their appearance suggesting that they would consider buying this kind of treatment if they could afford it. So consumers are likely to respond to the lower prices brought about by the shift in supply – a movement down the market demand curve. This sets up a new equilibrium at P_2 and Q_2 in Figure 7.6.

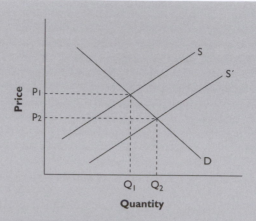

Figure 7.6 Effect of a change in technology

The next change is an increase in consumers' real income (due to the reduced cost of treatment) leading to an outward shift in the demand curve from D_1 to D_2 (see Figure 7.7). So there is a near equilibrium at P_3 and Q_3.

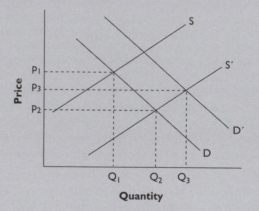

Figure 7.7 Effect of an increase in real income

Suppliers have reacted to the growth of consumer demand in exactly the way our theory predicts. Dentics has expanded its operations by opening more shops and providing more treatments.

Reduced costs and extra consumer demand have both led to the allocation of more resources to cosmetic dental treatment. (Remember from Chapter 5 that the final outcome will depend on how sensitive demand and supply is to factors such as a change in price.)

So our model has performed fairly well. But it suffers from being rather static.

A more dynamic view of the market

One thing the market is able to do very well is act as a powerful and efficient information system. Changes in consumers' tastes are quickly communicated to producers via market prices. The search for profits drives producers to offer new products or services and make them in more cost-effective ways. An example of this is the way in which consumers' concern over the link between high cholesterol and heart attacks has led to the appearance of cholesterol testing units at chemists and health food stores in the UK.

Competition and the need to respond to and, if possible, anticipate consumer demand lead to a system which provides the maximum choice for the lowest possible cost; a system which is flexible and dynamic but efficient.

Some economists argue that in the real world most markets will be in a constant state of flux – adjusting towards equilibrium but rarely actually reaching it. In this analysis, it is the market's ability to act as an information system that is important rather than its ability to produce a single equilibrium price.

Take the market for cosmetic dental services. If the market was free and competitive, then different dentists would offer different mixes of service, and some dentists would be more skilful than others. The skilful dentists offering the services consumers want would have lots of customers and would be able to charge higher prices than their competitors. This would force the other dentists to modify the services they are selling to try to capture back the consumers. This process of competition would be continuous, particularly as other factors influencing demand and supply such as levels of income, or the state of technology are likely to be also changing.

(Green 2007)

Activity 7.3

Can you think of any examples of free (or predominantly free) markets for particular health services operating in your country?

Feedback

Free or largely unfettered markets tend to be used for services that are deemed non-essential, such as cosmetic surgery, or services that do not require the involvement of a health professional, such as simple drugs available in retail pharmacies, or enhanced 'hotel' facilities when admitted to hospital.

Health care markets rarely meet the conditions of a perfect market. However, markets and market forces do exist in health care in spite of the typically extensive role of the state. Try answering the following question about markets as fully as possible.

Activity 7.4

What are the advantages of markets in the allocation of resources?

Feedback

Markets are a useful resource allocation mechanism for the following reasons.

1 In theory at least, markets automatically tend towards a situation of equilibrium where the output produced is exactly equal to the output used. You looked at this in the last activity.
2 Given a few specific requirements, markets will produce an output that is allocatively efficient – that is, each unit of output is produced when the additional benefit it brings exceeds its cost.
3 The market is dynamic: it is a 'powerful and efficient information system'. Changes in people's preferences are quickly passed on to and acted on by producers. Likewise, changes in the availability of and cost of resources are reflected in prices. Cheaper substitute resources are quickly opted for instead.

Summary

The economic framework of demand and supply is a useful way to think about factors that affect the use and provision of health services. In Chapters 3 and 4 you learned about demand. In Chapter 6 and in this chapter you have learned about the supply function and the effect various factors have on the supply curve. You also saw in this chapter how prices are determined and market equilibrium may be achieved. Examples were used to illustrate that markets do exist in the health sector but most are far from perfectly competitive.

References

CITIVAS (2009) *Markets in health care: theory behind the policy*, www.civitas.org.uk/nhs/download/Civitas_ Markets_in_healthcare_Dec09.pdf.
Green M (2007) *The economics of health care*. London: Office of Health Economics.
Palmer S and Torgerson DJ (1999) Definitions of efficiency, *British Medical Journal* 318:1136.
Smith A (1776) *The Wealth of Nations*, http://bookcoverarchive.com/adam_smith.

Further reading

Donaldson CK *et al.* (2004) *The economics of health care financing: the visible hand*. Basingstoke: Palgrave Macmillan, Chapter 5: 73–6.
Kikumbih N *et al.* (2005) The economics of social marketing: the case of mosquito nets in Tanzania, *Social Science & Medicine* 60(2):369–81.
Palmer S and Torgerson DJ (1999) Definitions of efficiency, *British Medical Journal* 318:1136.

Health care markets and efficiency

8

Lorna Guinness and Virginia Wiseman

Overview

So far you have looked at the behaviour of providers of health care (producers) and of patients (consumers) and have seen some ways in which knowledge of this behaviour can be used to inform health planning. In the previous chapter you learned how markets, when they are working well, are a highly effective system for the production and distribution of goods and services and about the necessary conditions for a perfectly competitive market. In this chapter you will consider whether these conditions can ever be met in the area of health care, different types of market failures in health care and mechanisms to counteract these failures.

Learning objectives

After working through this chapter, you will be able to:

- describe why monopoly power, externalities, public goods and information asymmetries constitute market failures
- explain the consequences for price, output and efficiency for each market failure
- suggest some strategies to address each health care market failure
- compare health care markets with the model of perfect competition

Key terms

Adverse selection. When a party enters into an agreement in which they can use their own private information to the disadvantage of another party.

Asymmetry of information. A market situation where all participants do not have access to the same level of information.

Deadweight loss. The loss in allocative efficiency occurring when the loss of consumer surplus outweighs the gain in producer surplus.

Externality. The cost or benefit arising from an individual's production or consumption decision which indirectly affects the well-being of others.

Market failure. A situation in which the market does not result in an efficient allocation of resources.

Monopoly power. The ability of a monopoly to raise price by restricting output.

Moral hazard. A situation in which one of the parties to an agreement has an incentive, after the agreement is made, to act in a manner that brings additional benefits to themselves at the expense of the other party.

Natural monopoly. A situation where one firm can meet market demand at a lower average cost than two or more firms could meet that demand.

Public good. A good or service that can be consumed simultaneously by everyone and from which no one can be excluded.

Social cost. The total costs associated with an activity including both private costs and those incurred by society as a whole.

Supplier-induced demand. The demand that exists beyond what would have been asked by consumers if they had been perfectly informed about their health problems and the various treatments available.

Transaction costs. Costs of engaging in trade – i.e. the costs arising from finding someone with whom to do business, of reaching an agreement and of ensuring the terms of the agreement are fulfilled.

Market failure

In Chapter 7 you learned that markets are useful resource allocation mechanisms because they are automatic, responsive to changes in consumer preferences and, under perfect competition, allocatively efficient. But what happens when perfect competition does not arise? In economics we refer to this as *market failure* as the market is unable to achieve an efficient allocation of resources. In fact, markets do not work well in all situations and health care is a very good example of this. Alongside equity and redistribution of wealth (see Chapter 17) and stabilization of the macro economy (Chapter 2), the correction of market failure is another reason for government intervention in the market. The health care market is characterized by a number of market failures: *monopoly, externalities, public goods* and *asymmetry of information*.

Monopoly

Monopoly is characterized by a single supplier in the market. A natural monopoly is a situation where one firm can meet market demand at a lower average cost than two or more firms could meet that demand. However, monopoly can occur as a result of other conditions:

- there are barriers to entry;
- there are few providers;
- there are few close substitutes.

Barriers to entry imply that it is difficult to participate in the market. In health care, barriers to entry exist in the form of professional bodies so that the supply of professionals is restricted. This in turn implies higher salaries than there would be if there were perfect competition – i.e. there is allocative inefficiency. The scarcity of hospitals in rural areas is also a good illustration of few providers. This might mean that hospital services are priced artificially high, which is inefficient. However, monopoly pricing may not occur if providers are non-profit-making. There are also few close substitutes for many health care goods and services such as an emergency Caesarean section or anti-retroviral therapy.

As a result of monopoly, firms are no longer price takers but have influence over the market price and the output level of production. Monopolies have an incentive to push up prices and restrict output produced. To maximize profit they will set output where marginal revenue equals marginal cost. Figure 8.1 illustrates the price and output decisions of a monopolist. A producer produces at the output where marginal cost equals marginal revenue because this is the output level where profits (total revenue minus total cost) are maximized. For a monopoly producer, marginal revenue is below the demand curve. This is because a one-unit increase in output increases revenue by the amount of the price of that unit (indicated by the demand curve) minus the loss in revenue on the other units caused by the associated fall in price. The corresponding output that they can produce at this point can then command a price, (Pmon) in the market. In a perfectly competitive market, the firm would have to produce at where MC = D on the graph where output is higher (Qcomp) and price is lower (Pcomp). This means that the monopoly is inefficient. Monopolies transform consumer surplus (see Chapter 3) into producer surplus (see Chapter 6). However, the loss in consumer surplus is greater than the gain in producer surplus. Therefore, there is an overall loss to society – the *deadweight loss* – a measure of loss in allocative efficiency.

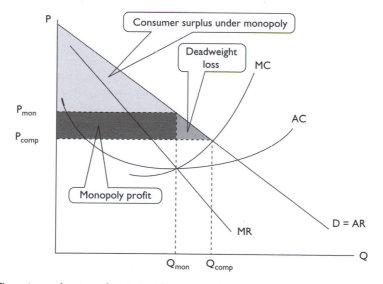

Figure 8.1 The price and output decision under monopoly

Sometimes, a monopoly producer will *price discriminate* so that marginal revenue is the same as the demand curve. Price discrimination means offering the same product at different prices to different people. For example, railways and airlines often charge lower prices to students, young people and elderly people. This is not an act of generosity. Quite the opposite, it is a way of maximizing profits. Parkin and colleagues note that 'by charging the highest price for each unit of the good that each person is willing to pay, a monopoly perfectly price discriminates and captures all the consumer surplus' (Parkin *et al.* 2008). In practice, monopolies are never able to perfectly price discriminate but they can discriminate between different groups of people where each group has a different elasticity of demand.

Activity 8.1

Many health services are delivered by hospitals or other central institutions that hold monopoly power. Drawing on your own knowledge and understanding of health care, can you think of any features of health care provision that are characteristic of a monopoly?

Feedback

In some cases there are close *substitutes* to health care. For example, if someone has influenza then they could take drugs for symptomatic relief. They could alternatively just spend some time in bed until the symptoms stop. In this case, rest is a substitute for medication. However, in most cases there are probably no substitutes: with a disease like appendicitis there is no real substitute for surgical treatment.

Health care professionals require a licence to practise. This licence is an example of a *barrier to entry* in the health care market. Patents are also barriers to entry because they prevent other manufacturers from producing a particular good. Patents are very common in the pharmaceutical industry.

Health care providers are not usually considered to be *natural monopolies*. It was noted in Chapter 6 that economies of scale exist only for small hospitals. It is unlikely, therefore, that a single provider can operate at a lower cost than would be achievable by several competing providers. However, in rural areas travel to other providers may be prohibitively expensive such that the local hospital is in effect a monopoly supplier for the local population.

Activity 8.2

In this example we are going to look at a hypothetical market for cervical cancer screening and an innovation that leads to a change in the market structure. The delivery of the cervical cancer screening was originally based on examining slides under a microscope. Then the government decided that private laboratories should carry out the laboratory work. There were 100 laboratories competing for this business. Since there are no significant economies of scale in this work, the firms carrying it out can be described in terms of the classic perfect competition model (see Figure 8.2). For the industry, the supply curve is the same as the marginal cost curve and the demand curve is as shown. The individual laboratory is a price taker and therefore faces a price P_e (set at the equilibrium point of the market). The laboratory produces a quantity of q_e, where MR = MC.

However, two years later it was agreed that the technology was no longer appropriate. It was decided that the manual reading of slides should be replaced by automated reading, which was found to be much more accurate. Since a patent exists on this technology and there are great economies of scale, the result will be that the (single) firm that holds the patent will provide all the services. The simple monopoly model in Figure 8.3 describes the new situation.

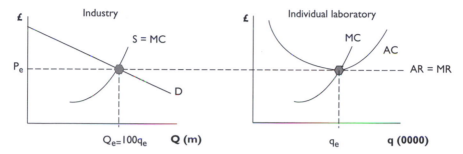

Figure 8.2 Hypothetical market for cervical screening before the introduction of new technology – a perfectly competitive market

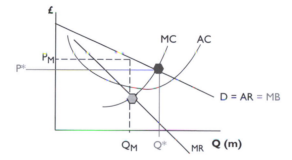

Figure 8.3 Hypothetical market for cervical screening after the introduction of new technology – a monopoly market
Q_M = Monopolist's profit-maximizing output
Q^* = Allocatively efficient output

Compare the pattern of price, cost and output in the two scenarios. Why is monopoly provision against the interest of users?

Feedback

In the competitive market MC = marginal social cost (MSC), MB (demand) = marginal social benefit (MSB). This means that the competitive market was allocatively efficient. With the new technology, a single provider could produce at a lower cost than multiple providers. This producer, if it was a profit maximizer, would have an incentive to produce at Q_M, which is below the allocatively efficient output (Q^*, where MC = MB). (Remember that there is no supply curve in the case of a monopoly, since quantity and price are determined by the interaction of demand and cost functions.) This is against the interests of consumers because units of output where the benefit exceeds the cost (MB > MC) would not be provided.

The advantage of the new technology is that *potentially* we can reduce costs, increasing the supply of the service. The disadvantage is that it allows a single provider to exert monopoly power. There are steps that the government can take to make sure that monopoly power is curbed and service provision is increased:

- they could make the market *contestable* – offering the monopoly to the provider that offered to cut prices the most;
- they could put a *ceiling* on the price to bring it down to the social optimum price, P* – where there is a monopoly, a price ceiling can lead to increased output (this is unlike a price ceiling in a competitive market, which will reduce the quantity supplied);
- they could break up the monopoly.

There is a particular problem when patent protection is involved. In this case, a supplier is allowed to be the sole provider of a good because it has developed the technology itself. Without patents, suppliers would not have the incentive to develop new, more efficient technologies because their competitors could adopt the new technology immediately without the expense of research and development costs. The downside of patents is that the firm is able to restrict output and raise price during the period that the patent is in operation. When anti-retroviral therapy was first found to be successful, the price set by the pharmaceutical firms was simply not affordable for low-income countries, in part because of patent protection.

It is sometimes suggested that monopolies are less able to achieve technical and allocative efficiency. It is argued that in spite of their profit maximizing motive, their incentive to reduce cost is diminished because monopolies have very large profits already. You have seen that markets with many suppliers tend to be very efficient (given that certain conditions are met) but that markets with only one supplier are allocatively inefficient. So what is the situation when there are a few suppliers? Such a system is called an *oligopoly*. Under oligopoly, the decisions of suppliers become very complicated. This is because the decisions of any one producer in the market will have consequences for all the other firms. Although the situation is complicated, it is safe to assume that the smaller the number of producers, the easier it is for them to restrict output and raise price, and therefore the less efficient is the market.

Externalities

Another form of market failure occurs when there are *externalities*. You may have heard the term 'externalities' but exactly what does it mean? An externality is a cost or a benefit arising from an economic transaction that falls on people who do not participate in the transaction. The normal interactions in the market take personal benefits into account, since private demand functions reflect self-assessed benefits to individuals. When there are external costs and benefits, the parties involved in the transaction do not take these costs and benefits into account. This failure to place a value on all costs and benefits can lead the market to under-provide or over-provide a good. A typical example of this divergence between the marginal private costs (or benefits) and the marginal social costs (or benefits), shown in Figure 8.4, is vaccinations.

The difference between the private and social benefit of vaccinations can be well described by the rise in measles cases in the UK. As a result of a media scare about the

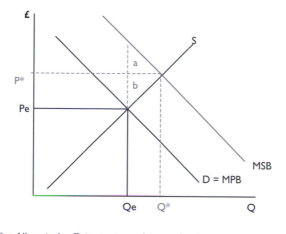

P*, Q* = Allocatively efficient price and output level
Pe, Qe = Profit-maximizing price and output level
D, S = Demand and supply
MPB = marginal private benefit (= demand)
MSB = marginal social benefit
Area a + b = the deadweight loss to society due to the market failure associated with
external benefits

Figure 8.4 An example of external benefits: the market for vaccination against measles

possible dangers to some children of the measles vaccine, there was a drop in vaccination rates. There are private benefits of being vaccinated: most children get a very high
immunity against measles, and thus are protected from the ill effects of the disease. In
addition there are benefits beyond this to society as a whole: vaccination reduces the
risk of others catching measles as well. As the vaccination rate fell, there was a rapid
reappearance of measles in the UK (confirmed cases in England and Wales rose from 56
in 1998 to 971 in 2007 – McIntyre and Leask 2008) posing a particular threat to more
isolated communities with traditionally low coverage who depend on 'herd immunity'.

The positive externality associated with vaccinations in general leads to governments introducing different ways to increase the consumption of vaccinations up to the
socially optimal level. These might include voucher schemes, a price subsidy or, as for
childhood vaccinations in most countries, state provision of vaccinations. In the UK a
catch-up campaign was launched by the government to bring vaccination rates back up.

Activity 8.3

When a good has unintended benefits, it is called a *positive externality*. If you relied on
markets to deliver goods with positive externalities like immunization, you would find
that the resulting number of immunizations would be less than the socially optimal
number needed to reach herd immunity levels. In other words, the market would
under-supply immunization.

There are also *negative externalities*. The classic example is smoking.

1 How is smoking a negative externality?
2 What might governments do to limit this externality?

Feedback

1 When people smoke there is a cost to themselves in terms of poorer health outcomes. However, there is also a cost to other individuals from second-hand smoke.
When people are weighing up the costs and benefits of smoking, they focus on the
impact on *them*. The market also doesn't consider the cost to others, and therefore
the market over-supplies the good. Another example of negative externality is pollution produced by a manufacturing company. The pollution affects the neighbourhood
around the company, but the company does not bear any direct costs from the pollution. So the company does not consider this a cost when it is deciding how much
of the good to produce. In these cases, the private cost is less than the social impact,
which causes individuals to underestimate costs and so over-supply.

2 Governments need to raise the price of smoking to reflect the cost to society. This
can be achieved through a specific form of taxation called a *Pigouvian tax*. Pigouvian
taxes aim to internalize the cost of negative externalities. Taxes work by increasing
the cost of the consumed goods, which will lead to a lower equilibrium quantity. In
the case of smoking, duties on cigarettes would be charged. Other examples might
be duties on alcohol and the more recent suggestion in the USA to tax junk food. In
the case of pollution, governments could introduce emission charges.

Public goods

Market failure and the suboptimal allocation of a good or service also occurs with
public goods. Parkin *et al.* (2008) provide the following definition of a public good:

> a good or service that can be consumed simultaneously by everyone (it is *non-rival*) and
> from which no individuals can be excluded (*non-excludable*). If the provider of a public
> good tries to ask people how much they are willing to pay to receive it, consumers say
> they don't want it. Why? Because the consumers know that once the good is provided
> they can consume it even if they don't pay for it. This is called the free-rider problem.
>
> (Parkin 2008)

A classic example of a public good is street lighting: all individuals on the street use the
lighting at the same time and no person can be excluded from using it. In addition, if
someone walks down the street this does not limit the lighting available to others on
the street. Such programmes will be under-provided by the market because people
hope to benefit without having to contribute to the cost. In other words, there are
incentives for free-riding.

So, is health care a public good? No, it isn't. For one thing, it is rival. If one person
consumes a drug (or a consultation, or a vaccination) then there is one drug (consultation, vaccination) less available for others to consume. Health care is also excludable
– providers can easily prevent individuals from consuming it. However, there are *aspects*
of health that *are* public goods, one of which is infection control such as malarial management through environmental measures (Mills and Gilson 1988). Everyone in the
community can benefit from having a malaria-free water supply without stopping anyone else from benefiting – it is non-rival. Furthermore, no one can be excluded from
this benefit. Information, something that is an integral part of many public health programmes, can also be considered a public good. However, this is only non-excludable
if individuals possess the *access goods* which enable them to receive that information

(e.g. TVs or radios). Non-excludability leads to free-riding so that individuals consume more than their fair share of the good. Non-rivalry leads to lower than socially optimal consumption. As a result, perfectly competitive markets under-supply public goods so that direct delivery or financing by government is required to reach a socially optimal level of output (Smith *et al.* 2003).

Health insurance

Demand for health care is often manifested as a demand for health care insurance. Insurance markets evolve as a natural response to the burden of risk. In fact, insurance is a response to the market failure related to the uncertainty around the timing of demand for health care. Insurance markets certainly complicate the model of demand you looked at in Chapter 4. Consumers, instead of demanding health care, demand health insurance. The insurance companies then demand the health care or else the individuals demand it and the insurers pay for it.

Activity 8.4

Read the following extract by Donaldson *et al.* (2005), and then try to answer the following questions:

1 Why do people take out insurance?
2 Why do people take out *health* insurance?

The article refers to 'actuarily fair premiums'. This means that the amount (premium) an individual pays for insurance reflects their personal likelihood of needing to use health care.

Uncertainty and the demand for insurance

For the individual, illness is unpredictable. In general terms, it may be possible to predict the prognoses associated with various chronic conditions and to predict in probabilistic terms how people of varying ages, circumstances, and pre-existing conditions will fare in terms of their future health status. But, at the level of the individual, future health status is likely to be uncertain.

It follows from this that one cannot plan one's future consumption of health care in the way that one could do so for commodities like food. As a result of this inability to plan when a future event will occur, an unregulated market would respond by developing insurance mechanisms, whereby an individual, or family, could make payments to some risk-pooling agency (usually an insurance company) for guarantees for some form of financial reimbursement in the event of illness leading to the insured person incurring health care expenses. Some insurance against loss of income may be taken out by the insured person, but, despite the desirability of doing so, it is difficult to insure against anxiety, pain and suffering resulting directly from illness. This is because of difficulties in valuing anxiety, pain and suffering in monetary terms, and because insurance companies could never obtain reliable and objective estimates of how much anxiety, pain and suffering an illness leads to. On the other hand, health care expenditures incurred are a fairly reliable signal that an illness has occurred and they are more readily quantifiable. Therefore, it is health care insurance which is mostly taken out by insured people, although it is commonly referred to as health insurance. People cannot insure against ill-health itself but rather the financial costs of ill-health. Thus, health care insurance embodies the wider concept of income maintenance.

If insurance policies are actuarially fair, premiums paid will equal health care expenditure incurred. However, this assumes that insurance companies make no profit and incur no administration costs. These assumptions do not hold, but people still take out (actuarially unfair) insurance, paying premiums which are 'loaded' so as to cover administration and profit. The reason for this is that, in general, people are risk averse; they do not like risk and gain utility from covering the uncertainty of large financial losses. This is a utility gain for which they are willing to pay.

For example, in a community of ten people it might be known that each person has a one-in-ten chance of incurring health care expenditures of £1,000 per annum. If all are risk averse, each would take out an insurance policy, paying £100 per annum each if it were actuarially fair. However, if administrative costs were £10 per annum, would each person be willing to pay the actuarially unfair premium of £101 each? The answer is probably 'yes'.

People are also more likely to insure against larger losses which are unpredictable than against smaller losses which occur more regularly and therefore more predictably. For instance, of those people who visit a dentist every six months for a check-up, some may not find it worth their while insuring against the predictable and inexpensive check-up itself, but would rather insure against the unpredictable and more expensive consequence of requiring treatment subsequent to the check-up. This does not mean, of course, that no one will insure against relatively small potential losses; many people do insure against such losses. The reason for this may be related not only to uncertainty itself, but also to the anxiety associated with incurring financial costs. However, as one would expect, the value of insurance is in providing cover against the uncertainty of financial losses – especially large ones.

(Donaldson *et al.* 2005)

Feedback

1 People who are risk averse are likely to take out insurance because insurance reduces the risks they have to face. They will take out insurance if the expected utility associated with doing so is more than the expected utility associated with bearing the risk themselves.

2 As Donaldson *et al.* point out, health insurance is not insurance against poor health per se. It is insurance against health treatment costs. If a person pays a health insurance premium then when they are ill they will not have to pay their health care charges. Alternatively, if they do have to pay then they pay at a much reduced rate.

Insurance therefore protects individuals from financial risk. However, the market for health care insurance is not necessarily allocatively efficient. Insurance markets are subject to particular market failures arising from asymmetry of information.

Asymmetry of information exists when one person in an economic transaction has more relevant information than the other person. It requires that the cost to the uninformed person of accessing this information is prohibitively high. This can lead to actions that work against the uninformed party and result in market failure. Under normal circumstances, the uninformed person would gather information so that they can minimize their loss. When the cost of information-gathering is so expensive that it would completely offset any benefits gained from the original transaction, it becomes inefficient to do so. You will now see how this occurs in health care insurance markets in the form of *adverse selection* and *moral hazard*.

Adverse selection

In the case of insurance, if someone thinks they are a low risk then they are less likely to take up insurance than someone who believes themselves to be a high risk. This will mean that only high-risk people will pool their risks and low-risk people will not. This is known as *adverse selection*. Of the informed group (individuals who know their own health risk), only those who will benefit most from an agreement will enter the agreement, to the detriment of the uninformed person (the insurer). The uninformed person cannot tell whether the agreement will be to their own disadvantage or not because they do not have the necessary information. In this case, the insurer will not be able to tell if those they insure are high or low risk. If the insurer could afford to gather information on the risk level of each person they insure then they could offer a premium that was beneficial to each person. As things stand there will be a sub-optimal level of insurance and as you will see in Chapter 11 this can lead to the collapse of the market as insurers select to cover risks adversely to themselves.

Activity 8.5

In a country where the main source of funding for health care is through private health insurance, are all groups in the population likely to be insured?

Feedback

Two groups of people remain uninsured. First, those who consider themselves to be of low risk but cannot find an insurance policy that reflects this low risk. This happens if the insurer is not informed of this low risk. This constitutes a market failure (adverse selection) because a premium acceptable to both insurer and insured could be found if asymmetry of information did not exist.

The other group who are likely to remain uninsured are those at high risk who cannot afford to pay an actuarially fair premium. Although not a market failure, this might be seen as unjust, in which case it may receive a lot of political attention. Even in the USA, which spends more money per capita on health care than any other country, there are an estimated 45 million people with no health insurance coverage at all. If many of these people have a higher than average health risk, a compulsory social insurance system might be justified on both efficiency and equity grounds (see Chapter 12). The idea of compulsory insurance is viewed critically by some in the USA because freedom of choice is a highly-valued ideal.

Moral hazard

Another form of market failure observed in both health care provision and health insurance markets is moral hazard. This occurs if the informed person, after the transaction has been agreed, uses their information to the disadvantage of the uninformed person. For example, someone who is insured may have an incentive to act recklessly (*consumer moral hazard*). This can manifest itself in less effort being made to avoid the need for health care – just like when individuals might take less care over locking up a bicycle when it is insured, people might not take exercise, might drink excessive alcohol or smoke. Under private or social insurance and tax-funded systems, the zero or subsidized price of health can also result in the over-consumption of health care when ill. Figure 8.5 shows how, in this case, consumers consume up to the point where their marginal benefit equals the marginal cost to them (the price) resulting in an overall welfare loss.

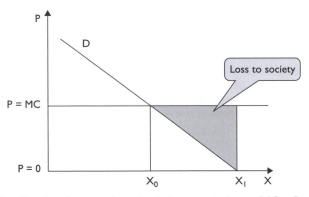

Figure 8.5 Potential welfare loss from setting price below marginal cost (MC – P > 0)

Insurers suffer financially from consumer moral hazard. To address this, the insurer could build a clause into the contract that disallows such behaviour but the *transaction costs* of monitoring whether the insured are adhering or not would be too high. There are two main methods used by insurance companies to reduce moral hazard. The first involves reducing premiums for people who have made no claims in previous similar transactions. This method helps to distinguish low-risk from high-risk persons and therefore gives the insurer the ability to offer premiums that reflect the risk levels of each group. The method will not be perfect, however, because some high-risk clients will not have made a claim yet, whereas some unfortunate low-risk clients will have already had to make a claim. Furthermore this cannot be applied when someone has never taken out a policy before or if it is not possible to verify whether they have made a claim or not. The strategy will provide insured people with an incentive to minimize their risk because if they do not and they then need to make a claim it will cause their future premiums to be increased.

The second mechanism is the introduction of different forms of user charges or cost sharing mechanisms, such as *deductibles* or *copayments*. These have been shown to reduce the utilization of health services and so potentially address this welfare loss (Lagarde and Palmer 2008; Thomson *et al.* 2010).

Activity 8.6

There are some drawbacks with user charges. What do you think these might be?

Feedback

- User chargers disproportionately affect low income groups.
- Demand is reduced for effective treatments as well as trivial health care.
- They may not reduce health care costs in a situation where there is *provider moral hazard*. Provider moral hazard (or supplier induced demand) occurs when a provider over-supplies services to maximize their income in the knowledge that the insurer (or third-party payer) will pay (see Chapter 10).
- In lower-income countries there may be no alternative to patient charges in order to raise funds for health care (fragile tax base, poorly developed insurance markets, etc.).

You will read more about different cost-sharing mechanisms under private insurance in Chapter 11.

Agency

Think back to the model of demand in Chapter 4. In the model, consumers (or, in the case of health care, patients) are said to be sovereign. In order to be so, they must:

- judge the costs and benefits of health care;
- bear the costs and receive the benefits;
- purchase those treatments where benefits exceed costs.

For many areas of health care, these conditions do not hold and patient sovereignty is limited. In most instances, the patient has health care insurance which means they do not bear the full cost. They also require a health care provider to act on their behalf in what economists refer to as an *agency* relationship. Economists often describe doctors as 'agents' because they act on behalf of the patient. The doctor (agent) is informed about a patient's health and their treatment options. The patient (principal) is relatively uninformed about these matters and therefore has to rely on the doctor to act in their (the patient's) best interests. A person will employ the services of an agent if they believe that their utility afterwards will be greater than without the help of the agent.

You will probably realize that this relationship is subject to information asymmetry – the doctor is usually better informed than the patient – and that this can give rise to moral hazard. In this instance, moral hazard occurs when an agent acts in their own interest at the expense of the patient or the third-party payer.

Activity 8.7

From your reading so far and your own experience and understanding, try to answer the following questions:

1 Licensing of doctors and other health care professionals is necessary and inevitable. Why might it be inefficient though?

2 In a system with third-party payers (such as social insurance), there are theoretically three asymmetries of information. One is the patient–payer relationship, which may lead to consumer moral hazard. What might be the other two?

Feedback

1 It was noted earlier that the existence of licensing is a barrier to entry into the health care market. As such it provides a potential for the exploitation of market power. In most countries there is a large number of doctors so we would expect the health care market to be competitive, but there are several reasons why this might not be the case.

a) Because doctors are much better informed than the purchasers of their services, they may be able to act as if they were a monopoly even though they are not. They can influence price because purchasers are uninformed about the relative quality of different providers. Patients who are uninformed about the effectiveness of services may, on the advice of their doctor, buy them at a price that is higher than the benefit they receive. This is called *supplier-induced demand* (see Chapter 10). Doctors will only have an incentive to do this if the financial reward for giving the service is relatively high.

b) Organizations that represent the interests of particular professions may have considerable power in a health service. It is important that these bodies do not have a role in setting fees for services. This would mean that doctors had control over both output and price in the health care market. If the fee was set relatively high then doctors would have incentives to increase provision beyond the allocatively efficient level (supplier-induced demand) – it is argued that there were efficiency gains in the US health care system after the powers of professional bodies were limited (Green 2007).

c) Specialist doctors may find that they really do have a monopoly on the services they supply. They will be able to supply their services to patients or employers at a very high price.

2 Table 8.1 outlines the possible asymmetries.

Table 8.1 Relationships with asymetric information

Informed party	Uninformed party	Market failure
Patient	Payer*	1 Consumer moral hazard 2 Adverse selection
Doctor	Patient	Imperfect agency
Doctor	Payer*	Provider moral hazard (supplier-induced demand)

* Payers may be private insurers, the social insurance system or the government

Asymmetry of information is not a market failure exclusive to the health care insurance market but is also found in health care services. The inefficiencies that arise because of the relationship between patient and doctor and doctor and payer are typical of an *agency* relationship.

Government intervention

So far in this chapter we have learned that market failures exist in both the health care market and the health insurance market. The presence of externalities and monopolies is a strong argument for government intervention. However, in the previous chapter a number of counter-arguments in support of markets in health care were made, including their facilitation of technical and allocative efficiency, innovation, resilience, voluntary cooperation and choice.

In this chapter you have also learned about initiatives that government and insurers can take to minimize the effect of these market failures. But what about government intervention – is this efficient? Government intervention will inevitably require some public funding (probably from taxation). If the government goes as far as taking over the health care market then huge amounts of finance will be required. Taxes are distortionary, whether they are on goods and services or on incomes. They change the equilibrium price and quantity, and can reduce social welfare in these markets. It is the *extent* of the market failure that is the important consideration. If market failures associated with health care are relatively minor, then health care should probably be left to the market.

Summary

You have read about the different types of inefficiency that occur in markets: monopoly, public goods, externalities and asymmetry of information, and the different mechanisms governments can use to control for their negative effects. You have also learned about the role health insurance plays in shaping the market for health care. In Section 4 you will bring together your reading from the first sections of the book to explore the area of health care financing.

References

Donaldson CK *et al.* (2004) *The economics of health care financing: the visible hand*. Basingstoke: Palgrave Macmillan.

Donaldson C *et al.* (2005) *Economics of health care financing: the visible hand* (2nd edn). Hampshire: Palgrave Macmillan.

Green M (2007) *The economics of health care*. London: Office of Health Economics.

Lagarde M and Palmer N (2008) The impact of user fees on health service utilization in low- and middle-income countries: how strong is the evidence? *Bulletin of the World Health Organization* 86(11): 839–48.

McIntyre P and Leask J (2008) Improving uptake of MMR vaccine. *British Medical Journal* 336:729, doi:10.1136/bmj.39503.508484.80.

Mills A and Gilson L (1988) *Health economics for developing countries: a survival kit*. London: London School of Hygiene & Tropical Medicine.

Parkin M, Powell M and Matthews K (2008) *Economics*. Harlow: Pearson Education.

Smith R, Beaglehole R, Woodward D and Drager N (eds) (2003) *Global public goods for health: health economics and public health perspectives*. Oxford: Oxford University Press.

Thomson S, Foubister T and Mossialos E (2010) Can user charges make health care more efficient? *British Medical Journal* 341:c3759.

Further reading

Gubb J, Lawson N, Smith S and Tomlinson J (2010) Will a market deliver quality and efficiency in health care better than central planning ever could? Debate. *British Medical Journal* 340:568–70.

Hanson K (2004) Public and private roles in malaria control: the contributions of economic analysis. *American Journal of Tropical Medicine and Hygiene* 71(suppl 2):168–73.

Hanson K, Kumaranayake L and Thomas I (2001) Ends versus means: the role of markets in expanding access to contraceptives. *Health Policy and Planning* 16(2):125–36.

Jack W (2001) The public economics of tuberculosis control. *Health Policy* 57(2):79–96.

Morris S, Devlin N and Parkin D (2007) *Economic analysis in health care*. Chichester: Wiley, Chapter 5, sections 5.1–5.3.5 and Chapter 6, sections 6.1–6.8.4.

SECTION 4

Health care financing

The changing world of health care finance

Lorna Guinness and Reinhold Gruen

Overview

This chapter introduces the question of where funding for health care comes from and how it is used. After an introduction to third-party arrangements and out-of-pocket payments, it examines the historical development of various countries' provision of health care, the distinction between public and private agents in the finance and provision of health services, and the question of the extent to which governments take responsibility for organizing health services.

Learning objectives

After working through this chapter, you will be able to:

- distinguish between the principal ways of funding health services
- identify historical and cultural factors that have influenced the evolution of health care finance
- identify factors which have determined the growth of health care spending
- distinguish between the different options of private–public mix in the financing and provision of health care

Key terms

Community financing. Collective action of local communities to finance health services through pooling out-of-pocket payments that can include a variety of payment methods such as cash, in-kind and partial or delayed payment.

Financial intermediary. An agency collecting money to pay providers on behalf of patients.

Fund pooling. The collection of funds that can be used for financing a given population's health care so that contributors to the pool share risks.

Out-of-pocket (direct) payment. Payment made by a patient directly to a provider.

Over the counter (OTC) drugs. Non-prescription drugs purchased from pharmacists and retailers.

Purchasing. The process of allocating funds to the providers of health care.

Regulation. Government intervention enforcing rules and standards.

Revenue collection. The raising of funds either directly from individuals seeking health care or indirectly through governments or donors.

Universal coverage. Extension of health services to the whole population so that they have access to good quality services according to needs and preferences, regardless of income level, social status or residency.

Unofficial payments. Spending in excess of official fees, also called 'under the table' or 'envelope' payments.

Health system financing

'Health system financing is the process by which revenues are collected from primary and secondary sources, accumulated in fund pools and allocated to provider activities' (Murray and Frenk 2000). Figure 9.1 locates the role of health system financing within the health system as a whole. Within the financing function of the health system there are three main activities. *Revenue collection* refers to the raising of funds either directly from individuals seeking health care or indirectly through governments or donors. *Fund pooling* refers to the collection of funds that can be used for financing a given population's health care so that contributors to the pool share risks. *Purchasing* is the process of allocating funds to the providers of health care.

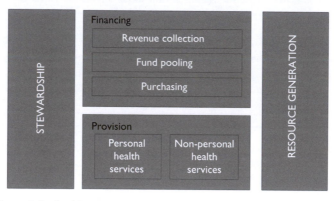

Figure 9.1 Functions of the health system
Source: Murray and Frenk (2000)

Ultimately, whether through out-of-pocket payments, taxation or health insurance, financing for the health system originates from households. In a most basic way, therefore, health care financing represents a flow of funds from patients to health care providers in exchange for services. As Figure 9.2 shows, there are two ways of paying for health services:

• *out-of-pocket payments:* this is the simplest and earliest form of transaction between patient and provider;

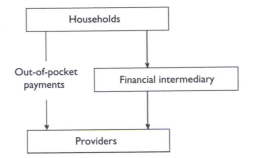

Figure 9.2 The flow of funds in health care provision

- *third-party payments:* where providers are paid by an insurance company or a government.

Much of this chapter focuses on the principal type of financing, through third parties. Beforehand it is appropriate to think more about out-of-pocket payments, which are a significant source of health care finance.

Activity 9.1

1 For which health services do you need to pay out-of-pocket for in your country?
2 Which expenses are unlikely to be covered out-of-pocket?
3 Do you think that out-of-pocket spending has increased during the past few years?

Feedback

1 In many countries out-of-pocket payments for health care play an important role. From low-income countries there is evidence that people who are not covered by insurance pay high amounts for health care in relation to their income. In Africa, more than 50 per cent of health care expenses come from directly paid private sources (Bennet *et al.* 1997). Types of out-of-pocket expenditure include the following.
   - Private consultations with doctors.
   - Over the counter (OTC) drugs.
   - Co-payments and user fees: where third-party payment is prevalent, cost sharing in the form of co-payments plays an important role. Co-payments and user fees may apply to prescribed drugs, hospital care, outpatient care and emergency transport.
   - Unofficial fees: besides official fees, unofficial payments to health workers are common in many countries. Additional payments to staff to get access to hospital care are common in some Asian countries. In a range of countries in central and eastern Europe, doctors used to expect unofficial payments as a supplement to their income.
   - Services not covered by insurance: transport costs, traditional or complementary medicine and luxury services such as cosmetic surgery.
2 These are expenses that are high in relation to income. For example, expensive therapies are unlikely to be paid out-of-pocket, as people would need to spend a

large proportion of their income or wealth on health care. Usually, individuals seek insurance to protect themselves against such potentially catastrophic losses. You may also think of services with characteristics of a public good which are financed publicly because they are not provided by private markets. Think of preventive services, such as health education, which the individual consumer may not be willing to purchase privately.

3 Overall out-of-pocket spending on health care is increasing. This is due to the growing proportion of OTC drugs and increasing cost sharing.

The evolution of health service finance

International comparisons show that countries use different ways of paying for health services. For example, France and Sweden have developed distinctly different practices to fund hospitals and to pay for doctors. Latin American countries have social insurance systems whereas in many African countries government funding is common.

To a large extent, these differences are due to historical factors. Analysing the historical context will make you aware that health finance today has been shaped by cultural and political factors from the past. It will explain why the approach to health finance differs between countries; this will help you to make more meaningful comparisons between countries and also enable you to understand the strengths and weaknesses of your own country's health system.

From private to social health insurance to universal coverage

Prior to the development of modern health care systems, *governments* or *charities* financed services for groups of the population for whom they perceived a duty of care. For example, hospitals for the poor existed in India, China, Arabia and medieval Europe (Abel-Smith and Campling 1994).

For the more affluent, *private* (or *voluntary*) *health insurance* was pioneered in Europe as early as the eighteenth century. In the nineteenth century, private insurance was developed throughout Europe and spread to North and South America. Meanwhile, *social* (or *compulsory*) *insurance* was introduced in Germany for industrial workers in 1883 by Otto von Bismarck (1815–98), building on the existing voluntary precedents. Payroll-based social insurance systems developed steadily in Europe, later in Latin America and Asia and now Africa.

Achieving universal health care coverage

Countries have used different means of making health care available to all: *universal coverage* is achieved either through the extension of social insurance or government provision to the whole population.

The Soviet Union extended coverage through government provision in 1938, and that example was followed by the countries of the Soviet bloc after World War II. The UK extended coverage to all in 1948. The British NHS was established as a major part of the social reforms recommended by William Beveridge with the aim of providing health services for the whole population. In the USA, private insurance has assumed a larger role than in Europe. But, even in the USA, publicly funded health care plays a large role for the elderly (Medicare), the poor (Medicaid), and armed services personnel, and the 2010 health care reforms aim to move the USA to universal coverage.

The health finance systems of low-income countries have been strongly influenced by their colonial past. In British colonies, government funded services for the armed forces and civil services provided the basis for further extension of health care, whereas in French colonies the model was provided by larger firms, which were required to provide services for their employees. To a variable extent, charitable organizations and missions also played a role in financing hospitals. In the post-colonial era these countries made efforts to extend services 'as far as economic growth and available resources allowed' (Abel-Smith and Campling 1994).

Activity 9.2

This activity gives you an opportunity to identify the current basis of the health finance system in your country.

1 What is the main way of financing health services in your country (out-of-pocket payment, private insurance, social insurance or taxation)? What were the precedents of the current funding system?
2 Approximately what proportion of the population is covered by each source of funding?

Feedback

1 The health finance systems in most countries can be traced back to one of the several means of funding which had evolved by the end of the nineteenth century. The earliest form of finance was by direct payment from those using the service to health care providers. Later, services funded by government or charities evolved, followed by private and social insurance. In many countries, voluntary schemes prevailed before social insurance or tax funded systems were introduced. In low-income countries, precedents of formal financing systems are services for the armed forces and civil service, and mission hospitals.
2 Having a large single source of funding doesn't necessarily mean that the whole population is covered. Most countries rely on several sources of funding, as they often retain some elements of previous arrangements when a new means of finance is introduced.

Increasing health care costs

As health systems have evolved and larger proportions of national populations are covered by health insurance, there has been rising concern about the increasing costs of health care. Figure 9.3 shows how growth in total health expenditure has outstripped GDP growth for OECD countries over the last 15 years. Why are health services getting more expensive? You need to be aware of microeconomic and political considerations when analysing changes in health care costs. There are a number of interrelated reasons that answer this question.

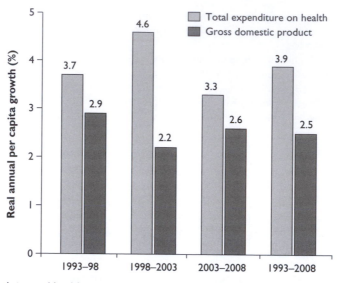

Figure 9.3 Growth in total health expenditure and GDP 1993–2008
Source: OECD (2010a)

Demographic factors

As well as *absolute population growth, relative changes within a population* affect health care costs. Relative changes can mean that the distribution of the population shifts towards groups with higher health care needs (the elderly, the very young, displaced populations).

Economic factors

As you read in Chapter 2, economic trends influence the health sector and the costs of delivering health services. In general, economic growth is associated with rising costs of health services. Economic recession has the opposite effect. But you need to be aware that unemployment and poverty are related to ill health and put additional strain on health services. When assessing cost escalation, you need to consider general price rises by taking into account the inflation rate. Supply factors also exert important pressures – for example, increasing numbers of doctors and hospitals or payment increases for health workers.

Health technology advances

At the beginning of the twentieth century, health services had only a few effective treatments. Since then, the number of effective interventions has steadily expanded – for example, antibiotics (1938), open heart surgery (1954), haemodialysis (1960) and computerized tomography (1973). Between one quarter and one half of health expenditure growth between 1960 and 2007 can be attributed to technological advances (Smith *et al.* 2009). Most recently, the use of expensive diagnostic tools, such as MRI and CT scanners have been driving up health care costs with an increase of over 100 per cent for MRI units per capita across OECD member countries between 2000 and 2008 (OECD 2010b).

Disease patterns

Why does the change of disease patterns, which has been observed in many low-income countries, affect health care costs? First, new diseases like HIV/AIDS increase the level of ill health in the population. Second, the relative increase in chronic diseases and long-term illness is related to higher treatment costs. With economic development, countries are likely to experience higher health care costs, as deaths among infants from communicable diseases decrease relative to adult deaths from chronic diseases. This trend has been described as the *epidemiological* (or *health*) *transition*. Note that in 2001, 60 per cent of all deaths in the world were from non-communicable diseases. But these figures are unevenly distributed among income groups: non-communicable diseases were responsible for only 36 per cent of the deaths among the poorest 20 per cent of the world as compared to 87 per cent among the richest. This indicates that inexpensive, effective interventions against communicable disease still have a high priority in improving the health of the poor (Mathers *et al.* 2006).

Evolution of the health system

Some authors (Relman 1988; Hurst 1992) have put forward a three-stage model to explain how health systems have changed during the last 60 years resulting in changing costs:

1 During the first stage, policies removed the existing financial barriers to health care. New funding arrangements increased population coverage and triggered the *expansion* of health services.
2 The subsequent increase in demand led to a rapid growth of health care expenditure. Often spending grew faster than the gross domestic product (GDP) and policy efforts were focused on *cost control*.
3 From the experience of ever-rising costs, it was realized that cost control alone is not effective. Policies of the third stage aim to *improve efficiency* of service delivery and use.

Political factors

Health budgets are inevitably based on political judgement. There may be additional 'cash injections' before elections or deviations from planned growth rates because of other priorities. Health funds may be diverted officially to support other purposes. Concerns about equity may improve access to services and increase costs. On the other hand, corruption of politicians, civil servants or health care providers may lead to substantial economic losses.

Some popular fallacies of the current debate

Be cautious with estimates of the effect of ageing on health care costs. Recent research has shown that the highest costs occur during the last year of life, irrespective of age.

Very old people may even tend to consume fewer resources than younger ones (Hamel et al. 1996; Werblow et al. 2007). In high-income countries, the increasingly high costs of dying seem to be a more important factor than the steadily increasing proportion of the elderly.

You should also be aware that, contrary to popular belief, *prevention and early treatment* can lead to increased costs in the long run. For example, lifetime health care costs are lower among smokers than among non-smokers, suggesting that early death from smoking prevents paying extra costs of treating other diseases (Barendregt et al. 1997). In addition, earlier death reduces the cost of paying retirement pensions.

Another fallacy is related to the effect of *new health care technologies*. New equipment may be expensive initially but may ultimately be more cost-effective than the older technologies it replaces. As you will learn later in the chapters on economic evaluation, new technologies can only be justified if they lower costs or improve outcomes and/or services. It is important to be aware that it is not technological advance per se that escalates costs, rather the failure to implement the rules of economic evaluation (Normand 1991).

The changing world of health services finance

The rising costs of health care mean that paying for health care is an issue of concern in most, if not all, countries. Governments are worried about the economic and political consequences of the increasing cost of providing health services and try to limit spending through tighter controls and other reforms. There is a large body of literature to suggest that many countries have been dissatisfied with the existing methods of finance and delivery of health services or, as in the case of the former Soviet Union, have been compelled into reform through massive political change and economic crisis. Although the motives and types of reform may differ, there have been some common themes:

- *separation of purchaser and provider responsibilities* whereby the underlying idea is that purchasers contract with those providers offering best value for money and that this increases the efficiency of service delivery;
- *redefinition of the role of the state* in responsibility for health care;
- *encouragement of the private sector;*
- *encouragement of competition between providers;*
- *alternative sources of funding*: budget constraints and political change in many countries has resulted in the health sector and governments seeking out alternative ways of mobilizing resources.

When considering the last of these it is helpful to distinguish between *macro-level* and *micro-level* changes. Micro-level changes do not affect the basic method of funding. Such changes include introduction of co-payments and changes in the way providers are paid. In contrast, macro-level changes involve a change in the basic principle of funding, such as the move in Italy and Spain from social insurance towards a system mainly based on taxation or the development of the tax-based universal coverage system in Thailand. Some of the most radical recent changes have occurred in the former Soviet Union and Eastern Europe (Davis 2010). A large number of former communist countries have undergone a change from government funded services to social insurance. Eleven countries passed social insurance laws between 1991 and 1996 (Ensor and Thompson 1997).

Radical changes have also been taking place in some low-income countries where the greater use of community financing and patient charges has been pursued. The term 'community financing' doesn't refer to a special finance mechanism; it is related to the way fundraising is organized by local communities. The collective effort of rural communities often has other targets than health, such as crop insurance or credit financing. Community funding for health care is more likely to develop where there are no free government services.

Developing methods to pay providers

Methods of paying health care providers have evolved along with the development of funding systems. Finding the optimal means of providing payment has been a constant source of political debate as it can be a key factor in managing costs (Bodenheimer 2005). Strategies used by doctors to gain favourable conditions have included boycotts and takeovers as well as the foundation of their own insurance organizations (Abel-Smith and Campling 1994). Conflicts between the medical profession and financing agents are related to issues of whether:

- doctors should be employed or act as independent contractors;
- payments should be based on a *salary*, on the number of patients cared for (*capitation*), on the items of care provided (*fee-for-service* – FFS), on the quality of their performance or on a combination of these options;
- patients should pay health care providers directly and then claim reimbursement from government or insurance companies or payments should be made directly to the providers by the funders.

Activity 9.3

Patients, trade unions, employers and doctors are important interest groups which have shaped the development of health care finance. For example, failure of the USA to achieve universal coverage has been related, among other reasons, to the influence of a medical profession with 'the power to use a political system, which responded to strong lobbies' (Abel-Smith and Campling 1994). To what extent has the medical profession influenced the way health services are paid for in your country? Think of the employment status of providers of health care and methods for paying them.

Feedback

You should be aware that many of the current ways of paying providers reflect political conflicts from the past. Along with the development of health care financing, doctors have employed strategies to achieve an independent status from the financial agent and more favourable payment conditions. This was less successful in countries where strong consumer and government interests shaped the organization of health care, such as in the Nordic countries, where employed doctors are common. In the USA, the dominance of private insurance companies has supported the trend towards independent practitioners who are paid by FFS. Many countries have mixed systems for paying doctors, for instance salaried doctors in hospitals and independent contractors in primary care. In the next chapter you will explore the impact of different methods for paying providers.

The public–private distinction

A common feature of all health systems is the distinction between public and private health care. This distinction refers to both the finance and the provision of health services. The concept of *ownership* is used to distinguish whether an organization belongs to the private or public sector.

The notion of a public agency refers not only to government organizations but also to public bodies with statutory responsibilities, like social insurance companies. The private sector can be divided into *for profit* and *not for profit* organizations. The former include the drugs industry and private hospitals or clinics in which some (sometimes most) of any financial surplus goes out of the organization to the shareholders. Not for profit organizations reinvest any financial surplus in their organization by developing facilities and training staff. The distinction from 'for profit' is not as clear-cut as some surplus in 'not for profit' organizations can also go out of the organization in the form of enhanced salaries and bonuses.

The following extract from Donaldson *et al.*'s (2005) book provides a framework for analysing the private–public relationship.

Public–private mix in finance and provision

The organisation of financial intermediaries may be on a monopolistic, oligopolistic or competitive basis. In a monopolistic system, the financial intermediary is usually a public agency such as a government, a quango[1] or a health corporation. In an oligopolistic system (i.e. one in which there are a small number of large intermediaries) finance can be controlled by public agencies or private agencies, such as insurance companies, or a combination of these. In a competitive system, a large number of small private intermediaries would exist ...

The provision of services, however, does not necessarily have to match the financial organisation. For instance, hospital care in many European countries represents a large, vertically integrated health system, in which finance and provision are combined within one organisation. Thus, both finance and provision are public as in the case of quadrant (1) [in Figure 9.4]. In many countries, general practice would fall into quadrant (2), such care being provided by self-employed doctors who, nevertheless, happen to receive almost all of their income from the public purse. Also, it is important to recognise that systems do not have to be vertically integrated in these ways: a third-party private payer, such as an insurance company, could also fit into segments (3) and (4). The basic point is that public finance does not have to match public provision, nor private finance match private provision. Public provision could be financed by private arrangements (private insurance, direct charges, etc.) and private provision by public finance (e.g. prospective payments made by government agencies directly to private hospitals).

There is a stronger case for government intervention in *financing* rather than in *providing* health care. Control of financial arrangements permits government bodies

[1] A quango is an organisation that is funded by the government but acts independently of it (i.e. a quasi non-governmental organisation).

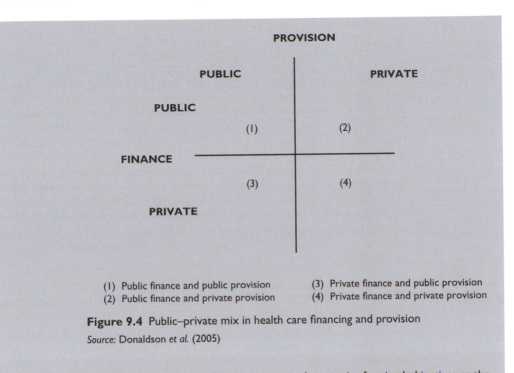

(1) Public finance and public provision   (3) Private finance and public provision
(2) Public finance and private provision   (4) Private finance and private provision

Figure 9.4 Public–private mix in health care financing and provision
Source: Donaldson *et al.* (2005)

more direction of the health care system in the pursuit of societal objectives: as the collective purchaser of care on the community's behalf, a public body can dictate terms of provision with equal power to both public and private providers. Simply providing public services does not guarantee use by those groups for whom they are intended, because less ill, rich or privately insured patients may be more 'attractive customers' for such hospitals than those more in need of care.

(Donaldson *et al.* 2005)

Activity 9.4

Focus on the different options for organizing health care and compare the examples given in the extract to the situation in your country. Consider where on Figure 9.4 the following services in your country would fit in terms of their finance and provision:

• primary care;
• hospital care;
• traditional/complementary medicine.

Feedback

You have probably discovered that both provision and finance can have a private and a public dimension. Sometimes it may be difficult to draw a clear dividing line between public and private. For example, in Germany, general medical practitioners are privately set up but they need to be members of a public body if they want to provide service to those who participate in social insurance. In many countries it is not uncommon for publicly employed doctors to engage in private practice and use – to a varying extent – government facilities. Under options (1) and (4) in Figure 9.4 the situation is straightforward, with both finance and provision being either public or private: for example, a government-owned hospital funded from social insurance (1) or a traditional healer paid by private fees (4). Category (2) applies to doctors who are self-employed but paid from public funds. Category (3), private finance and public provision, is not unusual – for example, pay beds in a public hospital.

Governments can organize finance, act as a purchaser, provide services and regulate health services. In many low-income countries, governments have historically had the major role in the provision of health care. Governments see it as the most efficient and equitable method of providing services. Though the private sector may play an increasing role, socioeconomic conditions are such that private care will not totally replace public services. In particular, primary health care in low-income countries is reliant on the public sector.

Activity 9.5

Contrast this view with the opinion presented by Donaldson *et al.* that there is a 'stronger case for government intervention in *financing* rather than in *providing* health care'.

Feedback

Donaldson *et al.* argue that simply providing government services does not ensure equity and efficiency. They favour the separation of responsibilities between purchasers and providers of care. As a purchaser of care, 'a public body can dictate terms of provision with equal power to both public and private providers'. Later in this book you will explore the options for state intervention in health care in more depth.

Summary

In this chapter you have learned about the different ways of funding health services, and how and why different systems have evolved in different countries. The reasons for increasing health care costs have been explored. Finally, the possible combinations of public and private funding and provision have been examined. In the following chapter you will consider the economics of different methods for paying providers. After that, the mechanisms of private health insurance and for achieving universal coverage will be investigated in Chapters 11 and 12 respectively.

References

Abel-Smith B and Campling J (1994) The history of the organization and financing of health services, in Abel-Smith B and Campling J, *An introduction to health policy, planning and financing*. London: Longman.

Barendregt J, Bonneux L and Van der Maas J (1997) The health care costs of smoking. *New England Journal of Medicine* 337:1052–7.

Bennet S, McPake B, and Mills A (1997) *Private health providers: serving the public interest.* London: Zed Books.

Bodenheimer T (2005) High and rising health care costs, part 3: the role of health care providers. *Annals of Internal Medicine* 142(12, Part 1):996–1002.

Davis C (2010) Understanding the legacy: health financing systems in the USSR and central and eastern Europe prior to transition, in Kutzin J, Cashin C and Jakab M (eds) *Implementing health financing reform: lessons from countries in transition.* Copenhagen: European Observatory on Health Systems and Policies.

Donaldson C et al. (2005) *The economics of health care financing: the visible hand.* Basingstoke: Palgrave Macmillan.

Ensor T and Thompson R (1997) Health insurance as a catalyst to change in former communist countries. Paper presented at the Annual Health Economics Unit Conference, Dhaka, Bangladesh.

Hamel MB et al. (1996) Seriously ill hospitalized adults: do we spend less on older patients? Support investigators. Study to understand prognoses and preference for outcomes and risks of treatments. *Journal of the American Geriatric Society* 44(9):1043–8.

Hurst J (1992) *The reform of health care: a comparative analysis of seven OECD countries.* Paris: OECD.

Mathers CD, Lopez AD and Murray CJL (2006) The burden of disease and mortality by condition: data, methods, and results for 2001, in Mathers CD et al. (eds) *Global burden of disease and risk factors.* New York: Oxford University Press.

Murray C and Frenk J (2000) A framework for assessing the performance of health systems. *Bulletin of the World Health Organisation* 78(6):717–31.

Normand C (1991) Economics, health and the economics of health. *British Medical Journal* 303:1572–7.

OECD (2010a) How much is too much? Value for money in health spending, in *Health policy studies: value for money in health spending.* Paris: OECD.

OECD (2010b) Growing health spending puts pressure on government budgets, according to OECD health data 2010. Paris: OECD.

Relman A (1988) Asessment and accountability: the third revolution in medical care. *New England Journal of Medicine* 319:1220–2.

Smith S, Newhouse J and Freeland MS (2009) Income, insurance and technology: why does health spending outpace economic growth? *Health Affairs* 28(5):1276–84.

Werblow A, Felder S and Zweifel P (2007) Population ageing and health care expenditure: a school of 'red herrings'? *Health Economics* 16(10):1109–26.

Further reading

Abel-Smith B and Campling J (1994) The history of the organization and financing of health services, in Abel-Smith B and Campling J, *An introduction to health policy, planning and financing.* London: Longman.

European Observatory on Health Care Systems (2002) Funding health care: options for Europe, policy brief 4. London: *European Observatory on Health Care Systems.*

OECD (2010) How much is too much? Value for money in health spending, in *Health policy studies: value for money in health spending.* Paris: OECD, Chapter 2.

Smith S, Newhouse J and Freeland MS (2009) Income, insurance and technology: why does health spending outpace economic growth? *Health Affairs* 28(5):1276–84.

World Health Organization (2000) Who pays for health systems? in *World Health Report.* Geneva: WHO, Chapter 5.

10 | Provider payments

Mylene Legarde

Overview

You will recall the debate on paying providers from Chapter 9. This chapter examines this issue in more detail. It identifies and explains the main payment mechanisms typically used to pay health professionals and hospitals, and the incentives created by these mechanisms. After presenting the concept of *incentives* in a general context, the theoretical frameworks that have been used by economists to analyse the various incentives that are present in the health system are described.

Learning objectives

After working through this chapter, you will be able to:

- define 'incentives'
- describe two agency relationships in the health care sector
- explain the role of incentives in the agency relationship
- describe the different types of payment mechanisms used to pay doctors and their resulting incentives
- describe the different types of payment mechanisms used to reimburse hospitals and their resulting incentives

Key terms

Agent. A person who acts on behalf of another.

Agency theory (or principal-agent theory). Describes the problems that arise under conditions of asymmetric information between two parties, the principal and the agent.

Capitation payment. A pre-determined amount of money per member of a defined population, served by the third-party payer, given to a provider to deliver specific services.

DRG (diagnosis-related group)/HRG (health care resource group). A case-mix classification scheme which provides a means of relating the number and type of acute inpatients treated in a hospital to the resources required by the hospital.

Fee-for-service (FFS). Payment mechanism where providers receive a specific amount of money for each service provided.

> **Incentive.**   Factor that motivates a particular course of action or encourages people to behave in a certain way.
>
> **Principal.**   A person on whose behalf an agent acts.

Incentives

You have learned that achieving allocative efficiency in health care systems is dependent on a number of factors, including the important market failure of information asymmetry. You have also read about the importance of the *principal* and the *agent* in influencing demand in health care markets (see Chapter 8). In this chapter you will look at the nature of the incentives created by the financing mechanisms in these relationships and their impact on provider behaviour. But first, let us look at what is meant by the term 'incentive'.

Generally speaking, an incentive can be defined as any factor that motivates a particular course of action or encourages people to behave in a certain way (usually in order to improve their own situation, where a disincentive is the reverse).

In health services, incentives might encourage health care providers to work more or less hard (both in terms of the quality and quantity of work provided). Certain incentives might also encourage health workers to try to increase the demand for health services. In turn, this can have important consequences for health care expenditures.

Although economics is mostly concerned with *financial incentives*, there are other types of incentive. Agents' behaviours can also be driven by *moral incentives*, when a particular choice is dictated by moral considerations or what they consider as the right thing to do. In a society, individual behaviours can also be driven by *coercive incentives* created by laws and legal rules which, if broken, will result in punishment or imprisonment.

How incentives can work ... and misfire!
In some schools teachers submit each week the names of students who are attentive listeners, and at the end of the week one of the names is drawn from a hat and that child obtains a prize of some sort. Such mechanisms create an incentive that encourages all children to behave nicely and listen to their teachers.

Some mechanisms can also unexpectedly create incentives that will encourage people to behave in a way that was not intended. For example, in a famous study on teachers' behaviours (Brian and Levitt 2003), economists showed how tests that had an important role in the assessment of teachers' performance could produce strong incentives for them to cheat and assist their students.

Agency theory

Description of the model

As you learned in Chapter 8, the principal–agent relationship relates to a situation where a first party, the agent, wants the second party, the principal, to perform a particular task on their behalf to achieve their objectives. The interests of the two parties are divergent, because the task should directly benefit the principal, but it is costly to the agent who has to exert some effort to perform it.

In addition to these divergent interests, the agency relationship is characterized by an asymmetry of information between the agent and the principal. In many instances it is very difficult to measure and evaluate the performance of agents objectively. The principal cannot observe the performance of the agent or does not know if the agent has performed in the best possible way he or she could. The question that lies at the heart of principal–agent theory, therefore, is how to motivate the agent to act in the interest of the principal, or how to design incentives that will align the interests of the two parties. There is a wide array of individual contracts that try to do this and link employee performance and remuneration. Such mechanisms include 'piece rates, [share] options, discretionary bonuses, promotions, profit sharing, efficiency wages, deferred compensation, and so on' (Prendergast 1999).

Agency theory in the health sector

A patient consults a health professional to act on their behalf and to prescribe the best course of treatment for their medical condition. Yet, instead of following the unique interest of the patient, the health care provider may seek to maximize their own utility. Assuming the health professional's utility is maximized through increased revenues and more leisure time, they are likely to minimize effort (e.g. the amount of time spent examining the patient) or provide unnecessary care or treatment where there are financial benefits from the additional services provided. Due to the patient's lack of medical knowledge, the diverse range of possible courses of action and the difficulty in measuring quality, the patient doesn't usually know whether the steps taken by the health professional are the most appropriate ones and in their own best interest. Instead the patient relies on the provider's recommendations for treatment or further tests.

Agency is also an important factor in the relationship between third-party payers and health care providers in the delivery of health care services. As in the first case, the objectives of the principal (third-party payer) and the agent (health care provider) are not necessarily aligned. The third-party payer typically expects the health care provider to provide good quality services using the most cost effective approaches. Yet the health professionals or medical clinics do not bear the financial costs of the health care services provided (and even often ignore them). In seeking to maximize their own utility/welfare there is an assumption that they minimize effort and/or maximize their revenue. As in the relationship between health professional and patient, there is an asymmetry of information. Only the provider has full information regarding the patient's condition and the medical knowledge to define the treatment required, while their performance is difficult to measure. Within a third-party payer system, the patient would have little or no incentive to monitor the unnecessary activities of the provider as the patient may only incur costs through a small rise in insurance premium or taxation relative to the care he or she receives. Due to the agency relationship, there is a risk that the optimal level of care will not be provided by the agent/health care provider.

Supplier-induced demand

As you have already seen, the asymmetry of information in the health provider–patient and payer–provider relationships permits the provider to potentially act in their own interest. One aspect of this is that health care providers may recommend medical examinations and treatments over and above the optimal level. This phenomenon is known as *supplier-induced demand*. It represents the demand that exists beyond what would have been asked by consumers if they had been fully informed.

Figure 10.1 provides a graphical illustration of the supplier-induced demand problem. S_0 and D_0 represent the initial supply and demand of health services, with the initial equilibrium (P_0, Q_0). If there is an increase of services provided by health professionals to S_1, the standard supply and demand analysis would predict the price to fall from P_0 to P_1 and the quantity demanded would increase from Q_0 to Q_1 (Figure 10.1a). Yet, according to the supplier-induced demand assumption, an increase in supply leads directly to an increase in demand (Figure 10.1b). The demand is no longer independent and stable at D_0 but instead health professionals use their influence to shift the demand outwards to a level such as D_{S1}, where the equilibrium price declines to P_{S1} with equilibrium quantity Q_{S1}. In practical terms, imagine a situation where a health professional

a) Classic approach

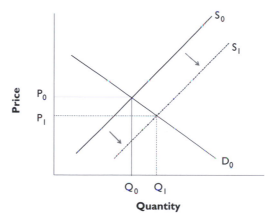

b) Supplier-induced demand

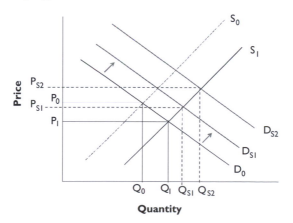

Figure 10.1 Supplier-induced demand

recommends to their patient, at the end of the consultation, that they should come back a few days later for a follow-up check, to make sure that the treatment is indeed working. Without the health professional's suggestion, it is likely that most patients would not come back for a follow-up visit. If health professionals manage to shift the demand a lot, such as to D_{S2}, the equilibrium may even rise above the initial price P_0 to P_{S2}, with equilibrium Q_{S2}.

Health providers' intrinsic motivation

The classical approach to agency theory has often been deemed too restrictive to account for the complexity of health professionals' motives (e.g. doctors' professional ethics as summarized by the Hippocratic oath). The model has been modified to account for the possibility that health professionals can also take the patient's well-being into account. In general, this is referred to as the 'intrinsic motivation' of health providers to perform efforts and seek to act in the patient's best interest. It means that they do not necessarily require a particular external pressure or incentive to act in ways that benefit patients.

Activity 10.1

A perfect agent from a societal perspective would maximize social welfare. From an individual perspective, a perfect agent would maximize a patient's utility. The factors that contribute to a patient's utility are:

- their health;
- information about their health and treatment;
- an appropriate level of participation in the decision-making process;
- process utility – respect from staff, pleasant environment, etc.;
- utility from non-health care consumption.

1 What do you think would encourage health care professionals to be perfect agents?
2 Consider what might be the major factors which feature in the utility function of a doctor.

Feedback

1 The factors that would limit the health care professional from acting in their own (personal) interest (besides their own interest in their patient's welfare) are:
   - if patients are relatively well informed;
   - the existence of peer review and other forms of professional regulation – the thought of being found out and embarrassed by their colleagues might be a very strong incentive;
   - their belief in a set of medical ethics; and
   - financial incentives in their contracts which encourage them to act in the interest of their patients.
   Although *patient utility* features in the health care professional's utility function, it is only one of several influences. The maximization of the health care professional's

utility is unlikely to occur at the same point as when the patient's utility is maximized.

2 You might have suggested:
  • their own income (and consumption);
  • their own leisure time;
  • the utility of their family and friends;
  • their professional prestige;
  • their patients' utility.

Despite the different factors that contribute to a health care professional's utility, empirical studies have shown that the uptake of health services is affected by provider characteristics, even after controlling for the other factors that affect demand (such as price, income and clinical needs). For example, incentives for self-referral (Hillman *et al.* 1990), physician attitudes towards earnings (Rizzo and Zeckhauser 2007) or payment mechanisms (Gosden *et al.* 1999) have all been shown to influence the utilization of health services. The findings of these studies confirm that different payment mechanisms create incentives that can affect the quality, quantity and costs of the care provided. As a result, how health care providers *should* be paid is a key issue in health care financing debates. The rest of this chapter explores this issue further by describing the main types of payment mechanism for health professionals and hospitals and their expected effects. You will also learn about the available empirical evidence in this area.

Paying health professionals

Health professionals are usually paid using one or, more often, a combination of the following four mechanisms: *fee-for-service, capitation, salary* or *performance-based payment*.

Fee-for-service

Fee-for-service (FFS) involves paying health professionals for each service provided to a patient (e.g. consultation, surgical act, X-ray, etc.). In other words, a health professional receives a fixed amount of money for every patient consultation. This method is widely used for paying health professionals in the private sector in many countries. For example, in the USA, physicians contracted by private insurers are usually paid FFS, as are GPs who provide primary care in France and Germany. Because this links the revenue of the health professional to the quantity of services provided, this mechanism creates an incentive for providers to increase their number of consultations or provide more services to each patient – i.e. supplier-induced demand. This kind of incentive can also be used to increase the volume of services where there is under-provision.

However, an FFS payment method does not always guarantee motivation to increase the volume of services. First, if the payment provided for a particular service does not exceed the cost incurred by the health professional, the converse will be true. The health professional may then decrease the volume of this service (or simply not provide it). Similarly, the differences in reimbursements offered to health professionals by Medicare and private insurance in the USA led practices to favour the treatment of privately-insured patients (Rice 1997).

Capitation

Under a capitation system, providers are paid a pre-determined amount per member of a defined population, to cover the provision of certain services on a continuous basis over a certain period of time (generally one year). Capitation is used as the main payment mechanism for GPs in the United Kingdom, but also in Italy and Spain (Langbrunner et al. 2005). Capitation payments are sometimes claimed to encourage providers to provide as little care as possible (e.g. minimize the number of patient visits to minimize the provider's effort and maximize their utility). This system can also lead to discrimination between patients in favour of those who require less attention; an activity described as 'cream skimming'. For example, there is evidence of a lower concentration of GP practices in poorer areas in the UK (Goddard et al. 2010). However, in the long-run, incentives are probably more complicated and effects on the quality of care can be positive. For example, if patients are free to choose their providers, a capitation system can encourage competing providers to improve the quality of the services to attract more patients, and increase their income.

Salary

In this approach, health care providers are employed by a particular organization (typically the national health system or the insurer) and receive a fixed salary every month. This form of payment is found in most low-income countries and in several western European countries, where physicians working in public health facilities are salaried (Langbrunner et al. 2005). As salaries are not linked to the volume of activities provided, there is no incentive to induce demand and there is even an incentive to under-provide services, as the salary is usually guaranteed at whatever level of outcome. However, mechanisms built into the salary system can counteract the lack of incentives. Some have argued that promotion (and associated increases in salary) is related to performance and can therefore introduce an incentive for increasing health professionals' efforts. In addition, unlike in a capitation system, there is no incentive for health professionals to compete for patients or select patients who require less effort. Despite this, systems in which health professionals receive salaries have been found to be associated with lower levels of health services (measured by tests, procedures and referrals) when compared with systems using other payment mechanisms (e.g. FFS and capitation – Gosden et al. 1999).

Performance-based payment

Faced with the limitations of the three traditional payment mechanisms presented above, payment mechanisms that link remuneration to particular desirable outcomes have been increasingly introduced in the health care sector, in particular in the USA (Christianson et al. 2007). These performance-based payments (also called pay-for-performance mechanisms) seek to align directly the interest of the agent (the provider) with the interest of the principal with a view to improving the quality of care. For example, in the UK GPs have been receiving an extra payment if the proportion of their patients who get vaccinated reaches a certain level. A danger here is that they may become target obsessed and neglect other important areas of care.

Part of the provider's remuneration is then directly linked to specific objectives, which can for example be defined in terms of use of services (e.g. proportion of women who are screened for cervical cancer – Kouides *et al.* 1998) or quality of services provided (e.g. time spent with each patient – Petersen *et al.* 2006). The following panel explores this approach further.

Perfomance-based payments in Rwanda
Examples of performance-based payment in low-income settings are still rare but they are gaining increasing attention from donors and governments alike as a way to improve the delivery of health care services by reaching more people with better quality services. Rwanda was one of the first countries to pilot such a mechanism in 2001. In the Kabutare district, the Ministry of Health and its operational partner, the non-governmental organization HealthNet International, introduced a form of performance-based financing, called the 'performance initiatives'. Before the introduction of the performance initiatives, staff at 15 health centres received a salary and annual fixed bonus, not linked to particular performance. Under the new approach, an output-based remuneration to the health centre replaced the fixed bonus system. Payments were set for the following services delivered by the health centres: curative care, ante-natal services, family planning, assisted deliveries and child immunizations.

Comparing productivity levels in 2001, when fixed annual bonuses were paid to staff, with levels in 2003, when an output-based payment incentive scheme was implemented, a study found significant increases in the productivity of health staff (Meessen *et al.* 2006). Despite methodological limitations, the study suggested that linking incentive rewards to verified performance led to increased pre-natal care, increased immunization coverage and increased assisted deliveries.

However, risks associated with this approach were also acknowledged. For example, as is often the case with FFS, users were induced to demand remunerated services. It was also observed that activities that were not remunerated were neglected and the quantity of remunerated services increased to the detriment of the quality.

Activity 10.2

This activity provides you with an opportunity to reflect on the current situation in your country.

1 How are health professionals paid in your country across different sectors?
2 What are the main advantages and drawbacks of each of the mechanisms used? (Think about the incentives created by each one, but also try to think about the implications of each mechanism for policy-makers/managers.)

Feedback

1 There are probably different systems coexisting in the same country. For example, GPs providing primary care might be paid by capitation, while doctors in hospitals might receive a salary. On the other hand, doctors in the private sector (e.g. self-employed having their own practice) will be paid by FFS. How doctors are remunerated in different contexts is often the result of political conflicts from the past

between different interest groups such as trade unions, consumers' interest groups and government bodies.

2 Table 10.1 lists some of the key advantages and drawbacks of the main four mechanisms used to pay individual providers.

Table 10.1 Advantages and disadvantages of the four main provider payment mechanisms

Payment	Advantages	Drawbacks
Fee-for-service	Provides a direct incentive to the doctor to increase effort (can be useful in some situations where there is an under-use of services)	Incentive to increase the provision of services beyond what is necessary (over-supply or supplier-induced demand); cost escalation
Capitation	No incentive to over-supply or induce the demand; strong incentive to improve efficiency of care delivery; improves continuity of care; ensures a good control of costs	Incentive to undersupply; increased efficiency may cause providers to sacrifice quality (however, not so much if patients are free to choose); 'cream-skimming' behaviours – doctors favour the enrolment of patients who are less sick
Salary	No incentive to over-supply or induce the demand; no incentive to compete for patients and/or select better-off and healthier patients; ensures a good control of costs	No incentive to improve efficiency; incentive to reduce services and/or quality of care
Performance-based payment	Increase the provision of specific (desired and targeted) services; increase the quality of care (when targeted)	'Gaming' behaviours (people trying to cheat by over-reporting); effort and attention is taken away from services that are not rewarded; potentially complicated system to monitor and enforce

Paying hospitals

There are essentially four mechanisms that have been used to reimburse hospitals for the health services they provide: line-item budgets, global budgets, payment per day or payment per case. As for individual payment mechanisms, each of these approaches is likely to have different effects on hospital behaviour.

Line-item budgets

This mechanism specifies a detailed budget for the main categories of inputs used in the delivery of health services (e.g. staff, medicines, food, etc.). Usually the allocation is based on the previous year's allocation and/or anticipated delivery of services. Due to their rigidity, line-item budgets provide limited incentives for efficient use of resources by hospitals. In addition they are typically only loosely related to actual services provided. Without linking the budget to a measure of quality there is no financial incentive to encourage the provision of good quality services.

This type of hospital payment mechanism was used in former communist countries as it allows a high level of control from the central level. It is still widely found in low-income settings where the lack of information on the costs, volumes of patients and patients' characteristics prevent governments from implementing more complicated payment mechanisms.

Global budgets

In this approach, hospitals receive a lump sum payment, which is expected to cover all their expenses to provide health services to the population over a given period of time (usually a year). Unlike line-item budgets, global budgets allow for flexibility in the management of resources as they provide some autonomy to hospitals. If they are allowed to keep any remaining surplus at the end of the period (or they are expected to cover any shortfall), hospitals can be encouraged to control costs and use resources efficiently. The danger is that they are also encouraged to ration health services and limit the services provided to make sure that their expenses will remain within their budget.

Global budgets have been widely used by many countries in the European Union as the main payment mechanism for hospitals. However, in most settings reforms have been introduced to facilitate some forms of case-based payments as well (see below).

Payment per day

With this payment mechanism, hospitals receive a set amount of money per bed-day. Because the costs of hospital care are usually higher during the early days of admission, and then diminish, the incentive created by payment per day is to keep patients longer so as to maximize revenue, especially when the payment per day is higher than the marginal cost of the bed-day. However, like FFS these incentives might be mitigated by other contextual factors. For example, if different payments per day apply for different patients, or if different insurers offer varying rates, hospitals might favour longer stays for some patients, while they might try to avoid the admission of others. Following the end of the communist regimes, per-day payments were introduced in hospitals in several eastern European countries, in an attempt to increase hospital admissions and efficiency of resource use simultaneously.

Payment per case

This involves prospectively paying providers a flat amount per hospitalization. In its simplest form, one standard payment is made for every case or discharge, regardless of the actual cost of care. Hospitals generate more revenue if they see more patients, so there are incentives to see more cases, especially if the case rate is higher than the actual marginal cost per case. This basic model encourages hospitals to be parsimonious in the use of resources (making sure that, on average, the resources used for a particular case are within the fixed envelope), but it can also lead to cream skimming whereby they increase admissions of less severe cases to the detriment of other more resource-intensive cases.

To limit these perverse incentives, most countries that have adopted this approach to pay for hospital services have introduced complex adjustments for case mix, to reflect variations in the efforts and costs involved by different pathologies.

Payment per case in case-mix models

In advanced health care systems, case-based payments for hospitals are based on classified systems of diagnosis often called diagnosis-related groups (DRGs), following the terminology used in the USA, where they were first introduced. In the UK, hospitals are paid according to a similar classification system, called HRGs (health care resource groups). DRGs classify patients requiring clinically similar treatments into standard groupings that consume comparable resources in hospital. DRGs are defined in advance and hospitals know the amount of money they will receive for each patient who falls into a particular DRG. Case-mix models reward hospitals for keeping costs within payment limits, and therefore to increase the efficiency of resource use. But they can also encourage hospitals to upgrade the severity of cases (also known as 'DRG creep'), and to discharge patients early and readmit them often. In practice, DRGs are complex to run and demand a lot of data. Evidence from transition countries in eastern Europe suggest these models are difficult to set up in health systems where the capacity might be limited (Langbrunner and Wiley 2002).

Summary

This chapter has explored the defining characteristic of the health care market of asymmetry of information that exists between those who supply the services (health care providers) and those who consume them or pay for them, and the impact of this relationship on payment mechanisms. The most common approaches to pay single providers have been salaries, FFS, capitation payments and more recently, performance-based payments. Historically, hospitals have been paid for their services through budgets (line-items or global) and payment per day or per case. Each payment mechanism creates a particular set of incentives, although these may be mitigated by characteristics of the health care market and particular features of the payment mechanism, and no single payment model is obviously superior. With this in mind, you will now go on to explore another aspect of health system financing in the form of insurance.

References

Brian J and Levitt SD (2003) Rotten apples: an investigation of the prevalence and predictors of teacher cheating. *Quarterly Journal of Economics* 118(3):843–78.

Christianson JB *et al.* (2007) *Financial incentives, healthcare providers and quality improvements: a review of the evidence.* London: The Health Foundation.

Goddard M *et al.* (2010) Where did all the GPs go? Increasing supply and geographical equity in England and Scotland. *Journal of Health Services Reseach & Policy* 15(1):28–35.

Gosden T *et al.* (1999) How should we pay doctors? A systematic review of salary payments and their effect on doctor behaviour. *QJM* 92(1):47–55.

Hillman BJ *et al.* (1990) Frequency and costs of diagnostic imaging in office practice – a comparison of self-referring and radiologist-referring physicians. *New England Journal of Medicine* 323(23):1604–8.

Kouides RW *et al.* (1998) Performance-based physician reimbursement and influenza immunization rates in the elderly. *American Journal of Preventive Medicine* 14(2):89–95.

Langbrunner J and Wiley C (2002) Hospital payment mechanisms: theory and practice in transition countries, in McKee M and Healy J (eds) *Hospitals in a changing Europe*. Maidenhead: Open University Press.

Langbrunner J et al. (2005) Purchasing and paying providers, in Figueras J, Jakubowski E and Robinson R (eds) *Purchasing to improve health systems performance*. Maidenhead: Open University Press.

Meessen B et al. (2006) Reviewing institutions of rural health centres: the performance Initiative in Butare, Rwanda. *Tropical Medicine & International Health* 11(8): 1303–17.

Petersen LA et al. (2006) Does pay-for-performance improve the quality of health care? *Annals of Internal Medicine* 145(4): 265–72.

Prendergast C (1999) The provision of incentives in firms. *Journal of Economic Literature* 37(1):7–63.

Rice T (1997) Physician payment policies: impacts and implications. *Annual Review of Public Health* 18:549–65.

Rizzo JA and Zeckhauser RJ (2007) Pushing incomes to reference points: why do male doctors earn more? *Journal of Economic Behavior & Organization* 63(3): 514–36.

Further reading

Gosden T et al. (1999) How should we pay doctors? A systematic review of salary payments and their effect on doctor behaviour. *QJM* 92(1):47–55.

Langbrunner J and Wiley C (2002) Hospital payment mechanisms: theory and practice in transition countries, in McKee M and Healy J (eds) *Hospitals in a changing Europe*. Maidenhead: Open University Press.

Langbrunner J et al. (2005) Purchasing and paying providers, in Figueras J, Jakubowski E and Robinson R (eds) *Purchasing to improve health systems performance*. Maidenhead: Open University Press.

Robinson JC et al. (2004) Alignment and blending of payment incentives within physician organizations. *Health Services Research* 39(5):1589–606.

Private health insurance

11

Sachiko Ozawa

Overview

Having explored sources and uses of health care finance in Chapter 9 you will now examine the strengths and weaknesses of private health insurance. This chapter provides an overview of the mechanisms of private health insurance and examines the measures insurers use to counteract the risks of moral hazard and adverse selection. You will begin by getting a global picture of private health insurance, revisiting the theoretical principles, and then looking more closely at how private health insurance and managed care work in practice.

Learning objectives

After working through this chapter, you will be able to:

- explain the economic rationale for insurance and how insurance works in health care
- give examples of how insurance companies try to counteract moral hazard and adverse selection
- distinguish between the main types of managed care organizations
- suggest reasons why private insurance can fail to provide equity and efficiency

Key terms

Actuarially fair premium. An insurance premium that is set where the expected payouts equal the premiums paid by the insured (plus the cost of administration).

Co-insurance. The percentage of a medical bill that the insured must pay, after deductibles and co-payments are met.

Community rating. Insurance premiums that are based on the pooled risk of a community. All individuals in the community pay the same premium, regardless of claims experience or personal level of risk.

Co-payment. A specified amount the insured must pay for each received service that can vary by service.

Deductible. A fixed amount of a health care charge that the insured must pay before the insurer begins payment for all or part of the remainder of the costs.

Experience rating.   Insurance premiums are based on the claims experience or risk level, such as age, of each insured group.

Managed care organization (MCO).   An organization with payment or delivery arrangements to control medical care costs and quality through utilization management, drug formularies and profiling participating providers according to criteria for appropriate use of medical services.

Underwriting.   The insurer's process of reviewing insurance applications, deciding what coverage to offer and determining the applicable premiums based on the health status of the applicant.

Private health insurance in context

Private health insurance is defined as a set of health services that are financed by a third-party through private non-income related payments called premiums. Enrolment in private health insurance is voluntary. Figure 11.1 presents private health insurance in the context of health care financing systems.

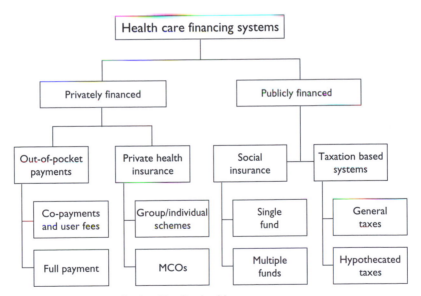

Figure 11.1 Public and private methods of funding health care

Activity 11.1

Private health insurance is one of the four major mechanisms used in financing health care and can take a number of different forms. However, in practice it plays a limited role in most countries. Look at Figure 11.2: what significance does private health insurance have in health care financing in OECD countries?

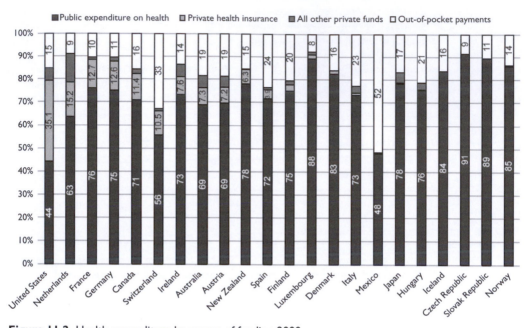

Figure 11.2 Health expenditure by source of funding, 2000
Source: Colombo and Tapay (2004)

Feedback

Figure 11.2 presents a list of OECD countries with total health expenditure broken down by funding sources, one of which is private health insurance (Colombo and Tapay 2004). On average, private health insurance represents a small share of total health expenditures among OECD countries. However, private health insurance also covers at least 30 per cent of the population in one-third of OECD countries. The USA is the only OECD country where private health insurance is a major funding mechanism for health care (> 35 per cent).

The proportion of health care expenditure on private health insurance varies around the world. In 2001, 39 countries worldwide had private health insurance markets contributing to more than 5 per cent of the countries' total health expenditures (Sekhri and Savedoff 2005). Almost half (46 per cent) were low- and middle-income countries (LMICs). Seven countries which funded more than 20 per cent of their total health expenditure through private insurance were Zimbabwe, Namibia, South Africa, Brazil, Chile, Uruguay and the USA. Although private health insurance takes a greater proportion of spending in high- and upper-middle-income countries (20 and 12 per cent of total health expenditures) than in low- and lower-middle-income countries (LMICs) (2 and 3 per cent of total health expenditures), it is still widespread in LMICs and an important form of protection for their middle classes (Sekhri and Savedoff 2005; World Health Organization 2010).

The mechanisms of private health insurance

Under private health insurance, voluntary premiums are paid in advance to the insurance company so that some health care costs can be covered at the time of illness. Insurance packages can be offered in the form of group or individual schemes as indemnity insurance, or in the form of managed care plans which we will cover later in this chapter.

There are various types of private health insurance coverage, depending on the health care system:

- *Principal* – if public health insurance coverage is not available, private health insurance will act as the person's main or principal coverage. This has been the case in the USA for individuals not eligible for public programmes such as Medicare (above 65 or severely disabled), Medicaid (poor or near poor) and SCHIP (poor children). Principal coverage is also common in LMICs;
- *Substitute* – if individuals can 'opt out' of mandatory public insurance coverage, private health insurance can replace or substitute coverage. In Germany, employees with an income above a certain threshold can opt out of the social sickness fund system;
- *Complementary* – if private health insurance covers co-payments incurred in the public system and not covered by public insurance, it is complementary. In France, Denmark and Sweden, both complementary and supplementary private health insurance schemes are offered;
- *Supplementary* – if private health insurance covers costs other than co-payments (e.g. drug costs) that are not covered by public insurance, it is supplementary. In Canada, private health insurance acts as supplementary coverage;
- *Duplicate* – if private health insurance covers providers that are already covered by public insurance, it is considered duplicate coverage. In the UK, private health insurance offers duplicate and supplementary coverage.

Activity 11.2

As you learned in Chapter 8, health insurance is a market solution to the market failure of temporal uncertainty in health care expenditures. What might be some of the factors that influence demand for voluntary health insurance? What proportion of the population in your country is covered by private insurance and who is likely to subscribe?

Feedback

People's demand for voluntary health insurance will be driven by:

- the level of risk aversion;
- the level of the potential income loss;
- other insurance options (or availability of substitutes) – if people do not have access to publicly funded or cheaper schemes, private health insurance may be the only option available;
- the level at which the premium is set (the price);

- ability to pay – since enrolment in private health insurance is voluntary, people have to have the means to pay the premium to enrol in the scheme; at actuarially fair premium, the premium is priced according to the risk, not ability to pay;
- risk of needing treatment – people who have a higher than average risk of needing hospital treatment may be more willing to purchase this scheme (i.e. adverse selection).

In most countries private insurance is a secondary source of financial protection, covering for example 13 per cent of the population in the UK in 2002 (Laing and Buisson 2003) and less than 2 per cent in most low-income countries (LICs). In these countries it attracts only the affluent members of the population, as enrolment is based on ability to pay. It contributes little to total health expenditure despite the growth of the private sector and increased competition between insurance agencies (Hsiao 1995).

Private health insurance, efficiency and equity

The market for health insurance is subject to three key forms of market failure: *adverse selection, moral hazard* and *diseconomies of scale*. Without government regulation in the market for private health insurance, these are likely to impact on both the efficiency and equity aspects of the health system.

Adverse selection

In practice, adverse selection arises from consumers having more complete information on their own health status than insurers, which may result in selecting plans that give them the greatest utility. Instead of using specific individuals' health histories to set the premium (i.e. experience rating), some governments have required insurance companies to underwrite premiums based on characteristics of the entire community, such as age and gender composition (i.e. community rating). In Ireland and Australia, community rating has been implemented on a national basis. However, community rating cannot survive in a price competitive market without banning experience rating or sometimes invoking compulsion (e.g. third-party car insurance). When consumers with different expected losses are charged the same premium, those with relatively lower expected losses (i.e. those that know they are less likely to fall ill or for whom the cost of illness is likely to be low) drop out of the insurance pool, leaving only individuals with relatively higher expected losses. This in turn can push up the premium, leading to further drop-outs of healthy individuals for whom the cost of the premium outweighs the benefit of being insured. If this continues unabated the market collapses.

Activity 11.3

Health insurance premiums are calculated by assessing the risk of ill health and the cost of projected illness or injury for an individual or a community. Suppose you are part of a community with an annual risk of 1 in 100 of needing hospital treatment and the average cost per case is £2,000 plus £10 for administration.

1 What is your annual actuarially fair premium?
2 What conditions need to be met for insurance to be offered at this premium?

3 In a competitive market, which groups of the population are not likely to be covered by this community-rated private health insurance?

4 What are the likely consequences of this lack of coverage?

Feedback

1 The premium P would be: $P = p \times c + a$ where p is the probability of the insured event, c is the cost to cover the loss and a is the administration cost. Inserting the above values results in: $(0.01 \times £2,000) + £10 = £30$, thus the premium would be £30 per year.

2 This formula is valid only under certain conditions:
- There needs to be a large number of subscribers to pool the risks. The larger the number of pooled events, the less likely unexpected costs will occur.
- The insured risks need to be independent. This means that the risk of falling ill is not caused by a single event which equally affects all insured individuals. This explains the difficulty of insuring risks due to wars or transmissible diseases in regions where large populations are at risk.
- The probability of the insured event must be less than one. It is therefore difficult to insure pre-existing conditions which will inevitably produce illness.
- People should not be able to influence their risk (moral hazard) and there should not be adverse selection.

3 If insurance in a competitive market sets a community-rated premium, those who perceive their risk as lower will opt out and take experience-rated insurance.

4 This will increase the average risk as more high-risk individuals will be insured than low-risk individuals. As a result, the premium for the remaining clients will increase, leading more low-risk individuals to drop out of the risk pool. This self-reinforcing mechanism will leave the chronically ill, the elderly and the poor without affordable insurance.

Insurance firms try to prevent the adverse selection described above by 'cream skimming' or 'cherry picking' where they actively seek healthy individuals to enrol in the insurance scheme. They often use clever tactics to select low-risk clients. For example, insurers know that a health care plan offering excellent obstetric care but poor oncology care will probably attract a healthier population than one that offers the opposite.

Moral hazard and diseconomies of scale

Whereas adverse selection is likely to lead to inequitable coverage, or no coverage if the market collapses as a result, moral hazard and diseconomies of scale have given rise to increasing health care costs. You read in Chapter 10 about the impact of provider moral hazard on costs. Insurance can also lead to consumer moral hazard. For example, individuals may see the doctor simply to socialize if insurance will pay for it.

Diseconomies of scale exist in the private health insurance market because there are usually many health insurance firms in the market, each with their own insured pool. Inefficiencies arise since it is not possible to spread the risks and share the fixed administrative costs over a large number of clients. Insurance involves high transaction costs related to marketing, claims processing, handling of reimbursements and fraud detection. In unregulated markets, administration costs account for between 10 and 14 per cent of total costs (Colombo and Tapay 2004).

Activity 11.4

This activity lets you apply your knowledge of private insurance to analyse patterns of private and public spending in the USA. Take your calculator and turn to the national health account of the USA, Table 11.1, and compare private and public expenditures.

Table 11.1 National health expenditure in the USA by source of funds and type of expenditure ($ billion 2008)

	Private consumer				Public			Total
	Private insurance	Out-of-pocket	Other	Sub-total	Federal	State & local	Sub-total	
Hospital care	259	23.2	27.1	309.3	330.7	78.3	409	718.3
Professional services	314.3	111.1	42.2	467.6	202.3	61.1	263.4	731
Nursing home and home health	16.1	43.5	6.2	65.8	101.9	35.4	137.3	203.1
Retail outlet sales of medical products	101.7	100	0	201.7	83	14.9	97.9	299.6
Government administration and net cost of private health insurance	92	0	1.7	93.7	45.5	20.4	65.9	159.6
Government public health	0	0	0	0	10.5	59	69.5	69.5
Research	0	0	4.7	4.7	33.5	5.4	38.9	43.6
Structures and equipment	0	0	89.2	89.2	9.5	15.2	24.7	113.9
Total	**783.1**	**277.8**	**171.1**	**1232**	**816.9**	**289.7**	**1106.6**	**2338.6**

Source: Center for Medicare & Medicaid Services (2010)

1 For which categories does public expenditure exceed total consumer expenditure? Suggest reasons to explain this.
2 Compare private insurance expenditure with out-of-pocket payments. For which categories do the latter exceed those financed through insurance? Discuss possible explanations.
3 Calculate programme administration costs as a percentage of total expenditure for public and private insurance spending, and compare the figures.

Feedback

1 Public spending exceeds spending through private health insurance for hospital care, nursing home and home health care. Elderly people who use these services are mainly covered by Medicare. Note that the government exclusively finances public health activities and bears the majority of research expenditure.

2 Out-of-pocket payments exceed insurance payments for nursing home care and are comparable for retail outlet sales of medical products. Private insurance plans usually fail to insure against the risk of long-term care. Many plans exclude coverage for common risks which are considered predictable, including products available in retail outlets, such as glasses.

3 Administration costs make up 12 per cent of private insurance (92/783.1) and 6 per cent of government spending (65.9/1106.6). These figures demonstrate the high transaction costs of private health insurance.

Rising costs present a huge burden on private health insurance systems. Lack of incentives to control costs and high levels of administrative costs highlight the inefficiencies of the system. Moral hazard and supplier-induced demand increase unnecessary costs. The USA is one of the few countries which depends on private health insurance as a major funding mechanism for health care, and is up against a significant challenge to control health care costs. The USA has the highest level of health spending among all OECD countries. While Americans have comparably few doctor visits and hospital days, their total expenditures are twice as high per capita as those of people in most other industrialized countries. Yet despite this enormous investment, the USA has failed to achieve improvements in life expectancy comparable to its peers. This gap between the investment and what is delivered in return suggests health services in the USA are less effectively deployed or come at a higher price.

Now read the following extract from Anderson and Squires (2010) and then try Activity 11.5.

Measuring the US health care system: a cross-national comparison
Based on analysis of OECD health data from 2008, the United States continues to differ markedly from other countries on a number of health system measures. Health care spending in the U.S. in 2006 was significantly higher than in other industrialized countries, both per capita and as a percentage of gross domestic product (GDP). The U.S. has a comparatively low number of hospital beds and physicians per capita, and patients in the U.S. have fewer hospital and physician visits than most other countries. At the same time, spending per hospital visit is highest in the U.S., and American patients are among the most likely to receive procedures requiring complex technology. The nation now ranks in the bottom quartile in life expectancy among OECD countries and has seen the smallest improvement in this metric over the past 20 years.

Previous cross-national analyses of OECD data have examined a number of explanations for why the U.S. has higher health spending per capita. These include administrative complexity, the aging of the population, the practice of 'defensive medicine' under threat of malpractice litigation, chronic disease burden, health care supply and utilization rates, access to care, and resource allocation.

These studies have consistently shown that, despite higher spending, the U.S. has, on many measures, lower health care utilization rates than most other OECD countries. The 2006 OECD data reveal similar findings—for example, in the high costs and low frequency associated with hospital discharges in the U.S. Some of these differences in average cost per discharge may be attributable to differences in patient case mix, the composition of the goods and services going into the treatment of a given medical condition, the prices paid by the hospitals for these goods and services, and the relative efficiency of hospitals. Furthermore, the administrative complexity in the U.S. health care system requires that American hospitals employ far larger staffs to handle billing requirements. While these issues require further investigation, one important difference may be the availability and use of technology in hospitals and other settings. U.S. providers have more access to expensive, high-tech medical technology in the treatment of patients and seem to perform more medical procedures involving sophisticated technology than do providers in other OECD countries.

Likewise, outpatient expenditures in the U.S. are also substantially higher than those in other OECD countries. One factor that could explain this large difference is that in the U.S., many expensive procedures are performed in outpatient settings, in contrast to most OECD countries, where they are more likely to be inpatient-based. For example, analysis of Medicare data shows that approximately half of beneficiaries receiving cardiac catheterization procedures, percutaneous translumi-nal coronary angioplasty, coronary bypass procedures, and knee replacements obtained them in outpatient settings. This heavy reliance on outpatient settings for medical procedures has two potentially negative consequences. First, it may be more difficult to ensure quality in the use of these technologies in the less tightly regulated ambulatory setting. Second, there is evidence that when physicians have a direct or indirect financial interest in outpatient facilities, the volume of these pro-cedures tends to rise significantly.

(Anderson and Squires 2010)

Activity 11.5

The USA has been one of the few countries that depend on private insurance as a major funding mechanism for health care. After you have read the extract from Anderson and Squires (2010) compare the cost of health care in the USA to that of OECD countries, highlighting the differences. Describe the problem and potential rea-sons for high health care costs in the USA.

Feedback

The USA faces a major challenge of rising health care costs. Although Americans spend twice as much as other OECD countries on health care, benefits are not observed in terms of higher levels of utilization or improvements in life expectancy. With private health insurance serving more than a third of the population, high levels of administra-tive costs, use of expensive technology and heavy reliance on outpatient treatment may be playing a role in rising costs. Consumer and provider moral hazard also add to these costs.

Combating market failure – the insurer

With consumers and providers facing incentives to exercise adverse selection, and moral hazard leading to increased costs and inadequate health care coverage, insurers and governments are faced with challenges to counteract them. To control consumer moral hazard, insurance companies use different cost-sharing mechanisms. These mechanisms act as a financial barrier to deter over-use of services, and can take the following forms:

- *co-payments* are a flat fee paid by the insured patient each time they access a medical service;
- *a deductible* (also known as 'excess') is the amount a person pays before insurance coverage begins to have an effect;
- *co-insurance* is a fixed percentage that the insured pays after the deductible is exceeded, up to the out-of-pocket maximum.

Patients with private health insurance typically pay a co-payment for each medical consultation, and are responsible for paying the deductible before the insurance coverage starts. Once they pay the deductible, co-insurance starts to apply where patients are responsible for paying a fixed percentage (often between 10 and 30 per cent) of the health care costs. The co-insurance ends when patients face the out-of-pocket maximum, after which they receive full insurance coverage until the coverage limit. Cost-sharing arrangements such as these can prevent people from seeking medical care that may not be necessary, but also discourage people from seeking necessary medical care.

Adverse selection can be controlled through better *underwriting*. Insurance companies try to better underwrite the risk by assessing the eligibility of a customer to receive health insurance and determine the premium to be charged according to risk. Although this may eliminate the potential collapse of the market associated with adverse selection, such a strategy may also have unfavourable effects. Underwriting (along with cherry picking and cream skimming) can lead to a situation where the sick cannot get insurance they can afford. The development of managed care plans has enabled insurers to implement some of these mechanisms to reduce supplier-induced demand and control health care costs.

Managed care

Managed care organizations (MCOs) were developed in the USA largely as a response to escalating health care costs. Managed care is a system in which a 'manager' intervenes to monitor and supervise the transactions between doctors and patients. The 'manager' may be a plan medical director, a trained utilization review nurse or a software program that identifies care that is potentially different from accepted clinical practice (Getzen 2007). The core functions of managed care include the sharing and management of financial risk, development and organization of provider networks, management of service utilization, received care and information flow, as well as measurement of quality and outcomes.

Managed care models can fall into one of three categories: *health maintenance organizations* (HMOs), *point of service* (POS) plans or *preferred provider organizations* (PPOs).

1 HMO – the most restrictive form of managed care organization. HMOs are responsible for both the financing and the delivery of health services, acting both as a health insurer and a health care delivery management system. In a staff model (or closed-panel) HMO, physicians are directly employed by the HMO, whereas in a group model, the HMO contracts with physician group practices to provide services to its members. The insurance only covers care provided by physicians who are part of the HMO, and referrals are necessary for most specialist care.

2 POS – similar to an HMO except that subscribers are allowed to see a non-HMO provider if they pay a significant out-of-pocket expense. The advantage is that subscribers are not locked into the HMO, though out-of-plan use remains low because of high cost-sharing.

3 PPO – a loosely organized MCO. The insurer negotiates contracts with a set of doctors and hospitals, which they consider the 'network', to obtain care at a discount. Patients can decide whether to seek care in-network for a small co-payment, or obtain care out-of-network and pay substantially more.

Figure 11.3 presents the increasing degree of cost and quality control, going from traditional indemnity insurance towards health maintenance organizations (Kongstvedt 2007)

Figure 11.3 The managed care continuum

Activity 11.6

What might be the advantages and disadvantages of HMOs and PPOs as compared with the traditional indemnity health insurance model?

Feedback

The main advantages of HMOs and PPOs are that there are fewer coverage limits regarding the amount of health care a patient can use, fewer out-of-pocket expense requirements, and prospective rather than retrospective payment. There is increased quality control of services, better follow-up of patients with chronic and behavioural conditions, and little incentive for providers to over-investigate and over-treat.

The disadvantages are that these systems can trigger adverse selection, place limitations on the choice of providers and may cause patients to fear being insufficiently investigated or treated as a result of efforts by the insurer to control costs.

Regulation of private health insurance markets

To protect consumers and prevent gaps in coverage, governments have put limits on premiums and profits of insurance companies, and set guidelines on benefit packages. Most industrialized countries have extended public insurance coverage or provided tax-funded services for the elderly and the poor. In many countries, governments have offered tax relief to firms who enrol their employees in private insurance or required employers with more than a certain number of employees to offer health insurance options.

The following measures merit attention:

- *Prohibit pre-existing condition exclusions* – to make private health insurance accessible for those who are already sick, governments may forbid insurance companies to exclude such individuals with pre-existing conditions from being denied insurance. This was one of the main provisions of the USA health reform of 2010.
- *Set a minimum package of benefits* – to ensure that insurance companies will not take away certain benefits to save costs, many governments have developed a minimum standard of benefit packages that all private health insurance must provide. LMICs with private health insurance often face the challenges of regulating benefit packages.
- *Risk equalization* – in some countries, private health insurance companies are legally required to use community rating. Governments of these countries require insurers to pay or receive a payment that equalizes the risk profiles in order to avoid insurer risk selection or cream skimming (e.g. South Africa, Australia, Ireland – Armstrong *et al.* 2010).

Following the recent trend towards economic liberalization (less state control and regulation), many LMICs have deregulated their private insurance markets. In Sri Lanka, for example, this has increased the number of insurance companies without substantially increasing coverage of the population. You have now seen how some level of government intervention is necessary to build a health system that is both efficient and equitable given the existing market failures in private health insurance.

Summary

Private health insurance offers voluntary coverage of health services where premiums are paid to an insuring organization to transfer the risk of incurring financial losses due to illness. In this chapter you have learned that private health insurance faces three key forms of market failure: adverse selection, moral hazard and diseconomies of scale. Adverse selection leads to inequitable coverage, where private insurance struggles to provide coverage for high-risk individuals and the poor. Moral hazard and diseconomies of scale contribute to system inefficiencies and rising health care costs. You have also read about various methods of cost-sharing that are used to discourage excess demand and to improve efficiency. Managed care was also developed by the insurance industry to control escalating health care costs. Finally, you explored how government intervention in private health insurance is necessary to prevent gaps in access to care and improve both the equity and efficiency of health systems. With this understanding of how the private insurance market functions, in the next chapter you will go on to consider different health care financing methods used for achieving universal coverage.

References

Anderson G and Squires D (2010) Measuring the U.S. health care system: a cross-national comparison. *Issues in International Health Policy* 1412(90):1–9.
Armstrong, J *et al.* (2010) Risk equalisation in voluntary health insurance markets. *Health Policy* 98(1):1–49.

Center for Medicare & Medicaid Services, Office of the Actuary, National Health Statistics Group, United States (2010).

Colombo F and Tapay N (2004) Private health insurance in OECD countries: the benefits and costs for individuals and health systems. *OECD health working papers* 15, DELSA/ELSA/WD/HEA(2004)6.

Getzen T (2007) Health economics and financing (3rd edn). Hoboken, NJ: John Wiley.

Hsiao WC (1995) Abnormal economics in the health sector, in Berman P (ed) *Health sector reform in developing countries*. Cambridge, MA: Harvard School of Public Health.

Kongstvedt P (2007) Essentials of managed health care (5th edn). London: Jones & Bartlett.

Laing W and Buisson W (2003) *Private medical insurance: UK market report 2003*. London: Laing & Buisson.

Sekhri N and Savedoff W (2005) Private health insurance: implications for developing countries. *Bulletin of the World Health Organization* 83(2):127–34.

World Health Organization (2010) *World health statistics 2010*. Geneva: World Health Organization.

Further reading

Drechsler D and Jutting J (2007) Different countries, different needs: the role of private health insurance in developing countries. *Journal of Health Politics, Policy and Law* 32(3):497–534.

Gottret P and Schieber G (2006) Voluntary health insurance, in Gottret P and Schieber G (eds) *Health financing revisited: a practitioner's guide*. Washington, DC: The World Bank: 103–21.

Achieving universal coverage | 12

Josephine Borghi

Overview

This chapter introduces the concept of universal coverage and explores the various combinations of health financing that can be used to achieve universal coverage along with their strengths and weaknesses.

Learning objectives

After working through this chapter, you will be able to:

- define the principles of universal coverage
- identify the key financing mechanisms through which universal coverage can be achieved
- describe the advantages and disadvantages of a tax-based system
- define the principles of social insurance and contrast it with tax-based funding
- assess the desirability of a universal coverage system based on private health insurance
- describe the significance of pre-payment schemes for health insurance in low-income countries

Key terms

Cross-subsidization. A situation arising when the funds of different population groups' risk pools are pooled.

Formal sector employees. Members of the population who are employed with a taxable income.

Fragmentation. A situation whereby there are many financing schemes which operate as separate risk pools with limited cross-subsidization.

Progressive. A financing mechanism is described as progressive if it consumes a greater proportion of the income of the rich than the poor.

Regressive. A financing mechanism is described as regressive if it consumes a greater proportion of the income of the poor than the rich.

What is universal coverage?

In Chapter 11, you learned about the principles of private health insurance. You identified that one of the key drawbacks in a system that uses predominantly private health insurance are problems of adverse selection and access to care for the poor. The focus of universal coverage is on providing protection from paying for health care out-of-pocket at the time of service use, and especially protection from incurring catastrophic health expenditures, or expenditures which exceed a certain proportion of income and can push a household into poverty. Ideally, the concept of universal coverage also implies that non-financial barriers, such as distance and acceptability of services, especially quality of care, should also be addressed (Ensor and Cooper 2004).

Universal coverage therefore implies *equity of access* and *financial risk protection*. It is also based on the notion of *equity in financing* – i.e. contributions are based on ability to pay rather than according to whether a person falls ill (WHO 2005). The following panels explore some of these equity concepts more closely.

Equity in health care financing

When considering who is bearing the burden of health care financing, it is common practice to compare contributions against ability to pay, measured in terms of income. Most people would agree that those who have greater wealth should contribute more of their income to health care than those who are poor. The extent to which contributions to health care vary with ability to pay is typically defined in relation to three concepts: progressivity, regressivity and proportionality.

- *Progressive:* contributions to health care are considered to be progressive if the richest segment of the population contributes a higher proportion of their income than the poorest. This is the principle underlying the system of income tax in most countries.
- *Regressive:* contributions are said to be regressive if the rich pay a relatively smaller share of their income than the poor.
- *Proportional:* if everyone is contributing the same proportion of their income then the contribution is said to be proportional.

Taking account of varying levels of need in the distribution of health benefits

When we talk about equity of health care utilization, access or expenditure, it is usually discussed in terms of 'need' (e.g. equal access for equal need). We know that the poorest groups in society have the greatest need for health care due to their economic vulnerability which makes them more prone to illness. Ideally then, we would expect the poorest 20 per cent of the population to get more than 20 per cent of the benefits of health care, in line with their need. Generally, if the poorest 20 per cent of the population get less than 20 per cent of the benefits and the wealthiest 20 per cent get more than 20 per cent of the benefits, we define the distribution of benefits as being 'pro-rich'. If the poorest 20 per cent of the population get more than 20 per cent of the benefits, with richer groups getting less than 20 per cent, we define the distribution of benefits as being 'pro-poor'. 'Pro-poor' policies that target disadvantaged groups by treating people differently according to their needs are underpinned by the principle of *vertical equity*. The notion of vertical equity as well as other aspects of equity will be discussed in Chapter 17.

In 2005, the World Health Organization World Health Assembly urged member states to develop health financing systems that aimed to achieve universal coverage (WHO 2005). Many countries are currently considering how their health financing systems can move towards or sustain universal coverage. There are many different ways to achieve universal coverage. Indeed, universal coverage may be financed through general taxation, through health insurance schemes or through a mix of financing sources. Universal coverage can be achieved through one national system or a number of different schemes. However, all forms of universal coverage require that pre-paid funds (either tax-based or premium-based) are pooled, ensuring that funds from richer groups are used, to varying degrees, to subsidize health care utilization of poorer groups.

The main challenge facing any financing system wishing to achieve universal coverage is to achieve an expansion of coverage in three dimensions (see Figure 12.1):

* the *breadth of coverage*: the proportion of the population who have access to affordable and quality care;
* the *depth of coverage*: the range of accessible quality services available to the population in need;
* the *height of coverage*: the proportion of health care costs covered by the financing system.

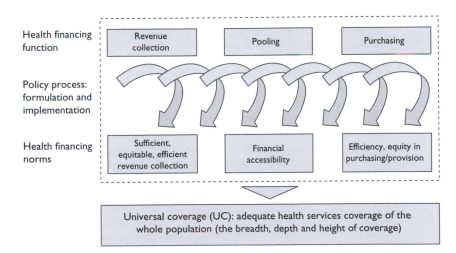

Figure 12.1 Relationships between health financing functions and universal coverage objectives
Source: Carrin *et al.* (2008); adapted by Honda (2010)

You have read briefly about the Beveridge and Bismarck models of health care financing in Chapter 9 as well as taken a detailed look at private health insurance in Chapter 11. You will now study these in relation to the aim of achieving universal coverage.

Tax-based systems (Beveridge model)

Where health care is funded primarily through general taxation, funds from those paying taxes are used to finance the provision of health services to the general population. Funds can flow directly to health providers or through an intermediary that purchases services on behalf of the population (ensuring a purchaser–provider split). For example, in the UK the principal fundholders in the NHS system have been the NHS Primary Care Trusts (PCTs). The PCTs commissioned (purchased) health care from hospitals and GPs and disbursed funds to pay for services on behalf of their enrolled patient population.

The advantage of tax-based systems of funding is that they are usually very progressive, meaning that the rich pay a higher proportion of their income than the poor. Tax is made up of multiple sources and income tax is typically very progressive as higher-income individuals pay a higher proportion of their income than lower-income individuals. In higher-income countries (HICs), income tax often constitutes a substantial proportion of total tax revenue. For example, across OECD countries in 2008, personal income tax represented 25 per cent of total tax revenue, followed by social security contributions (25 per cent) and VAT (19 per cent) (OECD 2010). In lower-income countries (LICs), the formal sector often forms a small proportion of the population. Hence, revenues from income tax may only constitute a relatively small proportion of total tax revenue. For example, in 2005, income tax represented 11 per cent of total tax revenue in Ghana and 14 per cent in Tanzania (McIntyre et al. 2008). Other forms of tax revenue include value-added tax (VAT), corporate income tax, excise tax (e.g. taxes on fuel, alcohol and cigarettes), and import and export duties, among others. The levels of these taxes, and their contribution to the overall tax base, vary by country. The progressivity of each tax also varies from place to place. In most HICs, for example, VAT is regressive, meaning that the poor pay a greater proportion of their income than the rich, the reason being that VAT is levied on most commodities which are consumed by the majority of the population. In contrast, VAT has been found to be progressive in some LICs, due to exemption policies for certain commodities which are consumed more by the poor, coupled with the fact that the poor often survive on a largely subsistence basis, producing many of their own consumption requirements.

Tax funding is typically used to finance exemption schemes in both HICs and LICs. These are schemes which ensure that certain population groups, deemed vulnerable, do not pay for services (e.g. children under 5 years of age, pregnant women, the poor). In the USA Medicare and Medicaid are government-funded bodies which finance the care of the elderly and disabled and the poor respectively. In the UK, schemes include government-funded 'Sure Start' centres providing child care, early education, health and family support to parents and children. While exemption schemes targeting specific population groups or services are typically relatively effective, schemes targeting the poor tend not to be, due to the difficulty and cost of appropriately and effectively assessing eligibility (Witter 2009).

In some countries, tax funding has been used to provide financial protection to the informal sector not covered by social health insurance, for example under the universal coverage scheme in Thailand. Tax funding can also be used to subsidize community or social health insurance. In Ghana, for example, a fixed 2.5 per cent levy on VAT funding is used to finance the national health insurance scheme.

Social health insurance (Bismarck model)

Social health insurance is typically operated by a public agency and financed through compulsory contributions from payroll. The amount is usually split between employers and employees. For example, if the total social security contribution of an employee is 6 per cent, this may be made up of a 3 per cent contribution by the employee and a 3 per cent contribution by the employer. In some cases, the employee will pay a higher share of their income than the employer. Contributions to social health insurance are normally progressive. However, the benefits from these contributions generally only reach the members of the insurance scheme, except in cases of cross-subsidization with other schemes. As contributions are a set percentage of income, this depends on there being an agreed measure of income, and works best among those in formal employment. In European countries social health insurance has succeeded in covering the vast majority of the population, allowing for a large risk pool. Germany has the world's oldest system, originating in 1883 when the government made health insurance compulsory for all. Insurance is funded by employee and employer contributions and government subsidies. In France the social security system (referred to as *La Sécu*) was created in the post-World War II period. Initially focused on workers, it was expanded to the informal sector (farmers and informal farm labourers) in the 1960s. In 2000 a system of universal coverage was finally achieved on the basis of residence in France. Such a situation allows for redistribution of resources from richer to poorer individuals, from younger to older, from the healthy to the sick. This is made possible through cross-subsidization, whereby better-off groups subsidize worse-off groups.

More recently, in LICs, such schemes have started within the government sector, covering only government employees (e.g. this was the case in Ghana, Kenya and Tanzania). Over time, these schemes may expand to cover the private formal sector (as happened in Ghana). In other settings, the private formal sector may be covered through a separate system, either of compulsory contributions matched by employers, or of private health insurance. It has been argued that in the African context, experiments with social health insurance have sometimes led to fragmented and inequitable situations, where the formal sector is insured and has access to a broad range of services, while the informal sector remains uninsured and largely reliant on poor quality public health services (McIntyre et al. 2008). Sometimes national health insurance schemes may receive tax subsidies, and sometimes the schemes may subsidize schemes for poorer groups.

In summary, social health insurance:

* has compulsory membership;
* involves payroll deduction of contributions;
* is run by public bodies, either single or multiple organizations;
* is based on redistributional policies;
* has clearly defined, earmarked resources;
* is usually complex and expensive to administer, relative to tax-based systems;
* can mobilize additional resources for the health sector.

Activity 12.1

A key choice facing countries seeking a transition towards universal coverage is whether to opt for a system of general tax funding or mandatory social health insurance, or a mix of the two. This activity lets you assess the differences between tax funding and social health insurance by using an example from Mills (2007). Read through Table 12.1 and then answer the following questions:

1 Identify the differences between tax funding and mandatory social health insurance in relation to covering hard to reach groups.
2 Compare the two schemes in terms of the demands on management.
3 Compare the two schemes in terms of the reliability of income available for health financing.
4 Overall what do you think are the advantages and disadvantages of social health insurance?

Table 12.1 Advantages and disadvantages of social health insurance and tax funding as the core approaches to financing universal coverage (Mills 2007)

Aspect	Tax funding	Mandatory social health insurance funding
Source of funding	Pools money from all who fall within the tax net (both direct and indirect taxation)	Employers and employees in the formal sector
Equity of financing	Generally progressive	Less progressive since progressivity is likely to encourage under-reporting of salaries and remuneration in kind
Population coverage	No limitations in theory	Absolute number of beneficiaries and growth normally tied to size and nature of formal sector
Coverage of hard to reach groups	No barriers in principle	Needs additional mechanisms and usually tax funding
Health care benefits	No required link between payment and benefits	Contributions and benefits closely linked
Demands on management	Does not require a beneficiary-specific system, hence lower management costs	Requires system for collecting revenue, identifying beneficiaries, paying for their care
Political	Share allocated to health is dependent on political decision-making process	Income earmarked for health
Economic implications	Dependent on taxation structure; does not need to be tied to employment	Increases cost of employment

Feedback

1 Tax funding is the only reliable method for covering hard to reach groups, be it through exemption policies or broader national commitment to funding the costs of the informal sector poor, such as the universal coverage scheme in Thailand.
2 It has been argued that increasing health sector revenue by raising taxes is feasible, and that it is not easier to collect social health insurance revenues than general tax

(Wagstaff 2007). The management demands of social insurance can be substantial, including tackling corruption and under-declaring of income (Yepes 2005), resulting in high administrative costs. Challenges can also be faced in ensuring funds are effectively transferred to providers (Dixon et al. 2004).

3 Although tax funding benefits from administrative simplicity, a key issue is ensuring that health continues to attract the necessary funds. The advantage of social health insurance is that funds are earmarked for health.

4 The principal advantages of social health insurance are:
   • funds for health care are clearly identified and do not have to compete with other demands on government such as defence, housing and social security;
   • people may be happier paying social insurance knowing that it will be spent on health care than paying taxes which may not be used for health care;
   • employee contributions mean that people may behave as better, more responsible consumers of health care, reducing the risk of moral hazard, and may be more likely to demand high-quality services from providers;
   • employer contributions mean that they have an incentive to ensure premiums are as low as possible, thus encouraging health care providers to be as efficient as possible.

The disadvantages are:

   • social insurance is a form of employment tax (i.e. it is paid by those in employment) and this may prove to be a disincentive for employers to create new jobs;
   • the amount raised will vary with the number of people employed so the health care system has no guaranteed income;
   • the cost of collecting funds from employees and employers (extra costs that do not arise with tax-based systems);
   • if there is more than one social insurance fund, there is the risk of adverse selection of subscribers.

Private health insurance

In a system of universal coverage, the purpose of private health insurance is typically twofold. Private insurance can be used to provide complementary cover for luxury or high-cost services, or a broader range of health care providers, not included in a social health insurance or tax-funded system. Private health insurance can also offer a means of faster access to care, in systems where waiting time for specialized public providers is significant, as in the UK. In countries where social health insurance is restricted to the public formal sector, private formal sector employers may purchase private health insurance for their employees. Private health insurance premiums are generally progressive, as private insurance tends to be used by richer groups who contribute more, but the benefits from private insurance are limited to those who contribute. Private health insurance can also increase health system inequity by removing richer population groups from the risk pool, and leading to fragmentation, as schemes generally operate independently of one another as separate, relatively small risk pools.

Activity 12.2

1 Should private health insurance play a role in achieving universal coverage?
2 Can private insurance promote equity?

3 Is private health insurance a feasible option for LICs as a means to achieving universal coverage?

Feedback (adapted from Mills 2007)

1 The reliance on private health insurance as a core element for achieving universal
   coverage is controversial due to concerns over equity. Private insurance cover is
   generally tied to employment for the formal sector, members of which tend to be better off. Premiums are risk rated which can make cover expensive for higher risk and
   vulnerable groups, which often leads to their exclusion. There are generally many different private insurance schemes and hence a fragmentation of risk pools, compromising the objectives of universal coverage (as illustrated in the USA and South Africa).
2 Private insurance can increase financial protection and access to health services for
   those willing and able to pay, but at a likely cost of compromising equity objectives.
3 Few LICs currently have a substantial private insurance market and the competen-
   cies needed to create such as market are in short supply. Private insurance is not
   likely to cover more than a small proportion of the population, especially in poorer
   countries. Thus it is not generally considered a desirable option for low- and middle-
   income countries (LMICs). However, as you will see below, small scale community-
   based voluntary health insurance schemes may be used as a stepping stone to the
   development of a national or larger-scale social insurance scheme.

Moving towards universal coverage: health care reform in the USA
In 2010, the Patient Protection and Affordable Health Care Act was signed into law in
the USA. With 45 million people (around 15 per cent of the population) without
insurance coverage, health care spending at 17 per cent of GDP and mixed quality in
services (Lyke 2009), health care reform was seen by many as critical. The reform
attempts to move the USA to a system of universal coverage. The Act itself will
require most US citizens and legal residents to have health insurance while providing
subsidies for low-income individuals/families and caps on their annual out-of-pocket
payments. Moves will be made to ban discrimination against people with pre-existing
conditions, to ensure that they are able to get health insurance, and tax cuts will be
offered to small businesses to help them pay for health insurance for their employees.
The reform will also create state-based American health benefit exchanges through
which individuals can purchase coverage, and separate exchanges through which small
businesses can purchase coverage, and will impose new regulations on health plans in
the exchanges and in the individual and small-group markets. The insurance sold on
the exchanges will all be private (BBC News 2010; Kaiser Family Foundation 2010).

Community health insurance

This is a form of voluntary health insurance, which places emphasis on community
ownership and empowerment. Such schemes generally target the informal sector in
which people are not covered by mandatory insurance, and have been introduced in
countries where user fees are charged. Community health insurance has been promoted as a means of offering financial protection to the informal poor, and has been

especially popular in rural areas of LICs. Such schemes can be operated by communities, government or non-governmental organizations and have often been created as an extension of a micro-financing scheme. These schemes generally operate on a relatively small scale, with a small risk pool and limited cross-subsidization. Premiums are usually a flat rate paid monthly or annually per individual or household, typically covering a basic package of public services. Community health insurance can face difficulties in enrolling the poorest, due to the affordability of premiums and a limited understanding of the concept of risk pooling. While schemes sometimes have an exemption provision for the poorest (as in Ghana and Tanzania), this can be difficult to implement.

Contributions to community health insurance are typically regressive due to the flat-rate premium and the fact the schemes generally operate in poorer rural communities, hence posing a greater burden on the rural poor. However, community health insurance played an important role in the evolution of European and Japanese universal coverage arrangements (Criel 1998; Ogawa *et al.* 2003), as well as the development of the national health insurance scheme in Ghana. It can serve to raise awareness of the insurance principle, create experience of risk pooling and offer financial protection when the public system does not offer free care.

The following summary relates to work conducted by Eklund and Stavem (1995) evaluating a community insurance scheme in 18 villages in Guinea-Bissau in West Africa.

Community health insurance through pre-payment schemes in Guinea-Bissau

The village health post prepayment scheme in Guinea-Bissau is an example of a simple community health insurance scheme that pools risks for basic primary health care services (particularly drugs), while simplifying management demands. Three components underpin the scheme: community participation; local resource mobilization; and a formal contract made between the village leaders and the Ministry of Public Health (MINSAP). This contract specifies the following roles for the village and government:

i. The village is responsible for setting fees (premiums), when these are paid and whether the payments are per capita, per adult or per household. The fees are uniform within each village.

ii. The village is responsible for ensuring funds are available from the scheme to ensure a continual drug supply.

iii. A local committee is nominated to manage the scheme's activities at the village level.

iv. The village is responsible for the building of the health post apart from a few specified items supplied by the MINSAP.

v. The government supplies some basic furniture, equipment and approximately six months' supply of drugs for the village. It also subsidizes future supplies of drugs purchased by the village.

vi. One or more villagers are trained as village health workers and midwives.

As the scheme does not use a system of user fees for services there is no need for systems of accounting and protection of the funds at the village level. The prepayments are collected at one time by the village committee treasurer and then sent up through the health system to be deposited in an earmarked account for drug purchases. In addition, no billing takes place as providers are not being reimbursed for services; and no risk assessment is required as premiums are community rated.

Eklund and Stavem (1995) describe their main conclusions from the evaluation as follows.

> Adverse selection is prevented by almost universal membership within each village participating. Moral hazard is avoided through the vigilance of village health workers and midwives, who dispense drugs only as needed, based on diagnosis, and by the pressure of the local community.
>
> Although the level of cost recovery is low, this understates the total amount of resource mobilization. Villagers provide construction materials for the USB and the labor of village health workers and midwives for implementation and management of the scheme – none of which is reflected in cost recovery figures. Further, respondents indicated their willingness to prepay greater amounts, provided that drugs could be made available on a timely basis. Drugs are heavily subsidized to the USBs, however, and their price is not regularly increased, to reflect inflation and devaluation. The degree of subsidization of USB drug supplies is thus increasing over time.
>
> The survey found that the level of satisfaction with the village health posts was high, despite evidence that drug stocks are rapidly depleted. Respondents' willingness to prepay was often linked to improvements in the quality of service, including greater availability of drugs and better training for village midwives. Yet, the quality of service that can be provided at village health posts depends critically on the extent of support from the rest of the health care system.
>
> (Eklund and Stavem 1995)

Activity 12.3

When you have read the information about the community insurance scheme in Guinea-Bissau, consider the following questions:

1 How do the schemes of the 18 villages vary in relation to the degree of cross-subsidization between adults and dependants?
2 How do rural pre-payment schemes control for moral hazard and adverse selection?
3 What has been the reported effect on drug availability and quality of care?

Feedback

1 Most schemes are based on fixed rates per adult or per household, which also cover children. Contributions are flat rates regardless of income, but the poor are exempt from payments.
2 Moral hazard is easier to control in small communities where villagers know each other and health workers know the needs of their patients. Adverse selection is prevented through nearly universal membership.
3 Although the availability of drugs continues to be uneven, the quality of care overall was perceived to be higher after the introduction of insurance.

Other sources of finance

Donor funding and out-of-pocket payments also constitute considerable sources of health care financing, especially in LICs. Direct provider payments are highly regressive, as payments are typically uniform and constitute a bigger burden to the poor than the rich. Typically these payments are higher and represent a higher proportion of total health funding in LICs. The degree of equity of the overall health financing depends on the share of each source of health financing in the overall system. A further issue is the extent to which funds are pooled across schemes.

Summary

You have learned about the principles of universal coverage and the principal financing mechanisms that can be used to achieve it. You have seen the relative advantages and disadvantages of social health insurance compared to general taxation to achieve universal coverage. You have also seen the potential role and limitations of voluntary health insurance, be it private health insurance or community health insurance. This chapter completes your consideration of the principal methods of funding health care: taxation, social insurance, private insurance and out-of-pocket expenditure. You will now consider economic evaluation.

References

BBC News (2010) *Q&A: US health care reform*, http://news.bbc.co.uk/2/hi/8160058.stm.

Carrin G, Mathauer I, Xu K and Evans DB (2008) Universal coverage of health services: tailoring its implementation, *Bulletin of WHO* 86:857–63, www.who.int/bulletin/volumes/86/11/07-049387/en/index.html.

Criel B (1998) Western European social health insurance systems: a two-sided coin? in Nitayarumphong S and Mills A (eds) *Achieving universal coverage of health care*. Bangkok: Office of Health Care Reform Project, Ministry of Public Health.

Dixon A, Langenbrunner J and Mossialos E (2004) Facing the challenges of health care financing, in Figueras J, McKee M, Cain J and Lessof S (eds) (2004) *Health systems in transition: learning from experience*. Buckingham: Open University Press.

Eklund P and Stavem K (1995) Community health insurance through prepayment schemes in Guinea-Bissau, in Shaw RP and Ainsworth M (eds) *Financing health services through user fees and insurance*. Washington, DC: World Bank.

Ensor T and Cooper S (2004) Overcoming barriers to health service access: influencing the demand side. *Health Policy Plan* 19(2):69–79.

Honda A (2010) Assessing efforts towards universal financial risk protection in low and middle income countries, workshop sponsored by AHPSR, Cape Town.

Kaiser Family Foundation (2010) *Summary of new health reform law*, www.kff.org/healthreform/upload/8061.pdf, accessed 27 March 2011.

Lyke B (2009) *Health care reform: an introduction*, congressional Research Service Report for Congress, R40517, http://assets.opencrs.com/rpts/R40517_20090729.pdf, accessed 27 March 2011.

McIntyre D *et al.* (2008) Beyond fragmentation and towards universal coverage: insights from Ghana, South Africa and the United Republic of Tanzania. *Bulletin of WHO* 86(11): 817–908.

Mills A (2007) *Strategies to achieve universal coverage: are there lessons from middle income countries?* A literature review commissioned by the Health Systems Knowledge Network. Geneva: WHO, www.who.int/social_determinants/resources/csdh_media/universal_coverage_2007_en.pdf.

OECD (2010) *OECD tax database* www.oecd.org/ctp/taxdatabase

Ogawa S *et al.* (2003) Scaling up community health insurance: Japan's experience with the 19th century Jyorei scheme. *Health Policy and Planning* 18(3):270–8.

Wagstaff A (2007) *Social health insurance reexamined.* Washington, DC: World Bank.

WHO (2005) *Achieving universal health coverage: developing the health financing system,* WHO/EIP/HSF/PB/05.01. Geneva: WHO.

Witter S (2009) Service- and population-based exemptions: are these the way forward for equity and efficiency in health financing in low-income countries? in Grossman M and Lindgren B (eds) *Innovations in health system finance in developing and transitional economies. Advances In Health Economics And Health Services Research* 21:251–88.

Yepes F (2005) Corruption in the health sector: the Colombian experience, in Nitayarumphong S *et al.* (eds) *What is talked about less in health care reform?* Nonthaburi, Thailand: National Health Security Office.

Further reading

Carrin G, Mathauer I, Xu K and Evans DB (2008) Universal coverage of health services: tailoring its implementation, *Bulletin of WHO* 86:857–63, www.who.int/bulletin/volumes/86/11/07-049387/en/index.html.

McIntyre D *et al.* (2008) Beyond fragmentation and towards universal coverage: insights from Ghana, South Africa and the United Republic of Tanzania. *Bulletin of WHO* 86(11): 817–908.

Schoen C *et al.* (2010) How health insurance design affects access to care and costs, by income, in eleven countries. *Health affairs* 0862.

Wagstaff A (2007) *Social health insurance reexamined.* Washington, DC: World Bank.

WHO (2005) *Achieving universal health coverage: developing the health financing system,* WHO/EIP/HSF/PB/05.01. Geneva: WHO, Chapters 1 & 2.

SECTION 5

Economic evaluation

What is economic evaluation and what questions can it help to answer?

13

Virginia Wiseman and Stephen Jan

Overview

So far we have learned that perfectly competitive markets provide the most efficient allocation of resources. We have also learned that markets in health care suffer from a number of 'failures' and for this reason (as well as equity concerns) governments intervene. Having no 'market' does not remove the central problem of allocating scarce resources. We will learn in this chapter and the subsequent three chapters that economic evaluation is one approach that can assist with resource allocation where markets do not exist.

We begin our exploration of economic evaluation by introducing some key concepts. You will encounter these concepts throughout the following three chapters so it is important that you understand them. This chapter will also give an overview of the types of economic evaluation and the sorts of policy questions they can address. Chapters 14 and 15 look at the *methods* for measuring and valuing costs and consequences while Chapter 16 discusses ways of *presenting and interpreting* information on costs and consequences to inform health care decision-making.

Learning objectives

After working through this chapter, you will be able to:

- define economic evaluation
- describe the different techniques of economic evaluation
- explain how economic evaluation helps to assess efficiency
- explain the main stages in economic evaluation
- describe how economic evaluation can contribute to answering policy questions

Key terms

Cost–benefit analysis. An economic evaluation technique in which outcomes are expressed in monetary terms.

> **Cost-effectiveness analysis.** An economic evaluation technique in which outcomes are expressed in health units such as life years saved.
>
> **Cost–utility analysis.** An economic evaluation technique where outcomes are expressed in health units that capture not just the quantity but quality of life.
>
> **Economic evaluation.** Compares the costs and consequences of alternative health care interventions to assess their value for money.
>
> **Sensitivity analysis.** The process of assessing the robustness of the findings of an economic evaluation by varying the assumptions used in the analysis.

A day in the life of a health minister

As free markets rarely exist in health care, decisions have to be made about which health services should be funded in the face of resource scarcity. These are difficult decisions to make especially when medical technologies are improving and expanding, real incomes are increasing and many countries have an ageing population.

A minister of health once remarked that 'the only thing a minister of health is ever destined to discuss with the medical profession is money'. There never seems to be enough money to do everything worth doing and ministries of health frequently encounter situations where each request for additional funding may be legitimate in that it will improve health but the budget often cannot cover all of the requests. For example, suppose a minister of health receives requests from two different programmes, one from the Tuberculosis Programme (TBP) and the other from the Expanded Programme on Immunization (EPI). The TBP wants additional funding for 'Directly observed therapy – short course' or DOTS. The EPI wants to add hepatitis B vaccine (HBV) to its routine programme. Without an increase in the overall budget, the new programmes could not be covered unless some other programmes are cut.

The question, then, is how can the minister decide which of the requests should be supported? Giving support for one, or possibly both, means that something else should be cut back – which programme should it be? Which interventions are 'worthwhile'? This is where economic evaluation comes into the picture.

Impact of health problems

A key priority of many societies around the world is the alleviation of health problems: disease, injury or a risk factor for one of these. The impact of such health problems can be manifested in different ways – physical disability, morbidity and mortality, emotional distress, social difficulties and isolation, and financial and economic losses. Each manifestation can be seen at the level of the individual, the family and household, the local community, and the rest of society. The impact of health problems can be measured as:

- the number of cases;
- the number of deaths;
- the amount of disability, pain or suffering;

- the number of people with a risk factor;
- the amount of money spent on a health problem;
- the amount of lost income due to a health problem.

For example, the death during childbirth of a mother who already has two children and who is the only schoolteacher in the village can be measured in various ways, such as:

- a 'case' of maternal mortality;
- the number of years of life she has lost by dying prematurely;
- the amount of her wages that her family will no longer receive;
- the effect of the loss of her wages, particularly on her school-age children who can't be educated because the money for school fees is no longer available;
- the loss to her husband who misses her company and her skills as a housekeeper and part-time farmer;
- the loss of her guidance and training for her young children;
- the loss of the investment her own parents made in training and educating her to be a teacher;
- the loss to the school system which now has to hire or train new teachers to replace her.

So, in economic evaluation the impact of health problems can be assessed using a variety of health measures such as the number of cases of illness, the number of deaths due to illness, the number of potential years of life lost due to illness or in monetary terms as the *cost of health problems* – the monetary value of resources spent or lost because of the health problem.

Resources needed for an intervention

You know in advance that you will never have enough money to do everything you would like – so knowing all the possible interventions available for a health problem is not enough. It means you also need to know what the interventions cost. Determining the cost of an intervention can sometimes be complicated. A first step is to know what specific resources are used to implement the intervention. Resources are the ingredients of health care interventions. They are also referred to as *inputs* or *resource inputs*. A useful approach is to divide the resources into seven categories:

- personnel;
- buildings and space;
- equipment;
- supplies and pharmaceuticals;
- transportation;
- training;
- social mobilization and publicity including information, education and communication.

Activity 13.1

Look at the photograph of a growth monitoring session in a low-income country. What resources are being used in the health intervention depicted?

Figure 13.1 A health intervention in a developing country
Source: Global Samaritans

Feedback

In the photo your attention was probably first drawn to the equipment, in particular the weighing scale. Then you will have noticed the staff – the nurse who is writing down the weights of the babies. She has been trained to carry out this activity. You may have forgotten the vehicle and driver – they are not in the picture. Other activities would include the maintenance of vehicles and equipment, the training of staff, the supervision by higher levels of staff at a health centre or wherever they are based. Another resource to keep in mind is the time of the mothers – they could be doing other activities instead of waiting for their babies to be weighed. And how did the mothers know that there would be a growth monitoring session in this place at this time? Resources have gone into informing and motivating the mothers to bring their babies.

Having identified the resources, you need to measure how much of each resource is used. This is what economists call production – how much of each resource or input is required to produce the growth monitoring service. Finally, you need to establish the value of each resource that you have used, so that you can calculate the cost of the intervention. The most straightforward way to value resources is to use money as the measure. Some costs will not be easy to determine – think of the time of the women who brought their children for the growth monitoring session. How would you estimate its value in monetary terms? For the moment it is enough that you begin to be aware that costing is not always a simple matter of collecting price information – it may require skill and judgement on the part of the economist. We will explore costs more closely in the next chapter.

Outcomes or consequences

The goal of an intervention is to reduce the impact of a health problem. For economic evaluations, you need to measure how much the impact is reduced. To figure out if the intervention has done enough good to justify its cost, you need to know how the health problem changes after the intervention. Specifically, you need to know what occurs *as a result of* the intervention, in other words, the outcome or consequences of the intervention.

You can assess this change by measuring the difference in the health problem in one of two ways. You can either measure the impact of the health problem before and after the intervention, or with and without the intervention. For this reason economic evaluations are often done alongside clinical trials or some other form of intervention evaluation where these impacts are being specifically assessed.

Since impact is assessed using either health measures (number of deaths, number of cases, etc.) or their monetary equivalent, and since outcome is merely the difference in impact, units used to measure outcome are identical to the units used to measure impact.

Take the example of the use of impregnated bed nets to prevent malaria. If you wanted to determine their impact, you could calculate the number of deaths in children aged 6 months to 5 years in a village where the nets were impregnated and compare this to the number of malaria deaths in villages of similar size and characteristics where the bed nets were not impregnated. Suppose that the results showed that:

- villages which did not receive the intervention had 73 deaths from malaria;
- villages where bed nets were impregnated (with the intervention) had 16 deaths from malaria.

As a result of the intervention, you could conclude that there were 57 fewer deaths from malaria. The *outcome* of the new malaria intervention then is a reduction of 57 deaths.

While health care's goal is to achieve as greater reduction in health problems as possible, your health care budget often won't allow you to implement all desirable interventions. This is exactly the same dilemma faced by the minister of health at the beginning of this chapter. He or she still faces the challenge of comparing the request for funding by the TBP for DOTS with the request for funding from the EPI to introduce HBV. Some decision must be made as regards the relative value of the interventions. This is how economics as a discipline can assist.

What is economic evaluation?

According to Drummond *et al.* (2005) two features characterize economic evaluation: it is a *comparative* analysis (i.e. it compares two or more different options), and it compares these options in terms of their *costs and their consequences*. Figure 13.2 illustrates this. Two alternatives are presented, A and B. When assessing programmes A and B, we compare the difference in costs with the difference in consequences. This is called an *incremental analysis*. Let us now begin thinking about comparing costs and consequences of different interventions in a practical way.

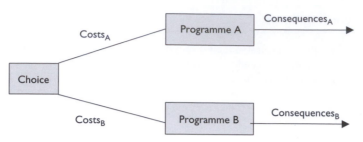

Figure 13.2 Costs and consequences
Source: Drummond *et al.* (2005)

Activity 13.2

Imagine that programme A is a community-wide programme distributing free insecticide-treated bed nets (ITNs) to control malaria. What alternative programmes might you want to compare this against?

Feedback

Here are some suggestions but you can probably think of others. We have concentrated on malaria but you might be interested in comparing your intervention with other infectious disease programmes or alternatively non-health programmes in the agricultural or education sectors.

- Do nothing (i.e. not implementing ITNs).
- Using ITNs only in target groups (i.e. pregnant women and children under 5).
- Social marketing of ITNs – social marketing projects encourage private sector distribution networks to make health products available to low-income people at subsidized prices. Products are sold, rather than given away free of charge.
- Distributing ITNs only in malaria endemic areas.
- Other forms of malaria control such as indoor residual spraying (IRS) or intermittent presumptive treatment (IPT) in pregnant women or infants.
- Treating malaria using different antimalarials.

Types of economic evaluation

Table 13.1 summarizes the different types of economic evaluation studies.

Cost–benefit analysis

Cost–benefit analysis (CBA) is a method of economic evaluation where the monetary value of the resources consumed by a health intervention (costs) is compared with the monetary value of the outcomes (benefits) achieved by the intervention. While the lay meaning of 'benefit' is 'something good', in CBA it means the 'monetary value of the outcomes' achieved by an intervention. CBA is appropriate when a decision-maker wants to know: is a single intervention policy or a number of intervention policies

Table 13.1 Types of economic evaluation

Type of analysis	Measurement/valuation of costs in both alternatives	Identification of consequences	Measurement/valuation of consequences
Cost–benefit analysis	Monetary units	Single or multiple effects, not necessarily common to both alternatives	Monetary units
Cost-effectiveness analysis	Monetary units	Single effect of interest, common to both alternatives, but achieved to different degrees	Natural units (e.g. life years gained, points of blood pressure reduction, etc.)
Cost–utility analysis	Monetary units	Single or multiple effects, not necessarily common to both alternatives	Healthy years (typically measured as quality adjusted life years)
Cost analysis	Monetary units	None	None

Source: Drummond *et al.* (2005)

worth implementing? (i.e. are benefits greater than the costs?) Two common cost–benefit indicators are:

- net present value (NPV): this result is expressed as a single number with monetary units;
- benefit–cost ratio (BCR): this result is expressed as a ratio of benefits to costs.

NPV is calculated by subtracting the cost of an intervention from its benefits. When the benefit is bigger than the cost, the net benefit will be greater than zero. This says that the value of the outcomes is worth more than the value of resources used up by the intervention, so the intervention is worthwhile.

Another way of comparing cost and benefit is the BCR. This is simply the benefits *divided by* the costs. The higher the BCR, the more worthwhile the intervention – and some interventions can actually be cost-saving, in other words, implementing them can save money for health services or for a society as a whole.

From a societal perspective, as long as net benefits are greater than zero, or benefits exceed costs (the BCR is greater than 1), the intervention should be implemented. For now, it is important to recognize that CBA's greatest appeal lies in the fact that it can be used to compare interventions with a range of different outcomes. These interventions can even relate to different sectors of the economy. In practice, however, the monetary valuation of benefits in CBA is difficult. Placing a value on human life and health can be extremely hard. Decision-makers can also find a single amount representing costs and benefits of a programme 'disconcertingly impenetrable' (Fox-Rushby and Cairns 2005).

Cost-effectiveness analysis

Cost-effectiveness analysis (CEA) is the most commonly used form of economic evaluation in the health sector. Under this method, the value of the resources spent on an intervention is compared with the quantity of health gained as a result. Unlike CBA, which compares monetary costs with monetary outcomes, CEA compares the cost of an intervention with the intervention's *health* outcomes.

Cost-effectiveness is typically expressed as a ratio of costs divided by health outcomes. The *cost-effectiveness ratio* (CER) of one intervention can then be compared with that of another. CERs typically come in the form of average cost-effectiveness ratios (ACERs) or incremental cost-effectiveness ratios (ICERs). ACERs relate to single interventions whereas ICERs compare relative costs and effects. ICERs are the ratio of the difference in cost between two alternatives to the difference in effectiveness between the same two alternatives. These two types of CER are shown in Figure 13.3.

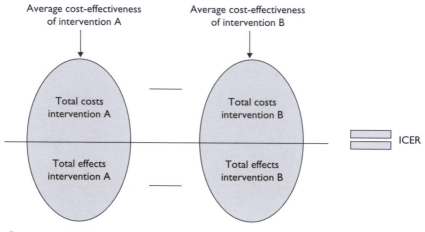

Figure 13.3 Comparative economic evaluation
Source: Fox-Rushby and Cairns (2005)

Where interventions are independent (i.e. the costs and effects of one intervention are not influenced by the introduction of another intervention(s)) then cost-effectiveness ratios can be calculated for each intervention and ranked giving those with a lower ACER higher priority. However, interventions are often not mutually exclusive, for example comparing two types of diagnostic testing for malaria. In this case we need to know what are the additional benefits to be gained from the new intervention and at what additional cost. This is where ICERs come into play. We will come back to CERs in Chapter 16.

CEA has been applied to many different types of health intervention. Its results – such as cost per life year gained – are often easily interpreted by planners and policy-makers. However, one of the key limitations of CEA is that it is restricted to comparisons of interventions that have a common single unit of effect.

Cost–utility analysis

Cost–utility analysis (CUA) is a broader form of analysis than CEA but a variant of that general approach (Drummond *et al.* 2005) and for that reason is often discussed under the heading of 'cost-effectiveness analysis'. Using CUA, one can assess the quality of, for example, life years gained, not just the crude number of years lived in a particular health state. This is especially useful for those interventions that may extend life but at the expense of side-effects (e.g. treatment for certain types of cancer). The most common measures of consequences in CUA are the quality adjusted life year (QALY) and the disability adjusted life year (DALY).

CUA was developed to address the problem of conventional CEA, which did not allow decision-makers to compare the value of interventions for different health problems. While this is a definite strength of the approach, some have questioned the ability of CUA to capture all the valued characteristics associated with an intervention. For example, QALYs do not capture differences in the process characteristics of interventions (such as respect, autonomy, provision of information, etc.), despite substantial evidence that patients *do* attach value to these (Mooney 1994; Howard *et al.* 2008).

Cost analysis or cost minimization analysis

Cost-minimization analysis (CMA) is a narrow subset of CEA. It is used to measure and compare input costs across alternatives where there is good evidence that outcomes are identical. Thus, the types of intervention that can be evaluated with this method are rather limited.

Activity 13.3

Now that you have gained an understanding of the main types of economic evaluation it is important to also learn how these techniques can be used to address policy questions. For each of the policy questions listed below, identify which type of economic evaluation would be most appropriate to use and explain why. The idea for this exercise came from a similar activity used by Fox-Rushby and Cairns (2005).

1 The Ministry of Finance wants to know whether it is worth investing further resources into malaria control or building new primary schools?
2 The Ministry of Health wants to compare the costs of receiving intravenous antibiotics in a hospital with receiving the same antibiotics (at the same doses) at home via a home health care service.
3 The Ministry of Health wants to compare the costs and outcomes of two interventions for the treatment of early stage breast cancer: mastectomy without breast reconstruction compared to breast conserving surgery and radiotherapy (breast conservation).
4 A malaria control programme wants to use economic evaluation to compare two different diagnostic strategies for malaria treatment: microscopy and rapid diagnostic tests.

Feedback:

1 CBA, as here we are dealing with the size of the budget and comparing interventions across different sectors of the economy.
2 CMA, as outcomes *should* be the same.
3 CUA, as there are likely to be differences in mortality and morbidity.
4 CEA, as there is likely to be a common unit of effect – e.g. cost per case detected.

Efficiency and economic evaluation

It is important to recognize that economic evaluation is *not* about choosing the cheapest option. According to Maynard (1987), 'The pursuit of efficient practices is not merely about reducing costs. If it were, the most "efficient" procedure would be to do nothing as that pushes costs to zero'.

The main forms of economic evaluation (i.e. CEA, CUA and CBA) can be used to pursue two types of efficiency: economic and allocative. We learned in Chapter 7 that economic efficiency enables assessment of the relative value for money of interventions with directly comparable outcomes. Put differently, economic efficiency is concerned with 'what is the least costly way to *achieve* a particular goal?'. Allocative efficiency describes a situation where resources are allocated and goods distributed in a way that maximizes social welfare. Allocative efficiency judges whether the goal itself is worthwhile pursuing. This requires us to take a 'societal perspective' and consider costs and benefits within and outside the health sector.

CEA and CUA are based on the production function approach (see Chapter 5) which focuses on the least cost way of producing a good whether it be a car or a hip replacement. These techniques compute the ratio of input to output (or vice versa) with inputs valued in monetary terms and is therefore a measure of economic efficiency. CEA considers only one measure of effectiveness and as a result often omits important social costs and benefits.

CBA can be used to measure both economic and allocative efficiency questions. It can be measured either within the health care sector or across other sectors of the economy because in principle it assesses all relevant costs and benefits that result from an intervention. While in theory this provides the most comprehensive form of economic evaluation, its use in the health sector has been limited largely due to the practical problems of measuring and valuing these benefits. In addition to economic and allocative efficiency, CBA is based on Pareto welfare optimization. In other words, the aim of CBA is to provide a framework for assessing the ability of an intervention or policy to offer a potential Pareto improvement (see Chapter 7 for an explanation of Pareto efficiency).

Stages of economic evaluation

There are four broad steps in undertaking an economic evaluation:

*   defining the decision problem (also known as 'framing the evaluation');
*   identifying, quantifying and valuing the resources needed;
*   identifying, quantifying and valuing the health consequences;
*   presenting and interpreting the evidence for decision-making.

You will learn about the second step in the next chapter, the third step in Chapter 15 and the fourth step in Chapter 16. For now we will concentrate on defining the decision problem.

Defining the decision problem

When defining the decision problem you will need to include clear statements on the purpose of the evaluation, intended audience, time frame, perspective and interventions for comparison.

Purpose

It is important to be very clear about *why* you are carrying out the economic evaluation. The statement of purpose should include the following information:

- the intervention(s);
- the health problem addressed by the intervention;
- the reason for conducting the evaluation and its importance;
- the units of analysis.

In terms of the last point, you want your analysis to have an impact on policy. Therefore it is important that results should be easy to communicate in terms that are both useful and understandable to the target audience. People want to know what they are getting for their money and this is most easily communicated when costs and outcomes are simplified to units that people can understand.

Audience

The main audience should be those attempting to use the information.

Activity 13.4

Can you identify what groups might use the results of an economic evaluation in their decision-making?

Feedback

Audiences can include:
- government (e.g. Ministry of Health);
- international health organizations (e.g. World Health Organization);
- multilateral development banks (e.g. World Bank);
- bilateral aid agencies (e.g. Swedish International Development Cooperation Agency – SIDA);
- non-governmental organizations (NGOs) (e.g. Oxfam);
- drug companies;
- global health partnerships (e.g. Global Fund);
- advocacy or special interest groups (e.g. tobacco control advocacy groups).

The audience will have an important bearing on the perspective of the analysis and in turn the different options being compared. An economic evaluation designed to inform a large international donor, such as the World Bank, about the cost-effectiveness of scaling up malaria control in the Africa region will be different to an evaluation for an NGO that wants to compare mechanisms for delivering antenatal care to women living in a remote area of Nepal. The main differences will lie in the way results are presented and the types of costs and effects taken into account. We will come back to this last point under 'perspectives'.

Time frame

Interventions often have different time patterns for their costs and outcomes; costs and outcomes are usually spread out over time (often a number of years) and, frequently, costs and outcomes change over time. It is quite common that the costs of the intervention are incurred at the beginning, while the benefits occur far in the future – an example would be an immunization programme for hepatitis B. A cost analysis must therefore consider the time course of interventions and outcomes separately and adjust for changes over time. *Discounting* is a procedure economists use to relate costs and outcomes occurring at different times to a common basis. We will learn more about this technique in the next chapter.

To understand how and why the costs of an intervention vary, think about dividing an intervention into start-up costs (those needed to set up the intervention) and maintenance costs (those needed to keep it going). If you do the cost analysis when beginning the intervention, it would be a mistake to assume that start-up costs (such as building a new clinic) are representative of the costs you will incur in later years. Conversely, if you begin the cost analysis after the intervention has begun, you cannot assume that everything put in place at the beginning of the project no longer has to be paid for and therefore has a value of zero.

Perspectives: whose costs and whose outcomes?

It is important to realize that health interventions frequently have costs and outcomes that affect different parts of a society. The perspective or viewpoint is like the lens through which costs and consequences are examined. It can be broad or narrow. Commonly used perspectives include:

* *Societal* – the broadest viewpoint possible which takes into account all the costs and all the outcomes of a health intervention, regardless of who incurs them or who gains from them. A societal perspective requires a vast range of micro and macro data and would be highly unlikely to address a specific audience;
* *Health system* – obviously a narrower point of view, this includes the costs borne and the outcomes received by the health sector.

Correctly thinking through the perspective can save large amounts of time and effort in performing the analysis because, depending on the perspective taken, some hard-to-measure costs and outcomes may not have to be considered.

The simplest example is the expenditure for a prescription drug. If the patient must pay 100 per cent of the cost of the drug, then the cost might not be important to the health service. On the other hand, if the health system must bear all of the costs of the drug, then this will directly reduce the funds available for other interventions and the health system might be very concerned with the drug costs – as the example below will show.

Should expensive drugs be provided free?
Consider a disease for which there is a drug treatment but the drugs are very expensive – e.g. they cost £10,000 to £12,000 per year for each patient. Citizens'

groups representing those affected by the disease are requesting that the Ministry of Health provide this medication free of charge to everyone with the disease. Now consider two contrasting perspectives: that of the Ministry and that of a group of citizens.

From the perspective of the Ministry, providing this drug will indeed help patients with the disease but the opportunity cost of these drugs is significant in terms of what could be provided for other patients. The budget is limited – what is the best use of available resources?

In contrast, the citizens' group will focus on the positive impact the drug is likely to have on people with the disease: they will be able to lead more normal lives of higher quality, perform their household duties and remain productive members of society, and their need to use the health services over any given period of time will be reduced. In contrast, if they do not get the drug they may not be able to work and consequently will be unable to support themselves or their families financially. From this perspective, supplying the drug will lessen the burden on the family and society.

You can see from the above example that the perspective you choose will dictate how you look at costs and outcomes.

Specifying the interventions/options for comparison

All the relevant interventions directly related to the health problem being evaluated should be included in the analysis. Interventions need to be described in enough detail that will allow all relevant costs and outcomes to be identified. For costs, this means asking who does what, to whom, where and how often (Drummond et al. 2005). For outcomes or consequences, it is important to examine which ones are measurable and in turn how they can be valued (Fox-Rushby and Cairns 2005). As you have learnt, the choice of outcome will dictate the type of economic evaluation undertaken (i.e. CEA, CUA or CBA).

Sensitivity analysis

For each stage of an economic evaluation it is important to document any assumptions made. You will have gathered by now that conducting an economic evaluation is far from an exact science. Lots of difficult questions are raised that do not always have clear-cut answers. Many of the procedures to estimate costs and benefits require estimates of data and preferences that are not known with certainty. For example, medical professionals are uncertain about the value of many preventive measures and their views can change as new evidence becomes available. There also tends to be considerable speculation over future drug costs. *Sensitivity analysis* is the process of deliberately varying these uncertain factors to examine their effect on the findings of a study. These type of assumptions will need to be tested under the final stage of an economic evaluation (i.e. 'presentation and interpretation of the evidence' (discussed in Chapter 16).

Summary

You have learned in this chapter that economic evaluation generates information on efficiency in non-market situations by comparing the costs and consequences of alternatives. There are three main forms of economic evaluation (CBA, CUA and CEA) and it is the way outcomes are expressed which distinguishes them. Under CBA outcomes are expressed in monetary terms, under CEA they are expressed in single health effects such as life years saved and for CUA multiple effects can be captured under measures such as QALYs. Establishing the purpose, audience, perspective, time frame and interventions for comparison are all important first steps in economic evaluation regardless of the type of tool being used.

References

Drummond MF, O'Brien B, Stoddart GL and Torrance GW (2005) *Methods for the economic evaluation of health care programmes.* Oxford: Oxford University Press.

Fox-Rushby J and Cairns J (2005) *Ecomomic evaluation.* Maidenhead: Open University Press.

Howard K, Salkeld G, McCaffery K and Irwig L (2008) HPV triage testing or repeat PAP smear for the management of atypical squamous cells (ASCUS) on PAP smear: is there evidence of process utility? *Health Economics* 17:593–605.

Maynard A (1987) Logic in medicine: an economist's perspective, *British Medical Journal* 295:1537–41.

Mooney G (1994) *Key issues in health economics.* Exeter: Harvester Wheatsheaf.

Neuhauser D and Lewicki AM (1976) National health insurance and the sixth stool guaiac, *Policy Analysis* 24:175–96.

Further reading

Drummond MF, O'Brien B, Stoddart GL and Torrance GW (2005) *Methods for the economic evaluation of health care programmes.* Oxford: Oxford University Press, Chapters 2 and 3.

Fox-Rushby J and Cairns J (2008) *Ecomomic evaluation.* Maidenhead: Open University Press, Chapters 1 and 2.

McPake B, Kumaranayake L and Normand C (2002) *Health economics: an international perspective.* London: Routledge, Chapter 12.

Counting the costs

Lorna Guinness

Overview

In Chapter 13, you learned that there are three steps in determining the cost of an intervention, once the decision problem has been identified: identification of the resources needed; quantification of the amount of each resource; and valuation of each resource. In this chapter you will focus on the third step: the valuation of resources to generate costs. You will learn about defining, calculating and comparing costs, known as cost analysis. In particular, you will learn about marginal costs – the cost of providing one additional unit of service.

Learning objectives

After working through this chapter, you will be able to:

- define and set up a cost analysis
- define and give examples of financial and economic costs
- define and give examples of capital and recurrent costs, fixed and variable costs
- calculate the following as they relate to an intervention: total costs, annual and annualized costs, average costs and marginal costs
- explain why discounting may be necessary

Key terms

Annual cost. The cost of an intervention, calculated on a yearly basis, including all the capital and recurrent costs.

Annualized costs. The annual share of the initial cost of capital equipment or investments, spread over the life of the project – usually modified to take account of depreciation.

Average cost. Total cost divided by quantity.

Capital cost. The value of capital resources which have useful lives greater than one year.

Direct cost. Resources used in the design, implementation, receipt and continuation of a health care intervention.

Discount rate.   The rate at which future costs and outcomes are discounted to account for time preference.

Discounting.   A method for adjusting the value of costs and outcomes which occur in different time periods into a common time period, usually the present.

Financial (budgetary) cost.   The accounting cost of a good or service, usually representing the actual (historical) amount paid – distinct from the economic (opportunity) cost.

Indirect cost.   The value of resources expended by patients and their carers to enable individuals to receive an intervention.

Intangible cost.   The costs of discomfort, pain, anxiety or inconvenience.

Marginal cost.   The change in the total cost if one additional unit of output is produced.

Overhead cost.   A cost that is not incurred directly from providing patient care but is necessary to support the organization overall (e.g. personnel functions).

Recurrent cost.   The value of resources with useful lives of less than one year that have to be purchased at least once a year.

Shadow price.   The true economic price of a good that reflects its value to society.

Time preference.   People's preference for consumption (or use of resources) now rather than later because they value present consumption more than the same consumption in the future.

Total (economic) cost.   The sum of all the costs of an intervention or health problem.

Costing – not as simple as it may look

It is important to know the cost of things you buy in the health sector. Every time a decision is made to implement one intervention instead of another, it is the same as making a purchase. The cost of the intervention becomes a very important part of the decision to use one intervention rather than another. But figuring out the cost of an intervention is often not easy. First you need to establish an inventory of costs based on a clear description of the intervention, identification of the resources used and organisation by type of resource. Next there is valuation and calculation of the costs. Finally you will need to carry out a sensitivity analysis. This chapter will take you through issues to consider at each of these steps.

Drummond *et al.* (2005) provide a list of questions that need to be answered when specifying interventions. They suggest that to identify costs you need to ask:

• Who are the people providing care (e.g. doctors, nurses, village health workers, volunteers, etc.)?

- What are the different activities of the intervention (e.g. training, drug distribution, etc.)?
- To whom is the intervention directed (e.g. different age groups, socioeconomic groups, ethnic groups or gender)?
- Where is each part of the intervention delivered (e.g. inpatient and outpatient care)?
- How long will the intervention run (e.g. weight loss programme for six months versus HIV prevention monitoring sexual behaviour over a 10-year period)? How often will individuals or populations be seen (e.g. monthly antenatal check-ups)?

Once the intervention is specified and resources identified (as described in Chapter 13) we turn to the valuation of those resources to generate costs. When economists talk about cost, they are referring to the opportunity cost of producing a good or, in this case, a health service. In perfectly competitive markets price will equate to opportunity cost (remember that you learned in Chapter 6 that the supply curve is equivalent to the marginal cost curve). Consequently price is often used as a proxy for costs. If this is the case, once you know the quantity of resources required, costing sounds easy: many types of resource have a readily obtainable price. However, given that most markets are not perfectly competitive, price may not be a good proxy. Think of the resource which is most scarce for some people – their time. How would you value the time of individuals? Or the difference in the prices of goods purchased on the black market from those purchased through official channels? In addition, the price of a resource may not be easily available. It may be that there are no records about what was paid, the purchase was made long ago and the resources have declined in value or the people who have the information are not willing to share it. This means costing requires both skill and judgement on behalf of the economist in valuing or estimating the price of a resource.

Financial and economic costs

Let's look at the case when the price is available, but it does not reflect the true value of the resource to society. If a resource is donated, the price paid is zero but the value of the equipment is not zero. Similarly, taxes or subsidies result in the price paid for a resource differing from its opportunity cost. Remember that opportunity cost is the level of benefit we would receive in the next best alternative option. When valuing resources economists use this definition to obtain the value of the resource to society. Where price does not reflect opportunity cost, the inputs are valued using a *shadow price*, reflecting the true value to society. Opportunity costs are also referred to as *economic costs*. They are used in economic evaluation and the weighing up of alternatives in health service delivery.

Financial costs are defined as the actual money spent on resources. They are used in programme planning and budgeting, as revenues must be generated to cover these financial outlays if a programme is to be sustained. Examples of financial costs include the price paid for supplies, maintenance, personnel, electricity and rent. The following activity will give you an idea of why the distinction between financial and economic costs might be important.

Activity 14.1

You are costing a primary health care project and have been asking around for the prices of resources which include imported vaccines. From a well-informed local source, you find out that the official prices of some resources do not seem to reflect their real value. Specifically, you are given the following information (Creese and Parker 1994):

- wages paid in the private sector for nurses and nurse assistants are US$1,350 and US$1,050, respectively;
- the driver is paid the national minimum wage, but in the informal sector, drivers are paid only US$300;
- although the project is able to buy fuel at official prices, there is always a shortage of fuel and in the black market the price is four times the official price;
- the official exchange rate is 50 shillings = US$1, but on the black market the average rate is 250 shillings;
- space which is given free would rent for US$300 on the private market;
- some community women have volunteered their time – most of them are house-wives and earn extra money by cooking for the market for which they would normally earn about US$300 in a month.

In Table 14.1 you will find the financial costs already calculated. Use the information above and, if necessary, the financial costs in the table to calculate the economic costs in the last column. What is their total? And which are the 'big ticket' items? Which resources are undervalued in terms of their financial costs, and which are overvalued?

Table 14.1 Monthly financial costs of an identified primary health care project

Resource	Financial cost (US$)	Economic cost (US$)
Staff:		
• nurse	900	
• nurse assistant	700	
• driver	600	
• volunteer helpers	0	
Vaccine	5,000	
Vehicle fuel	3,000	
Building space	0	
Total cost		

Source: Creese and Parker (1994)

Feedback

Check the economic costs you calculated by comparing them with those shown in Table 14.2.

You can see that the actual value to the economy and society of many of these resources is greater than their financial price – especially in the case of nursing staff, who are paid relatively poorly compared to the private sector. The driver, by contrast, is overpaid. The fuel and vaccines are also undervalued by comparison with their scarcity value in the economy.

Table 14.2 Financial and economic costs of an identified primary health care project (solution)

Resource	Financial cost (US$)	Economic cost (US$)
Staff:		
• nurse	900	1,350
• nurse assistant	700	1,050
• driver	600	300
• volunteer helpers	0	300
Vaccine	5,000	25,000
Vehicle fuel	3,000	12,000
Building space	0	300
Total cost	10,200	40,300

Source: Creese and Parker (1994)

Types of cost

Direct costs

Direct costs are resources used in the design, implementation, accessing or continuation of the intervention(s) being evaluated and are usually the main focus of a cost analysis. They are the costs of providing or accessing health services and can be incurred by either the provider or patient. Both should be included unless the study perspective dictates otherwise. Direct costs can be further classified as direct health care and direct non-health care costs.

- Direct health care costs are those costs essential to the implementation, receipt and continuation of the health service. They are the resources spent on health care;
- Direct non-health care costs are resources used in connection with the health service but are not health sector costs. Examples include the cost of transport to and from the facility or catering in hospitals.

Activity 14.2

Imagine that the minister of health has proposed that seven primary health care centres (PHCs) be built to decrease demands on a regional hospital. In Table 14.3 you will

Table 14.3 Resources used to establish and run seven new PHCs

Resource	Type of cost
Building the seven PHCs	
Education of parents on how to prevent exacerbation of asthma	
Laboratory equipment for PHCs	
Lunch while waiting at PHCs	
PHC health education to prevent smoking	
Salaries of intervention personnel	
Soap for hand washing in PHCs	
Training PHC teams	
Transportation to PHCs	
Vehicles to carry vaccines for PHCs	

see a list of the resources identified as necessary for this project. Consider the resources listed and, in the right-hand column, write down whether each is a health care or a non-health care cost.

Feedback

The classification of costs would be as shown in Table 14.4.

Table 14.4 Cost classification of resources used in setting up and running seven new PHCs

Resource	Type of cost
Building the seven PHCs	Direct health care
Education of parents on how to prevent exacerbation of asthma	Direct health care
Laboratory equipment for PHCs	Direct health care
Lunch while waiting at PHCs	Direct non-health care
PHC health education to prevent smoking	Direct health care
Salaries of intervention personnel	Direct health care
Soap for hand washing in PHCs	Direct health care
Training PHC teams	Direct health care
Transportation to PHCs	Direct non-health care
Vehicles to carry vaccines for PHCs	Direct health care

Indirect costs

In addition to direct costs, other resources might be used as a result of the health intervention. Indirect costs refer to resources like the patient's time that is taken up going to the hospital, rather than working. Similarly, other family members may also have to change their work schedules to take over some of the jobs that would have been done by the patient, or to accompany the patient to receive care. The time of other family members used for these reasons is also counted as an indirect cost.

Indirect costs are commonly measured using wages and earnings lost. If wages and earnings are not available or the person is not working, alternative methods can be used to find the value of their time – you will read more about different techniques for valuing people's time in Chapter 15.

Intangible costs

Some interventions may themselves cause pain and suffering such as side-effects from treatment or anxiety about whether the treatment will be effective. The value of pain and suffering is termed an intangible cost. Because measuring intangible costs is a difficult task, most economic evaluations do not calculate them. However, you should bear in mind that intangible costs could be major factors affecting the patient's and society's decision regarding treatment options.

Activity 14.3

Consider the following aspects of the problems posed by polio in a society. Classify the items in Table 14.5 as direct health care, direct non-health care, indirect or intangible costs of the health problem or intervention, noting your classification in the right-hand column.

Table 14.5 The costs of polio

Resource	Type of cost
Polio vaccine	
Salary of physical therapist who treats polio victims	
Loss of wages due to polio	
Loss of wages due to vaccine-induced polio	
Bus fare for family members visiting child at hospital	
Pain and suffering following a case of polio	
Cost of care of siblings to enable mother to take ill child for rehabilitation	
Time lost taking child to clinic for immunization	
Salary of nurse who runs immunization clinic	
Hospital cost for child with vaccine side-effects	

Feedback

The classification of the resources devoted to the problem of polio could be described as shown in Table 14.6.

Table 14.6 The costs of polio classified

Resource	Type of cost
Polio vaccine	Direct health care
Salary of physical therapist who treats polio victims	Direct health care
Loss of wages due to polio	Indirect
Loss of wages due to vaccine-induced polio	Indirect
Bus fare for family members visiting child at hospital	Direct non-health care
Pain and suffering following a case of polio	Intangible
Cost of care of siblings to enable mother to take ill child for rehabilitation	Indirect
Time lost taking child to clinic for immunization	Indirect
Salary of nurse who runs immunization clinic	Direct health care
Hospital cost for child with vaccine side-effects	Direct health care

Schemes for classifying costs

Classifying costs into different schemes helps ensure that you include everything necessary in the cost analysis. Different schemes serve different purposes and there are three main schemes for thinking about costs.

The most commonly used system for classifying direct health care costs is the functional classification scheme you learned about in Chapter 13. In this, resources are classified according to their use or function within a health programme (e.g. buildings, personnel and equipment). Alternatively, resources can be classified according to the activity for which they are used (e.g. training, outreach, treatment and administration). The two remaining schemes most commonly used and that you will read about here are capital and recurrent costs, and fixed and variable costs.

Capital and recurrent costs

An important way to classify costs, that can help determine the sustainability of a programme, is to classify according to the time period over which the resource will be used. Capital costs are generally defined as the costs of those resources such as equipment, vehicles, buildings and one-off training programmes that have a useful life of more than one year. Capital costs are often equated with start-up costs because they are paid for at the beginning of a programme but these resources are defined according to their useful life, not when they are purchased.

In contrast, recurrent resources are those with useful lives of less than one year and have to be purchased at least once a year – yearly, monthly, weekly, daily or irregularly but frequently. Recurrent costs are the value of recurrent resources. Any given capital investment will require some recurrent funds to keep it running. The sustainability of a health service depends heavily on whether funds are available to cover these recurrent costs. The recurrent cost coefficient (r-coefficient) is used to estimate the approximate amount a given capital investment will require to run adequately. Typically, r-coefficients in the health field run from about 0.25 for a basic clinic to 0.33 for a more high-technology referral hospital.

In economic evaluation, it is normal to calculate the annual cost of a health service. Capital costs are included in this calculation by converting them into a recurrent cost by spreading them out over time in a process called *annualization*. This is just like when you obtain a loan from a bank. When you obtain the loan you spread a one-time cost over years and your annual payment to the bank is a recurrent cost. The simplest method to obtain an annualized cost is straight-line depreciation, which simply divides the initial cost by the number of years of useful life. For example, a £10,000 X-ray machine which has a useful life of 10 years has an *annualized cost* of £1,000 per year.

Most economists prefer a slightly more complex method that takes account of the opportunity cost of money – the interest that would be earned if it were invested in the bank. This is called the *annualization method*. Banks calculate payment schedules by the annualization method.

Activity 14.4

Suppose you were calculating the annual costs of a family planning clinic. Calculate the annual cost of the resources in this example, using straight-line depreciation. The expected useful lives of the different resources are shown in Table 14.7.

Table 14.7 The costs and expected length of life of resources used in a family planning clinic

Resource	Useful life (years)	Total cost (£)	Annual cost (£)
Equipment	5	8,650	
Buildings	30	54,080	
Land	50	31,150	
Vehicles	5	8,165	
Initial training (nurses and midwives)	30	48,321	

Feedback

The annual costs of these items, using straight-line depreciation are shown in the right-hand column in Table 14.8.

Table 14.8 The annual cost of resources for a family planning clinic (solution)

Resource	Useful life (years)	Total cost (£)	Annual cost (£)
Equipment	5	8,650	1,730
Buildings	30	54,080	1,803
Land	50	31,150	623
Vehicles	5	8,165	1,633
Initial training (nurses and midwives)	30	48,321	1,611

Fixed and variable costs

Take a look at Chapters 5 and 6 to remind yourself about the classification of resources and costs by fixed and variable. This scheme is most often used when looking at issues of scale and how costs might vary with different levels of output, as described in Chapter 6.

Some items have both a fixed and variable cost component. These are termed semi-variable costs. A good example is a telephone. You will have to pay the monthly line rental whether or not anyone makes any calls – this part is fixed. A variable amount is payable depending on the amount that it is used.

Allocating shared costs

In many situations, a resource will be used for a number of purposes. This is particularly true for overhead costs. For example, a hospital administrator works on all the different activities of the hospital. One aspect of a cost analysis will be to determine a fair allocation of shared resources among the different activities which use the resource. One method is to attribute to a specific intervention the percentage of the resource which is used by the intervention. Typically, the following are used for calculations:

- *buildings* – the percentage of floor space used for activities related to the intervention;
- *staff* – the percentage of their time that staff spend on the intervention;
- *equipment* – the percentage of time the item of equipment is used for the intervention;
- *utilities (water, electricity, gas)* – the percentage of floor space used by the intervention;
- *maintenance* – the percentage of floor space used by the intervention.

However, using the percentage of floor space may be misleading. A storeroom and an operating theatre in a hospital may occupy the same floor area but the latter would consume much more in the way of utilities and maintenance. An alternative is to use the number of staff as a proxy for the percentage use – in this case it would be many times greater for the theatre. This would be a more realistic reflection of the resources used in the theatre.

Obtaining estimates of personnel time may be difficult. In some cases it is possible for an administrator to make a list of who works where and for how many hours per week. In other cases, staff can keep a log of where they work. If estimates of personnel time are not available, you could perform time and motion studies, which entail the use of a trained observer to determine the amount of time personnel actually spend performing tasks related to the intervention.

Activity 14.5

A new roof at a hospital costs £1 million and is expected to last 20 years. The TB ward occupies one floor in this 10-storey hospital. What is the share of the total annual cost of the roof which should be attributed to the TB ward?

Feedback

First, the total cost of the roof of £1 million should be annualized. With straight-line depreciation, the annual cost is £50,000 (£1 million/20 years = £50,000). There are 10 floors, so the percentage use of the shared input (the roof overhead) for the TB ward is 10 per cent – only 10 per cent of the annualized cost of the roof should be attributed to the TB programme. So £5,000 is the annualized cost of roof for the TB programme (10 per cent of £50,000 = $5,000).

Calculating costs

So far you have learned about framing the study and making an inventory of the costs. Finally you have reached the last of the three main steps – calculating the costs.

Activity 14.6

Explain each one of these four commonly used measures of costs:

1 Total cost
2 Annual cost
3 Average cost
4 Marginal cost

Feedback

1 Total cost is the sum of all costs. This gives an indication as to how much the intervention costs overall – taking account of the value of all the resources used.
2 Annual cost is the cost of the intervention calculated on a yearly basis – including all the annualized costs of capital expenditures as well as the yearly recurrent costs. Annual costs will vary from one year to another – in the first year, the start-up costs will be greater whereas after the intervention has been in operation for a while, the recurrent costs may form a higher part of the annual cost.
3 Average cost is the total cost divided by the total units of activity or outcome. Average cost gives an indication of how efficiently, on average, different providers are functioning.
4 Marginal cost is the change in the total cost if one extra unit of output is produced. Marginal cost can also be used to calculate how much would be saved by contracting a service. In practice you can see that often it is more than a change of only one unit of output which is of concern but rather a group of 10 or 100 extra units. In this case the correct term for the cost of the change is *incremental cost*. You may see some applications where the term incremental cost is used, rather than marginal cost.

The following activity is drawn from a real-life situation and shows an application of the incremental cost (and incremental benefit) concept to decision-making.

Activity 14.7

An evaluation of a sexually transmitted disease (STD) clinic found that while the service was much appreciated by the clients who were using it, quite a few people with STDs were not able to come during its opening hours, from 9.00 a.m. to 5.30 p.m, because they worked or were in school. A decision was made, therefore, to extend the opening hours to 7.30 p.m. on Monday and Thursday nights on a trial basis. This meant that staff would have to be paid more for the overtime and the managers were interested to know what the impact would be on the overall attendances at the clinic. The costs per week of the clinic *before* the extension of the hours are shown in Table 14.9.
The number of clients seen on average each week was 20 per day, or 100 per week.

Table 14.9 Costs per week of the clinic before the extension of the hours

Cost	£
Rental of premises	200
Staff:	
• receptionist	300
• practice nurse	385
• doctor	595
Medicines, etc.	270
Electricity, gas, etc.	55
Other operating costs	580
Total	**2,385**

Option 1: evening hours

After opening for an extra two hours on Monday and Thursday evenings each week, the following additional costs were incurred: staff £115, medicines £80, electricity £25 and other items £130. During the trial period, the clinic was very busy in the evenings, and an additional 15 patients were seen on Monday evenings and 12 on Thursdays.

1 What was the average cost per patient seen in the clinic?
2 What was the incremental (or marginal) cost per patient seen in the evenings?
3 What was the new average cost per patient of the clinic?
4 What recommendation would you make to the health authority about whether to maintain these new evening opening hours of the clinic?

Feedback

1 The average cost per patient at the beginning of the period was £23.85.
2 The incremental cost of the patients seen in the evening was £12.96 (£350 marginal costs/27 extra patients).
3 The total costs now (including evening hours, Option 1) are £2,735 (£2,385 + £350), the number of patients now attending is 127, so the new average cost is £21.54 (£2,735/127).
4 The evening hours seem to be a success – the incremental cost is below the average cost so the costs are still going down. Keep the new hours.

Option 2: Saturday hours

The clinic management held a meeting and decided that perhaps it would be good to open on Saturday mornings from 8.00 a.m. to 12 noon as well, to serve especially young people who come from outlying areas. The additional costs of opening on Saturdays were £250 for staff, £27 for medicines and £120 for other costs. The clinic was not as popular as predicted, with only five people coming on average on Saturdays.

5 What was the total incremental cost of this option?
6 What was the incremental cost per client of this additional group of clients?
7 What was the overall average cost per client (with options 1 and 2)?
8 Overall, with the information you now have about the opening hours (options 1 and 2) what recommendation would you make to the management regarding the best combination of opening hours of the clinic?
9 Now consider this: if the costs of opening on Saturday afternoons are the same as Saturday morning (£397), how many patients would you estimate are needed to make it worthwhile?

Feedback

5 The new incremental costs of Saturday opening (option 2) are £397.
6 The new incremental cost per patient is £79.40 (£397/5 patients).
7 The new total cost of the original clinic hours plus options 1 and 2 is £3,132, and the new average cost per patient is £23.72 (£3,132/132 total patients).

8 Evening hours were a success but the incremental costs of £79.40 per Saturday patient are high. Either give up on Saturdays altogether – or try Saturday afternoons!

9 It seems unlikely that the same incremental cost could be obtained for the Saturday hours as for the evening hours. The evening hours cost only around £13 per patient so ideally Saturday hours would give the same result – this would require about 30 patients (£397/13). If the average cost per patient could be kept at or near the average with option 1, this would mean that the clinic was still operating efficiently and therefore 17 patients would make this worthwhile (£397/21.54 = 16.7). This seems attainable if the clinic is well situated, user-friendly and the Saturday opening hours are made known to the teenage target group.

Some practical considerations

Until now the discussion has assumed that you are doing 'bottom-up' costing – starting from scratch and building up the costs, in the same way as you build up a budget. But sometimes you are faced with a situation of retrospective costing, whereby you have information on total expenditures by line item and most of the costs are joint costs – used by several activities. If it is not possible to go back to get the information on individual units of resources that were used or the costs of those resources, you can use the aggregated information and break this down by activity or 'cost centre'.

By now you may be wondering where you will find all the information you need. There are a number of sources, depending on what exactly you are trying to cost.

Health services costs

If you are costing the activities of a health facility such as a hospital, there is probably an accountant or financial officer who can provide much of the financial information you need, although you will still need to estimate the economic cost which may differ from the financial cost. Information on personnel allocation can often be obtained from the nursing manager or sister, from the medical director and from the administrator who is responsible for the non-medical and non-nursing staff of the facility. Information on supplies and drugs can be found either on invoices or from catalogues of equipment and drugs; if the drugs, for example, were donated, you will probably need to refer to an international source of information to find out the international market price. Vehicles and vehicle costs can often be obtained from the person responsible for managing the fleet of vehicles.

A handy hint in doing costing is to concentrate on the more expensive items and those which constitute the biggest fraction of the total – the 'big ticket' items, usually vehicles and vehicle running costs, personnel, drugs and supplies. Often half or more of the total cost will be spent on personnel, so getting good information on the wages and benefits and the allocation of staff will be a good start in getting an overall cost. Vehicles and drugs may be another major expenditure category, and time spent getting precise measures here may enhance the accuracy of your overall estimates.

Don't spend too much time chasing a detailed piece of information when the decision will not be affected by it. It is unlikely that time spent getting precise estimates of the allocation of electricity and cleaning supplies, for example, will make much of a difference in the overall total.

Patient and family costs

The time of patients and their families is an essential input into the delivery of health services. For example, in order to receive treatment a patient and family members will:

- spend time and money getting to the service;
- spend time in activities other than the ones they would normally be doing, in order for them or their household member to be able to use the service.

There are a number of ways to estimate these costs and it can be complex, involving the estimation of shadow prices for work and leisure time (Posnett and Jan 1996). The best way is to carry out a survey of the patients. However, you may not have enough time to carry out a full survey, and if this is the case you could ask a small sample of patients and make some estimates of their expenditure, the time they have spent, and of their lost wages.

Calculating the value of wages lost can prove problematic – should you use the minimum wage, the average wage or some estimate of the wage of the actual patients? There is also seasonal variation in the value of time in many agricultural areas. The important thing is to include patient costs if appropriate – too often the difficulty of calculating patients' costs has meant that they have simply been left out of the analysis altogether and this clearly leads to a misleading result – effectively costing the patients' costs as zero.

Which price should you use?

One issue which you may face is which price to use – say, for example, you are costing a project which used a vehicle. If the vehicle was purchased five years ago and the market price then was £10,000 but a new one now has a market price of £15,000, which price should you use to estimate the opportunity cost? This depends on the purpose of your analysis. Here are three possibilities.

- If you are looking 'for historical purposes' at the past cost of an intervention which will not be repeated, you could safely use the original price of £10,000.
- If you wanted to know the annual cost of running the programme for the past five years, you would use the annualized cost of the original expenditure: £2,000 per year.
- But if you wanted to know the cost of replicating the programme in another location, you should use the present replacement price of £15,000. The annual cost of running the project in the future would use the annualized cost of £3,000 per year, assuming you expect it to last five years.

Time preference and discounting

In general, individuals have a preference for utility (from consumption) that happens now as opposed to in the future and they value consumption-derived utility less as it occurs further into the future. Why? People live for today and the future is uncertain. In addition, as someone's earning potential increases over time, the value of a single unit of currency will be worth less to them in 10 years' time than it is now. In the same way we might value our health today more than being healthy in 10 years' time. Let's look at the example of a trainee nurse with approaching exams: a trainee nurse might be happy to pay £50 now to know that they are going to be healthy all of June because they have an exam during that time. However they are less likely to be willing to pay £50 now to know that they will be healthy for all of June in 10 years' time. This is because they actually value their health in the future less. Similarly, although the nurse is willing to pay £50 to be healthy in June this year, they might be willing to agree to pay $100 in 10 years' time so that they will be healthy in June in 10 years' time. This is because they value the utility that would be derived from the consumption that money would enable in the future less.

Because people do not place equal value on costs or outcomes that occur this year with those that occur in later years, economic evaluations must give different weight to costs and health outcomes that occur at different periods in time. While there are theoretical and practical problems in doing so, many economic evaluations are performed using some sort of adjustment for the occurrence over time, or *discounting*, both for the costs and for outcomes. Discounting is used to convert a value in the future (either costs or health outcomes) to today's equivalent or present value using a *discount rate*. National and international guidelines recommend using a 3 per cent discount rate, after controlling for inflation. In some countries, such as the UK, central government imposes a specific real discount rate for economic evaluations of publicly funded projects. In other countries where no specific rate is imposed, economists frequently choose one rate and then perform a sensitivity analysis to ensure the conclusions are stable with respect to the assumption about discount rates.

Sensitivity analysis

Cost estimates calculated using the methods described in this chapter should be seen as mean (average) values. As with most parameters in an economic evaluation, costs are also subject to uncertainty and we should explore the way cost uncertainty affects the result of the economic evaluation in a sensitivity analysis.

Summary

In this chapter you have learned about different ways of defining costs and why costing is rarely a straightforward and simple exercise. In addition you have gained an understanding of how to calculate the different cost measures: total cost, annual cost, average cost and marginal cost. You have learned about the difference between financial and economic costs and when it is appropriate to use each of these. Next you read about the different types of costs that might be considered for inclusion in a cost analysis: direct, indirect and intangible costs; and the ways in which these might be classified: by function or activity, recurrent and capital, and fixed and variable. Finally, some practical difficulties were discussed concerning obtaining data, allocating shared costs among different activities, identifying which costs to use and people's time preferences.

References

Creese A and Parker D (1994) *Cost analysis in primary health care: a training manual for programme managers.* Geneva: WHO.

Drummond M *et al.* (2005) *Methods for the economic evaluation of health care programmes.* Oxford: Oxford University Press.

Posnett J and Jan S (1996) Indirect cost in economic evaluation: the opportunity cost of unpaid inputs. *Health Economics* 5:13–23.

Further reading

Creese A and Parker D (1994) *Cost analysis in primary health care: a training manual for programme managers.* Geneva: WHO.

Drummond M *et al.* (2005) *Methods for the economic evaluation of health care programmes.* Oxford: Oxford University Press, Chapter 4.

Johns B, Baltussen R and Hutubessy R (2003) Programme costs in the economic evaluation of health interventions. *Cost Effectiveness and Resource Allocation* 1.1 doi: 10.1186/1478-7547-1-1.

Palmer S and Raftery J (1999) Opportunity cost. *British Medical Journal* 318(7197):1551–2.

Walker D and Kumaranayake L (2002) Allowing for differential timing in cost analyses: discounting and annualization. *Health Policy and Planning* 17(1):112–18.

Identifying, measuring and valuing consequences ◼ 15
Shunmay Yeung, Kristian Hansen and Lorna Guinness

Overview

This chapter starts with a brief review of the different consequences or outcomes that arise from health interventions and their suitability for economic evaluation. This is followed by a detailed exploration of the different non-monetary and monetary methods for measuring and valuing consequences. Some pros and cons of these methods are also considered.

Learning objectives

After working through this chapter, you will be able to:

- recognize the wide range of outcomes that arise from health interventions (both health and non-health)
- explain which type of outcome measure is most suitable for use in each type of economic evaluation
- identify different ways of *measuring* health in economic evaluation
- compare different approaches for *valuing* health and non-health outcomes
- define and give examples of health outcomes in monetary terms

Key terms

Disability adjusted life year (DALY). A measure of health based on the length of a person's life weighted by the level of disability they experience.

Human capital approach. An approach that uses market wage rates to measure the value of productivity lost through illness.

Quality adjusted life years (QALY). A health outcome measure based on survival weighted by quality of life, where quality of life is scored between 1.0 for full health and zero for death.

Willingness to pay (WTP). The monetary value, representing the maximum amount an individual would be prepared to pay out of his or her own income, to gain an improvement in health.

Defining and measuring health consequences

You will recall from Chapter 13 that there are three main types of economic evaluation: cost-effectiveness analysis (CEA), cost–utility analysis (CUA) and cost–benefit analysis (CBA). Each of these involves the comparison of different alternatives in terms of both their costs and consequences (Drummond *et al.* 2005). However, they differ in terms of the type of consequences they attempt to measure and value. In this chapter we explore these different methods, starting with those used to measure health consequences in CEA and CUA. Some outcomes of health interventions are more obvious than others. Immunizing a baby against diphtheria, pertussis and tetanus protects him or her from these potentially life-threatening diseases. In this case, outcomes might include: cases prevented, life years saved, number of vaccines delivered. Using radiotherapy as part of a treatment package to cure a woman of breast cancer potentially increases her life span, and a patient's poor adherence to anti-TB chemotherapy may result in treatment failure. These examples are all fairly obvious. However, there are many less obvious outcomes – intended and non-intended – and potentially negative as well as positive. For example, the positive externality derived from immunizing a baby (i.e. the herd immunity); the fact that the radiotherapy used as part of many cancer regimens is associated with negative adverse effects (intangible costs); and the negative externality of the risk of developing drug resistance due to poor adherence to anti-TB chemotherapy. Some of these outcomes may result in the need for additional expensive treatments.

Activity 15.1

For each of the interventions below, list any positive and negative outcomes that you can think of:

1 Improving access to clean water and sanitation in a rural village.
2 Screening pregnant women for HIV infection.
3 Neonatal intensive care for extremely pre-term infants.

Feedback

1 Decreased incidence of diarrhoeal disease, less time taken to fetch water (and therefore more time available to do other things).
2 For those found to be HIV positive, early treatment for the mother and decreasing risk of transmission to the infant. Potential negative consequences include psychological stress in considering the test and especially, in rare cases, false positive tests.
3 Increased survival but high risk of short- and long-term complications including neurological disability.

It is perhaps worth bearing in mind that the most useful measures for economic evaluation will be those that are 'tangible' and allow any changes to be quantified and compared across interventions and diseases.

Measures of health consequences

Health can be measured in a number of different ways.

Mortality

Mortality can be measured as the 'number of deaths averted' or 'number of life years gained'. This is a tangible and quantifiable measure that can be used across diseases and interventions. It is useful for preventative and curative interventions which impact on potentially life-threatening injury and disease but not for those which may cause significant morbidity but rarely death.

Morbidity

Several measures can be used here, as outlined below.

- *Number of cases cured or disease incidence*: these measures are particularly useful in measuring acute illnesses (e.g. malaria or acute respiratory infections). They indicate presence or absence of disease but not duration or impact and are therefore not good for chronic or disabling conditions such as diabetes or arthritis. In addition they can only be used to compare interventions where the type of outcome is identical;
- *Disease-specific indices*: for a number of chronic conditions, there are disease-specific indices or profiles which aim to capture severity of disease and/or impact on quality of life (e.g. an arthritis impact measurement scale). The advantage of these measures is that they are tangible, however, as above, they can only be used to compare interventions where the type of outcome is identical;
- *Generic health measures (indices and profiles)*: these are designed to be broadly applicable across different types of disease and interventions and to summarize core concepts of health and quality of life. Profiles like the Nottingham Health Profile (Hunt *et al.* 1985) present different dimensions of health separately (e.g. mobility, pain, emotional well-being). Health indices such as the Sickness Impact Profile (Gilson *et al.* 1975) provide a single summary index score. The advantage of an index is that it allows for the possibility of comparing health across interventions, diseases and populations. Aggregating scores to produce a single value can be done with or without taking into account people's preferences. Taking people's preferences into account allows the calculation of measures of utility such as the quality adjusted life year (QALY) or disability adjusted life year (DALY), used in CUA.

Intermediate measures

Sometimes it is not possible to measure actual health outcomes, especially in preventative interventions when the health outcome may be significantly 'downstream'. For example, if the intervention results in the reduced risk of an individual developing a certain illness. In this case an intermediate measure may be used. For example, the relationship between blood pressure (BP) and the risk of cardiovascular disease (CVD) is well described. Therefore, in measuring the impact of BP-lowering treatment on CVD, BP can be used as an intermediate measure of the risk of CVD. Intermediate measures are only useful when comparing similar interventions.

Process measures

This refers to activities which are known to or are believed to have a direct bearing on the outcomes achieved by the intervention – e.g. length of hospital stay or correct diagnosis.

Money

Monetary values can also be assigned to health outcomes. This is explored further later in this chapter.

Activity 15.2

1 For each outcome below decide what kind it is, and consider how useful the outcome is for economic evaluation.
   a) Number of patients that quit smoking as a result of a health education campaign.
   b) Number of (i) deaths averted and (ii) disability adjusted life years (DALYs) averted by treating severe malaria with the drug artesunate instead of quinine.
   c) The average blood flow density lipoprotein (LDL) cholesterol level after treatment with cholesterol-lowering drugs.
2 Now apply this thinking to a more practical situation. Assume you are a civil servant working in the Ministry of Health and one day you are called to the minister's office. You are informed that you must conduct an economic evaluation of several interventions including the distribution of free insecticide-treated bed nets (ITNs) to pregnant women. The finance department has already provided estimates of the costs to the public health care sector of running an ITN programme. It will be your duty to provide estimates of the outcomes of such a programme. Fortunately, a recent randomized controlled trial in your country captured data on health outcomes over two years among a group of pregnant women given an ITN and another group of pregnant women not normally sleeping under a net. Health outcomes registered include the number of maternal deaths, anaemia cases, low birth weight (LBW) babies born, infant deaths and malaria episodes among mothers and their newborns. The minister suggests to you that reduction in maternal deaths could be used as an outcome measure of the ITN programme. What will you reply?

Feedback

1 a) This is an intermediate measure. It can be directly linked to a final health outcome (i.e. lung cancer cases prevented).
   b) (i) This is a measure of mortality. It is a good measure in that it is tangible and can be used to measure across other acute injuries and deaths. (ii) This is a general health index. It fulfils all the criteria for a good outcome measure for economic evaluation.
   c) This is an intermediate measure. The ultimate goal is to reduce mortality from CVD. It is only useful for comparing with other cholesterol-lowering drugs or interventions.
2 You may reply that reduction in maternal mortality is too narrow a measure since there are other adverse health outcomes worth avoiding such as malaria episodes and LBW babies. You may suggest choosing a health measure which can incorporate different adverse health states in addition to premature maternal death, such as QALYs or DALYs. In addition, a broader health measure will be needed if the costs and consequences of an ITN programme must be compared to interventions aimed at other diseases.

Valuing changes in health using non-monetary approaches

At first glance the distinction between *measuring* and *valuing* benefits may appear pedantic, but as the following extract from Richardson *et al.* (1998) illustrates, it is actually quite important.

The measurement of benefits in economic evaluation involves two steps that are conceptually distinct and normally distinct in practice. The first is the measurement of the consequences of a health-related intervention as measured in natural units such as additional years of life, change in blood pressure, etc. Second, there is the determination of the *value* of these changes. Economics is concerned with the second of these steps and it is the role of epidemiologists or clinical researchers to determine outcome (consequence) in natural units. This implies that economic evaluation does not compete with or intrude upon clinical or epidemiological research. Rather the two forms of evaluation are complementary.

(Richardson *et al.* 1998)

All of the valuation techniques to be discussed in this section are designed to elicit 'utility weights' or, simply, 'utilities', that reflect an individual's preferences for different health states. In health economics, utility weights are most commonly used to generate QALYs and DALYs for use in CUAs of health care interventions. They allow the different characteristics of health (such as symptoms or ability to do activities) to be valued on a single scale and compared. There are two broad ways of estimating values for health states: those estimated from patients using *direct* valuation methods, and those estimated *indirectly* using 'off-the-shelf' values from the literature. We describe the different elicitation techniques for valuing health states a little later but first let's look at how QALYs and DALYs are constructed.

QALYs

By now you will be aware that QALYs are a health indicator which measures the amount of years of life lived, taking into consideration that some of those life years are lived in less than perfect health. An individual will have more QALYs the longer he or she lives and the better health he or she enjoys during those years. QALYs are therefore a measure of health gain, which is a 'good' of which an individual wishes to have as much as possible. Levels of health are described using a scale with anchor points of 0 (death) and 1 (full health) and the principle of combining the quantity and quality of life years. The example below illustrates how the calculation is made.

Utility weights and QALYs

Let us assume that there are two treatments for an illness. Both treatments extend the life expectancy of an individual by 10 years. However, treatment A results in the individual surviving the years in full health (represented by a utility score of 1 on a *cardinal scale** while death is shown by zero) compared to treatment B which results in the individual surviving the years in a state that only has a utility score of 0.5.

Treatment A has led to a gain in QALYs of 10 (10 × 1), twice that of treatment B which has led to a gain in QALYs of 5 (10 × 0.5).

Note that similar calculations are made under the DALY approach. Each state of health is assigned a disability weighting on a scale from 0 (perfect health) to 1 (death). To calculate the burden of a certain disease, the disability weighting is multiplied by the number of years lived in that health state and is added to the number of years lost due to that disease.

*A cardinal scale is a specific form of an interval scale with '0' reflecting states of health equivalent to death and '1' reflecting perfect health. This means that an interval from 0.2 to 0.3 has the same meaning to the individual as the interval from 0.7 to 0.8. (see page 176 of Drummond *et al.* 2005 for further explanation of cardinal scales).

Being able to measure *differences* in preferences in this way is fundamental to economic evaluation (in particular CUA) which is, as we have already learned, a *comparative* analysis. We are purely interested in differences between alternative interventions. Once the difference in preferences has been measured, these are combined with utility weights to calculate QALYs.

Discounting can also be important in the calculation of QALYs. In a CUA using QALYs, an analyst may decide to discount future life years (in full or compromised health), in a similar way to discounting costs, to incorporate the observation that most individuals prefer to experience good things sooner rather than years into the future. This means that a life year will be considered to be of a progressively lower value the further into the future this life year is experienced.

DALYs

DALYs were developed as part of the Global Burden of Diseases (GBD) study which was aimed at comparing disease burdens across all regions of the world (Murray and Lopez 1996). DALYs are a measure of healthy time lost caused by diseases in an individual or a population. This indicator combines the life years lost due to premature death with years lived in a health state less than full health. An individual will suffer a larger burden of DALYs lost the shorter he or she lives and the worse health he or she experiences. DALYs are therefore a measure of the health gap between actual health and a defined ideal for health achievement. This gap is a 'bad' which an individual or population would strive to minimize. DALYs in the original GBD study were characterized by four explicit value choices:

1 Premature death defined relative to a model life table corresponding to the highest observed life expectancies globally.
2 An unequal age weighting applied with relatively higher values attached to the middle years of an individual's life span, compared to early childhood and old age. The rationale for this is that because of the different social roles an individual plays during life, it is particularly important to be healthy in the middle years with many dependants in the form of young children and older family members.
3 Discounting of future life years whether in full or compromised health using an annual discount rate of 3 per cent.
4 Disability weights attached to diseases reflecting their severity using an inverted scale between 0 for full health and 1 for death. Disability weights were derived for

specific health problems, such as blindness or watery diarrhoea, from a group of international public health experts using the 'person trade-off technique' (you will read more about this technique later).

The value choices around disability and age weighting in the original DALY calculations have been the subject of much debate. Updates to the DALY calculations use equal age weights and are moving away from the expert panel approach for obtaining disability weights to one using a combination of community and expert-based assessments (World Health Organization 2004; Harvard University *et al.* 2009). Analysts wishing to use DALYs and QALYs as part of a CUA should subject their estimates to sensitivity analysis. In the case of DALYs the value choices might be varied, for example: using life expectancies from an analyst's own country rather than the standard life expectancies chosen for the DALY approach; equal rather than unequal age weights; and discount rates other than 3 per cent. In the case of QALYs, the assumptions underlying the calculations can also be varied.

Direct methods for valuing health states

Direct valuation can be a resource-intensive endeavour requiring the development of relevant health state descriptions and experienced interviewers. Direct valuation also requires high levels of respondent concentration and sound cognitive functioning (Rashidi *et al.* 2006). Participants in these types of valuation exercise have been members of the general population, patients suffering from the diseases under study or health sector personnel. To assess an individual's level of utility, they are asked to rank their preferences, making trade-offs between health states and alternatives (Sinnott *et al.* 2007). The *standard gamble* (SG), *time trade-off* (TTO), *person trade-off* and *visual analogue scale* (VAS) are direct methods widely used to estimate utility weights for economic evaluation.

Standard gamble

The SG method is a way of measuring preferences that is most consistent with conventional economic theory. It presents respondents with a choice between health outcomes involving uncertainty. A respondent is asked to imagine living in a compromised health state for a number years, for example 30 years. This compromised health state is carefully described to the participant to enable him or her to picture living in this way. The participant is then presented with a treatment option which will restore a patient to full health with probability P or immediate death with probability 1-P, as described in Figure 15.1. The probability of treatment success versus death is subsequently varied until the respondent is unable to say whether living in the compromised health state or having a treatment with P chance of full health is the better option. This specific P is interpreted as the respondent's valuation of the compromised health state. The more undesirable a health state is, the more willing a respondent is likely to accept a treatment option with a low chance of success. A key obstacle to utilizing the SG is that the concept of 'probability' is often difficult for respondents to understand. Despite this, the SG arguably mimics best the choices people face in 'real' clinical situations because it factors the uncertainty around events into respondents' choices.

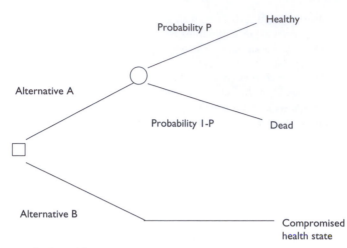

Figure 15.1 The standard gamble

Time trade-off

In the TTO technique, the respondent must indicate their preferred choice between two alternative health scenarios where alternative A is living in a specific compromised health state for X years followed by death and alternative B is living for a shorter amount of years, T, in full health followed by death (see Figure 15.2). The length of time, T, in full health is then varied until the respondent judges the two alternatives to be equally desirable. This particular duration, T, is then used to estimate this respondent's valuation of the compromised health state as T/X. For example, if an individual deems living 30 years in a specific compromised health state as equal to living 20 years in full health, the value of living one year in the compromised health state is 20/30 = 0.67.

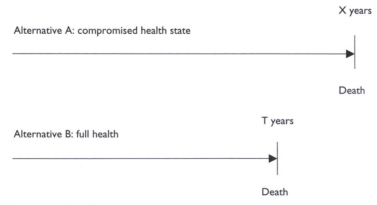

Figure 15.2 The time trade-off

Visual analogue scale

The VAS method utilizes a thermometer-type instrument such as that shown in Figure 15.3 to help respondents attach values to different health states. A number of different health states are described to respondents who are then asked to place these on the scale with mild health problems near the top of scale and severe health states near the bottom. Endpoints of the scale are typically framed as 'best imaginable health state' and 'worst imaginable health state' or 'full health' and 'death'. While the VAS has often been used for direct measurement of health states, it has some limitations. Many respondents have difficulty assigning interval scale values to health states and tend instead to merely rank them. Moreover, the method does not give the respondent a choice between two alternatives and therefore does not reflect the strength of preference necessary for economic evaluation. There is also a concern that rating scales are subject to measurement biases such as end-of-scale bias, where respondents tend to avoid the extremes (e.g. 0 or 100) (Sinnott *et al.* 2007).

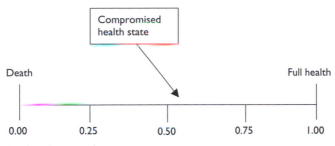

Figure 15.3 The visual analogue scale

Person trade-off

A respondent exposed to this technique is asked to imagine that he or she is a decision-maker who has been allocated a budget which is only enough to offer one of two mutually exclusive health care interventions, each improving the health of a certain group of patients. The choice is therefore effectively between two groups of individuals. A specific version of this approach was used to elicit disability weights for DALYs in the GBD study, as mentioned earlier, and the example below is based on this (Murray 1996).

Intervention A will extend the lives of 1,000 healthy individuals for exactly one year, at which point they will all die. If you do not choose this intervention, they will all die today.

Or alternatively:

Intervention B will extend the lives of n (≤ 1,000) blind individuals for exactly one year. If you do not choose this intervention, they will all die today.

If a respondent is presented with the choice between intervention A and intervention B where there are 1,000 individuals in each group, the hypothesis is that most respondents will opt for saving the 1,000 healthy individuals for an additional year. However, increasing the number of blind individuals saved in intervention B will increase the desirability of this intervention as compared to intervention A. If for instance a respondent deems the two alternative interventions as equally worthy when the number of blind individuals is 1,700, then the value of living one year as blind is 1,000/1,700 = 0.59.

Indirect methods (i.e. 'off the shelf' values)

The second method for valuing health states involves using pre-existing values. Respondents complete a multi-attribute health questionnaire for which each health state has a pre-assigned value or utility obtained from general population surveys (Gray et al. 2011). Exercises to obtain utility weights for QALYs are typically not aimed at specific diseases but rather health states as described using levels in a number of health dimensions. For example, the commonly used EuroQol-5D classification system uses the dimensions mobility, self-care, usual activities, pain/discomfort and anxiety/depression with three levels in each dimension to describe health states (a sample questionnaire is shown in Figure 15.4). For mobility, these levels are: I have no problems walking about, I have some problems walking about, I am confined to bed. Other assessment systems that are commonly used in valuing QALYs are the SF-36, developed in the USA, and WHOQOL, developed for use in low- and middle-income countries (Fox-Rushby and Cairns 2005).

Care must be taken when using these weights from the literature as the type of valuation method used (e.g. TTO, SG, etc.) has been shown to significantly influence results and preferences for health states across population groups (Jansen et al. 2000; Drummond et al. 2005; Sinnott et al. 2007). Consequently, there is a focus on developing the QALY weights based on the values of either the general population or patients in the setting where an economic evaluation is intended. Significant resources are required for capturing preferences in the general population involving a large number of participants. For instance, a total of 3,395 individuals from the UK participated in a TTO exercise to assign weights to 245 health states from the EuroQol classification system (Dolan et al. 1996). Once obtained, utilities are typically combined with survival estimates and aggregated across individuals to generate QALYs or DALYs.

So far we have discussed key approaches to measuring health outcomes using non-monetary values and explored two utility indices in detail. In the next section we examine why and how consequences are measured in terms of money.

Valuing changes in health and non-health consequences using monetary approaches

Health utility indices such as the QALY or DALY are useful for describing improvements in *health* across different health interventions. However, they may not capture the full value of health interventions, particularly if there are outcomes that may not be strictly 'health' (e.g. productivity gains, convenience and information) or there is value to others (e.g. public good, externality). Fox-Rushby and Cairns (2005) identify a long list of additional benefits that might arise from health care interventions ranging from satisfaction with services through to changes in current and future access to care. These are benefits that might arise from health care interventions but are not measured using health indices.

By placing a tick in one box in each group below, please indicate which statements best describe your own health state today

Mobility

I have no problems in walking about ❏

I have some problems in walking ahout ❏

I am confined to bed ❏

Self-Care

I have no problems with self-care ❏

I have some problems washing or dressing myself ❏

I am unable to wash or dress myself ❏

Usual Activities (*e.g. work study housework family or leisure activities*)

I have no problems with performing my usual activities ❏

I have some problems with performing my usual activities ❏

I am unable to perform my usual activities ❏

Pain/Discomfort

I have no pain or discomfort ❏

I have moderate pain or discomfort ❏

I have extreme pain or discomfort ❏

Anxiety/Depression

I am not anxious or depressed ❏

I am moderately anxious or depressed ❏

I am extremely anxious or depressed ❏

Figure 15.4 The EQ-5D-3L descriptive system

Source: Reproduced with kind permission of the EuroQoL Group

One way of capturing all such benefits is using the common unit of money. As we learned earlier, the monetary valuation of benefit is required to conduct CBA and can be compared against costs for informing decisions of resource allocation across all sectors. CBA has been widely used in areas such as environmental, transport and agricultural economics. In health economics the idea of putting a monetary value on human lives and quality of life has always been controversial.

Key approaches for eliciting monetary values of health

There are a number of different methods used to value the benefits of health care interventions in monetary terms. Some of the key ones are discussed below.

The human capital approach

This approach attempts to quantify the loss of a person's marginal productivity as a result of ill health – i.e. the marginal loss in economic output that results from a person not being able to work. The human capital approach has been used for many years and is based on the assumption that each individual contributes to a society's productivity. The monetary value of lost productivity due to ill health is calculated by multiplying the duration of illness by the amount that person would be earning (i.e. the 'market price' of their labour) during that time if they were not ill. Now try the next activity that shows how the human capital approach can be used to value the benefits of health care.

Activity 15.3

A man used to be a coal miner, a physically demanding job for which he was paid $80 per day. Due to a respiratory illness he can no longer go down the mine and instead works in the post room, a less demanding job for which he only gets paid $40 per day. Assuming that for each job the working week is five days and there are 45 working weeks in a year:

1 What is the annual indirect cost of illness?
2 What if the retired father of the miner became ill with the same illness? What would the indirect cost of illness be then?

Feedback

1 Annual earnings as a miner: $80 × 5 × 45 = $18,000
   Annual earnings as a post room clerk: $40 × 5 × 45 = $9,000
   Annual indirect cost of illness = $18,000 – $9,000 = $9,000
2 There is no straightforward answer here. You may have concluded that the indirect cost of illness was zero as the father was retired or you might have used the wage of a miner or a post room clerk as a 'proxy' for what the father could have earned had he been in productive labour.

There are a number of problems with the human capital approach.

- *It may not be equitable* because higher-wage workers will be deemed to have a higher indirect benefit than lower-wage earners. Also, the wage rates may themselves reflect inequities such as discrimination by gender or race.
- *There may be no labour market and therefore no 'market price'* for many groups including homemakers, the elderly and children. Some economists use proxies – an example of this is using the wage of domestic workers as a proxy for the time of homemakers. There is also an ongoing debate as to whether leisure time should be valued the same as working time (Posnett and Jan 1996).
- *Intangible costs are not included.* Most cost of illness studies exclude intangible costs such as the psychological cost of pain and suffering, despite these being potentially significant.

- *The relationship between health status and productivity is complex and can be two-way.* For example, someone who is unemployed or who is in a low-wage job will have fewer financial means to obtain the same quality of health care as someone earning a higher wage.

The friction cost approach

As you read above, the human capital approach does not take into account the complexities in the relationship between productivity and ill health. During production processes, everyone can be replaced in the short term. This implies that there may be no impact on productivity but increases in costs associated with replacing workers. The friction cost approach to measuring indirect costs has been used as an alternative to the human capital method and takes account of the fact that productivity losses from absences can be reduced in the short term by using excess capacity in the workforce and in the long term by replacing workers with unemployed persons or reallocating employees (Koopmanschap and van Ineveld 1992; Brouwer and Koopmanschap 2005).

Observed (or 'revealed') preferences

Observed preference studies examine the actual choices (i.e. preferences) that decision-makers or individuals express in real life. These are interpreted as revealing the relative value placed on different consequences and risks. An example of decision-makers' observed preferences is using the value of court awards in injury cases as a way of estimating the monetary value of that injury. An example of individuals observed preference is examining the amount paid for risk-reducing goods or services (e.g. bicycle helmets) and multiplying this by the change in risk (e.g. of severe head injury). Another example is the wage–risk approach where the difference in wages between jobs (e.g. miner and factory worker) is multiplied by the difference in risk of injury or death.

Each of these approaches has its problems. For example, using court awards as a way of estimating the monetary value of injury is problematic because the results will vary from situation to situation, and the amount awarded is not only a reflection of the compensation for injury but other factors including the earning potential of the individual and punishment of the defendant. Estimates of individual observed preference also suffer from the problem that individuals' values cannot be assumed to be the same across different situations.

Stated preferences

An alternative approach for estimating indirect costs and benefits uses surveys to elicit the maximum amount individuals are willing to pay (WTP) to receive something or to avoid something. While less common, surveys may also measure willingness to accept (WTA), which is the minimum monetary amount necessary for an individual to forego some good, or to bear some harm. In health care, stated preference studies have been used to estimate the value of new interventions or services for which there may not be a market, in order to assess whether the cost of the proposed intervention justifies the potential benefit to society. They are also used to guide the level at which goods or services need to be subsidized – for example, socially marketed mosquito nets or antimalarials to prevent and treat malaria (Onwujekwe et al. 2002; Wiseman et al. 2005) or government subsidized community insurance schemes (Mathiyazhagan 1998; Onwujekwe et al. 2009).

Two of the main methods for eliciting stated preferences are contingent valuation (CV) and discrete choice experiments (DCEs). While it is beyond the scope of this book to look at these in much detail it is important to gain a basic understanding of these methods. DCEs involve asking individuals to state their preference over hypothetical alternative scenarios. Each alternative is described by several attributes (e.g. convenience, quality of service). Price is treated as one of these attributes and therefore marginal WTP for an attribute can be derived. Contingent valuation seeks to describe a hypothetical market for a 'good'. Respondents are then asked about the maximum value they are willing to pay 'contingent' on this hypothetical market (Ryan et al. 2008). Stated preference surveys must be carefully designed in order to ensure validity of the results (Smith 2007). In particular, it is important to be clear about the type and extent of uncertainty. In most situations there is some uncertainty about the consequences or outcomes of a programme or intervention.

A final word of warning about eliciting monetary values of health. There is the potential for double-counting of benefits in cost-benefit analysis. For example, a person's reduced ability to work due to asthma may be included in the calculation of the cost of illness using the human capital approach or an observed or stated preference technique. This can be included in the cost–benefit calculation as a benefit or as a cost-offset deducted from the total costs (Drummond et al. 2005). Importantly, the effect on a person's ability to work should only be considered once.

Now that you have a better understanding of the different monetary approaches, try Activity 15.4 which focuses on one of these, WTP.

Activity 15.4

Suppose you want to introduce a new water container to reduce morbidity from diarrhoea but find it difficult to measure the benefits of the programme. Haddix et al. (1996) asked 100 households in a village about their willingness to pay to avoid diarrhoea. The villagers understood that the trade-off was between buying the container and coping with diarrhoea in the household. The results of the survey are shown in Table 15.1.

Table 15.1 Benefits of a new water container

Maximum WTP ($)	No. of households	Total 'benefit'	Cumulative % of households
25	5	125	5
20	10	200	15
15	50	750	65
10	15	150	80
5	15	75	95
0	5	0	100

1 Theoretically, what percentage of households would be willing to pay at least $10 for the water container?
2 If it was decided to supply the containers at $10 each, what would be i) the total cost to the village, ii) the total benefit and iii) the net benefit?
3 What factors might affect a villager's willingness to pay?

Feedback

1 80 per cent of the households would be willing to pay at least $10 for the water container.
2 i) The total cost to the village would be $10 × 80 households = $800
   ii) The total benefit = ($125 + $200 + $750 + $150) = $1,225
   iii) The net benefit = $1,225 − $800 = $425
3 A range of factors could influence their willingness to pay including the level of education, their understanding about the cause of diarrhoea and how much they perceive it to be a problem as well as their income. There are probably others that you thought of!

Willingness to pay studies are popular because they have a number of strengths:

- they can be applied to any situation and therefore can be used to elicit preferences for a theoretical intervention or service;
- they can be used to estimate directly any change in net social welfare – i.e. the benefit to all of society, and not just the individual patient;
- the desired scenarios can be set up exactly as the analyst would like;
- money is the denominator and because it is tangible and has a universally accepted value it can be easily understood.

However, there are also a number of challenges:

- the technique is open to bias because respondents can find the hypothetical situation difficult to understand;
- WTP tends to be positively related to the income of the respondent. It may be necessary to adjust WTP estimates to take account of income effects.
- the practical problems in conducting any survey (e.g. low response rate and deciding how much information to give);
- the people who respond may not be representative of the population as a whole (it is often the better educated who participate);
- the estimates are based on what people *say* they would do and not what they actually *do*;
- many people are unwilling or feel it is impossible to value lives; they frequently place an infinite value on life when responding to surveys and if this is the case then all interventions which save lives will have infinite benefits which will invariably exceed their costs and will always be worthwhile.

Summary

In this chapter we have explored a wide range of both health and non-health outcomes that arise from health interventions. Particular attention was paid to utility measures such as DALYs and QALYs used in CUA, a form of cost-effectiveness analysis. We also revisited the role of CBA and the direct and indirect approaches used to value health outcomes in monetary terms, including the popular human capital approach.

References

Brouwer WBF and Koopmanschap MA (2005) The friction-cost method: replacement for nothing and leisure for free? *Pharmacoeconomics* 23(2):105–11.

Dolan P, Gudex C, Kind P and Williams A (1996) The time trade-off method: results from a general population study. *Health Economics* 5(2):141–54.

Drummond MF, Sculpher MJ, O'Brien B and Torrance GW (2005) *Methods for the economic evaluation of health care programmes* (3rd edn). Oxford: Oxford Medical Publications.

Fox-Rushby J and Cairns J (2005) *Economic evaluation.* Maidenhead: Open University Press.

Gilson BS *et al.* (1975) The sickness impact profile: development of an outcome measure of health care. *American Journal of Public Health* 65:1304–10.

Gray A, Clarke P, Wolstenholme JL and Wordsworth S (2011) *Applied methods of cost-effectiveness analysis in health care.* Oxford: Oxford University Press.

Haddix AC *et al.* (eds) (1996) *Prevention effectiveness: a guide to decision analysis and economic evaluation.* Oxford: Oxford University Press.

Harvard University, Institute For Health Metrics And Evaluation at the University of Washington, Johns Hopkins University, University of Queensland and World Health Organization (2009) *Global burden of disease study operations manual,* www.globalburden.org/GBD_Study_Operations_Manual_Jan_20_2009.pdf.

Hunt SM, McEwen J and McKenna SP (1985) Measuring health stats: a new tool for clinicians and epidemiologists. *Journal of the Royal College of General Practitioners* 35(273):185–8.

Jansen SJ *et al.* (2000) Unstable preferences: a shift in valuation or an effect of the elicitation procedure? *Medical Decision Making* 20(1):62–71.

Koopmanschap MA and van Ineveld BM (1992) Towards a new approach for estimating indirect costs of disease. *Social Science and Medicine* 34(9):1005–10.

Mathiyazhagan K (1998) Willingness to pay for rural health insurance through community participation in India. *International Journal of Health Planning and Management* 13(1):47–67.

Murray CJL (1996) Rethinking DALYs, in Murray CJL and Lopez AD (eds) *The global burden of disease: a comprehensive assessment of mortality and disability from diseases, injuries and risk factors in 1990 and projected to 2020.* Boston, MA: Harvard University Press.

Murray CJ and Lopez AD (1996) *The global burden of disease: a comprehensive assessment of mortality and disability from diseases, injuries and risk factors in 1990 and projected to 2020.* Boston, MA: Harvard University Press.

Onwujekwe O *et al.* (2002) Altruistic willingness to pay in community-based sales of insecticide-treated nets exists in Nigeria. *Social Science and Medicine* 54(4):519–27.

Onwujekwe O *et al.* (2009) Willingness to pay for community-based health insurance in Nigeria: do economic status and place of residence matter? *Health Policy and Planning* 25(2):155–61.

Posnett J and Jan S (1996) Indirect costs: valuing unpaid inputs into health care. *Health Economics* 5:13–23.

Rashidi AA, Anis AH and Marra CA (2006) Do visual analogue scale (VAS) derived standard gamble (SG) utilities agree with Health Utilities Index utilities? A comparison of patient and community preferences for health status in rheumatoid arthritis patients. *Health and Quality of Life Outcomes* 4:25.

Richardson J *et al.* (1998) The measurement and valuation of quality of life in economic evaluation. Centre for Health Program Evaluation working paper 97, ISSN 1325 0663.

Ryan M, Gerard K and Amaya-Amaya M (2008) *Using discrete choice experiments to value health and health care.* The Netherlands: Springer.

Sinnott PL, Joyce VR and Barnett PG (2007) *Preference measurement in economic analysis: guidebook.* Menlo Park, CA: Health Economics Resource Center, http://www.herc.research.va.gov/files/BOOK_419.pdf.

Smith RD (2007) Contingent valuation in health care: does it matter how the 'good' is described? *Health Economics* 17(5):607–17.

Wiseman V *et al.* (2005) Differences in willingness to pay for amodiaquine+artesunate,amodiaquine+ sulfadoxine-pyrimathamine, artemether-lumefantrine or monotherapy: experiences from Tanzania. *Bulletin of the World Health Organization* 83(11): 845–52.

World Health Organization (2004) *World health report 2004*, http://www.who.int/whr/2004/en/report04_ en.pdf.

Further reading

Dolan P (2000) The measurement of health-related quality of life for use in resource allocation decisions in health care, in Culyer AJ and Newhouse JP (eds) *Handbook of health economics*. Amsterdam: Elsevier: 1723–60.

Drummond MF, Sculpher MJ, O'Brien B and Torrance GW (2005) *Methods for the economic evaluation of health care programmes* (3rd edn). Oxford: Oxford Medical Publications, Chapters 5–7.

Fox-Rushby J and Cairns J (2005) *Economic evaluation*. Maidenhead: Open University Press, Chapters 8–12.

Gold MR, Stevenson D and Fryback DG (2002) HALYS and QALYS and DALYS, oh my: similarities and differences in summary measures of population health. *Annual Review of Public Health* 23:115–34.

World Health Organization (2008) *Global burden of disease: 2004 update*, www.who.int/healthinfo/global_ burden_disease/2004_report_update/en/index.html.

16 Economic evaluation and decision-making

Damian Walker

Overview

You have been given frameworks to use when comparing costs and consequences of interventions, and you have learned how to calculate these costs and consequences. This chapter will enable you to describe the process of allocating resources using different types of economic evaluation, and discuss the uses of economic evidence in policy, including the factors influencing the uptake of economic evaluation evidence. It will also help you develop an awareness of the critical assumptions made in an economic evaluation.

Learning objectives

After working through this chapter, you will be able to:

- describe the process of allocating resources using different types of economic evaluation
- understand the uses of economic evidence in policy
- discuss areas of application of economic evaluation
- display an awareness of the critical assumptions made in an economic evaluation
- discuss the factors influencing the uptake of economic evaluation evidence

Key terms

Average cost-effectiveness ratio (ACER). Ratio of the difference in cost to the difference in effect of a single intervention against its baseline option (e.g. no programme or current practice).

Benefit–cost ratio (BCR). Ratio of total monetized benefits divided by total costs. An indicator used in cost–benefit analysis (CBA).

Incremental cost-effectiveness ratio (ICER). Ratio of the difference in costs between two alternative programmes to the difference in effectiveness between the same two programmes.

Marginal cost-effectiveness ratio (MCER). Ratio of the difference in cost and effect resulting from the expansion or contraction of a programme.

Net present value (NPV). Total monetized benefits minus costs. An indicator used in CBA.

Evidence-based practice

Limited health care budgets have emphasized the need to use resources effectively and efficiently. In order to achieve this there has been a growing interest in implementing evidence-based policy decisions. Consequently, in recent years economic evaluation has acquired greater prominence among decision-makers, who need to know which interventions represent 'value for money'. You will recall from the preceding chapters that economic evaluation can help provide the necessary information by comparing the value of the *costs* and *benefits* from competing interventions. Exactly how decision-makers then use this information to allocate scarce health care resources is the focus of this chapter.

The process of allocating scarce health care resources using cost–benefit analysis

Having assessed the costs (Chapter 14) and consequences (Chapter 15), the next step in an economic evaluation is to bring together these results in a simple and understandable form for the audience, to provide an overall indication of value for money in a way that will inform decision-making.

You will recall from Chapter 13 that two summary measures typically used in cost–benefit analysis (CBA) are:

- net present value (NPV);
- benefit–cost ratio (BCR).

Let's now look at these in a bit more detail. NPV is calculated by summing the monetized benefits and then subtracting all of the costs, with discounting applied to both benefits and costs as appropriate. The formula for the NPV is:

$$NPV = \sum_{t=0}^{n} \frac{(\text{Benefits} - \text{Costs})_t}{(1 + r)^t}$$

where:

r = discount rate
t = year
n = analytic horizon (in years)

The BCR represents the ratio of total benefits over total costs, both discounted as appropriate. The formula for calculating the BCR is:

$$BCR = \frac{PV_{\text{benefits}}}{PV_{\text{costs}}}$$

where:

PV_{benefits} = present value of benefits
PV_{costs} = present value of costs

A CBA will yield a positive NPV if the benefits exceed the costs. Implementing such a programme will generate a net benefit to society. An equivalent condition is that the ratio of the present value of the benefits to the present value of the costs must be greater than one. However, if there are two or more mutually exclusive interventions that have positive NPV then there has to be further analysis. From the set of mutually exclusive interventions the one that should be selected is that with the highest NPV or highest BCR ratio.

Activity 16.1

Table 16.1 is a summary of a CBA study for two competing interventions, A and B.

Table 16.1 Costs and benefits

Project	A	B
Costs (£ million)	2	4.7
Benefits (£ million)	10.2	15.5

Assuming that all costs and benefits are present values, and were computed for the same time period:

1 Compute the BCRs for each project.
2 How would you interpret the results to the policy-maker, using layman's language?
3 Based solely on the results from the preceding question, which project would you recommend?
4 Compute the NPV for each project.
5 Interpret the results of the answers to the previous question.
6 Based on those results, what would be your recommendation?
7 Do these results change your previous recommendation? Why or why not?

Feedback

1 $BCR_A = 10.2/2 = 5.1:1$
  $BCR_B = 15.5/4.7 = 3.3:1$
2 £1 spent on Project A returns £5.1.
  £1 spent on Project B returns £3.3.
3 Project A has a higher return per pound spent so we would recommend it over Project B.
4 $NPV_A = 10.2 - 2 = £8.2$
  $NPV_B = 15.5 - 4.7 = £10.8$
5 Project A gives us a net benefit worth £8.2 million. Project B gives us a net benefit worth £10.8 million
6 Society gains more from Project B than from Project A. Therefore we would recommend Project B.
7 Yes. However, other relevant factors need to be taken into consideration:
  • Project B has more than twice the capital outlay of Project A.
  • Society might not be able to implement Project B because of limited resources.
  • Political or societal support might also play a part.

The process of allocating scarce health care resources using cost-effectiveness and cost–utility analysis

There is considerable antipathy in the general public to the idea of placing a monetary value on human life. Therefore, in health care decision-making, cost-effectiveness analysis (CEA) and cost–utility analysis (CUA) are more common evaluative frameworks. In CEA/CUA, the next step is to bring together the costs and effects, in the form of a ratio, to provide an overall indication of cost-effectiveness in a way that will inform decision-making. Depending on the study question and comparison undertaken, there are three types of cost-effectiveness ration. You have already learnt a little about two of these.

1 *Average cost-effectiveness ratio (ACER)*: an ACER deals with a single intervention and evaluates that intervention against its baseline option (e.g. no programme or current practice. We saw in Chapter 13 that it is calculated by dividing the total cost of the intervention (C) by the total number of health outcomes prevented by the intervention (E).

$$ACER = \frac{Total\ Costs_{Intervention\ A}}{Total\ Effects_{Intervention\ A}}$$

2 *Marginal cost-effectiveness ratio (MCER)*: the MCER assesses the specific changes in cost and effect when a programme is expanded or contracted (e.g. the additional costs and effects of vaccinating an additional child). In practice it is rare for output to change by one unit, so the marginal CER of a particular programme is often approximated by dividing the additional costs associated with a larger change in production than one unit, by the change in production. An example might be the cost of extending the same vaccination service to another village and dividing this by the additional number of vaccinations in order to approximate the marginal cost per additional child vaccinated.

$$MCER = \frac{Total\ Costs_{Intervention\ A+1} - Total\ Costs_{Intervention\ A}}{Total\ Effects_{Intervention\ A+1} - Total\ Effects_{Intervention\ A}}$$

3 *Incremental cost-effectiveness ratio (ICER)*: an ICER compares the differences between the costs and health outcomes of two alternative interventions that compete for the same resources, and is generally described as the additional cost per additional health outcome. You will recall from Chapter 13 that the ICER numerator includes the differences in programme costs. This can also include the averted disease costs and averted productivity losses depending on the choice of perspective. Similarly, the ICER denominator is the difference in health outcomes.

$$ICER = \frac{Total\ Costs_{Intervention\ A} - Total\ Costs_{Intervention\ B}}{Total\ Effects_{Intervention\ A} - Total\ Effects_{Intervention\ B}}$$

It should be noted that the terms MCER and ICER are often used interchangeably in the literature. And while many believe that an ACER provides no useful information for decision-makers, the World Health Organization (WHO) has argued for their use as part of 'generalized cost-effectiveness analysis' (Murray *et al.* 2000; Hutubessy *et al.* 2002). Generalized CEAs require the evaluation of a set of interventions with respect to the counterfactual of the null set of the related interventions – i.e. the natural history of disease. Thus data on the relative *average* cost-effectiveness of interventions, which do not pertain to any specific decision-maker, can be a useful reference point for evaluating the directions for enhancing allocative efficiency in a variety of settings. WHO's framework does not preclude the analysis of *incremental* (or *marginal*) cost-effectiveness; rather it allows the identification of current (via the use of ACERs) allocative inefficiencies *as well* as opportunities presented by new interventions (via the use of ICERs).

Activity 16.2

1 Calculate the MCER for expanding the programme:
   - Total cost$_A$ = £5,000
   - Total cost$_{Ax}$ = £10,000
   - Total outcomes$_A$ = 3
   - Total outcomes$_{Ax}$ = 5

   where subscripts:
   - A refers to the original programme and
   - Ax refers to the expanded programme.

2 Calculate the ICER for two alternative programmes, A and B, competing for resources, given:
   - Total cost$_A$ = £5,000
   - Total cost$_B$ = £26,000
   - Total outcomes$_A$ = 3
   - Total outcomes$_B$ = 10

   where a programme outcome is the number of disease cases attributable to the programme for the same-sized patient population.

Feedback

1 The MCER is the ratio of the differences in total costs and total outcomes between the initial programme level and expansion level.
   MCER = (£10,000 – £5,000) / (5–3)
   MCER = £5,000 / 2
   MCER = £2,500 per outcome

2 The ICER is the ratio of the differences in total costs and total outcomes between the two programmes.
   ICER = (£26,000 – £5,000) / (10 – 3) ICER = £21,000 / 7
   ICER = £3,000 per disease case prevented

Comparing interventions

When the choice is between a new intervention and the status quo, the analyst should begin by applying the principle of dominance (sometimes called 'strong' dominance). Dominance favours a strategy that is both more effective *and* less costly. Either the new intervention or the status quo may be preferred using this principle.

When one of these is both more effective and more costly, the decision-maker must decide if the greater effectiveness justifies the cost of achieving it. This is done by calculating a cost-effectiveness ratio.

In studies that compare multiple mutually exclusive interventions – i.e. if somebody receives one of the interventions they cannot receive the other – an additional dominance principle should be applied. The analyst should first apply the principle of strong dominance; any of the competing interventions is ruled out if another intervention is both more effective and less costly or vice versa. The analyst should then apply the principle of extended dominance (sometimes called 'weak dominance'). The list of interventions, trimmed of strongly dominated alternatives, is ordered by effectiveness. Each intervention is compared to the next most effective alternative by calculating the ICER. Extended dominance rules out any intervention that has an ICER that is greater than that of a more effective intervention. The decision-maker prefers the more effective intervention with a lower ICER. By approving the more effective interventions, quality adjusted life years (QALYs) gained or disability adjusted life years (DALYs) averted, for example, can be purchased more efficiently. Note that dominance principles can be also applied by ranking interventions in the order of their cost; the same finding will result. Dominance principles can be applied when outcomes are measured in units other than QALYS or DALYs. It is important to note that while this approach is technically correct, other criteria shape policies in addition to efficiency.

Comparing the costs and effects of multiple, mutually exclusive interventions

Assume there five interventions (A–E) available in addition to the standard of care. The average cost and QALYs per patient are shown in Table 16.2.

Table 16.2 Average cost and QALYs in a hypothetical comparison of interventions

Intervention	£ per patient	QALYs per patient
Standard care	50	1.0
A	120	1
B	100	2.0
C	250	3.0
D	350	4.0
E	550	5.0

We can exclude intervention A as it is strongly dominated by intervention B, i.e. intervention B is both cheaper and more effective. Removing intervention A from the table, each intervention is now compared to the next most effective alternative by calculating the ICER. This results in Table 16.3.

Table 16.3 Hypothetical comparison of costs and effects of interventions (continued)

Intervention	£ per patient	QALYs per patient	ICER (£)
Standard care	50	1.0	–
B	100	2.0	50
C	250	3.0	150
D	350	4.0	100
E	550	5.0	200

We can exclude intervention C as it is weakly dominated by interventions B and D. For example, if 100 patients were given intervention C it would cost £25,000 and 300 units of effect would be gained. However, 300 units (50 × 2 + 50 × 4) can be gained at a cost of £22,500 (50 × £100 + 50 × £350) if 50 patients are given intervention B and 50 patients are given D. Or alternatively, 320 units (40 × 2 + 60 × 4) can be gained at a cost of £25,000 (40 × £100 + 60 × £350) if 40 patients are given intervention B and 60 patients are given D. Weak or extended dominance requires two strong assumptions: 1) that treatments are perfectly divisible; and 2) that there are constant returns to scale. In other words, it has to be possible to deliver alternatives B and D to smaller numbers of patients without any change in cost-effectiveness. The final results are shown in Table 16.4.

Table 16.4 Final results of the hypothetical cost-effectiveness analysis

Intervention	£ per patient	QALYs per patient	ICER (£)
Standard care	50	1.0	–
B	100	2.0	50
D	350	4.0	125
E	550	5.0	200

Interpreting cost-effectiveness data: the cost-effectiveness plane

The incremental cost-effectiveness ratio represents a measure of how efficiently the proposed intervention can produce an additional unit of effect (e.g. DALY averted or QALY gained). By using this standard method, the cost-effectiveness of alternative interventions can be compared, helping policy-makers decide which they should adopt. The goal of the decision-maker is to adopt all health interventions that represent efficient ways of averting morbidity and/or mortality or, conversely, of gaining health.

The incremental cost and incremental effect can be represented visually using the incremental cost-effectiveness plane. The horizontal axis divides the plane according to incremental effect (positive above, negative below) and the vertical axis divides the plane according to incremental cost (positive to the right, negative to the left). This divides the incremental cost-effectiveness plane into four quadrants through the origin (see Figure 16.1).

Each quadrant has a different implication for the decision. If the ICER falls in the south-east quadrant, with negative costs and positive effects, the new intervention dominates and is always considered cost-effective. If the ICER fell in the north-west quadrant, with positive costs and negative effects, the new intervention is dominated and is never considered cost-effective. If the ICER fell in the north-east quadrant, with positive costs and positive effects, or the south-west quadrant, with negative costs and negative effects, trade-offs between costs and effects would need to be considered. These two quadrants represent the situation where the new intervention may be cost-effective compared to current practice, depending upon the value at which the ICER is considered good value for money.

In order to decide if an intervention offers 'good' value for money, the ICER must be compared to a specified monetary threshold. This threshold represents the maximum amount that the decision-maker is willing to pay for health effects. The intervention is deemed cost-effective if the ICER falls below this threshold and not cost-effective otherwise. For example, if a decision-maker is willing to pay an additional £50,000 for a year of life, the intervention is considered cost-effective if the ICER is below £50,000 per life year gained. In situations where a threshold is not stated explicitly, the act of decision-making implies a value for the threshold. Based on the recommendation of the Commission on Macroeconomics and Health (World Health Organization 2001), WHO classifies interventions as 'highly cost-effective' for a given country if results show that they avert a DALY for less than the per capita national gross domestic product. Several countries have their own thresholds. For example, $50,000 per QALY gained (1982 US$) is commonly used as the threshold in the USA (Hirth et al. 2000). Likewise, in Canada the range of values proposed is CAN$20,000–120,000 (1990 CAN$) (Laupacis et al. 1992). In the UK, £20,000–30,000/QALY is commonly used in economic evaluation as the ceiling ratio. These thresholds all apply to decision-making at the national level; however, decisions may be made at the international, sub-national or individual hospital levels and decision-makers may wish to define thresholds according to their own contexts.

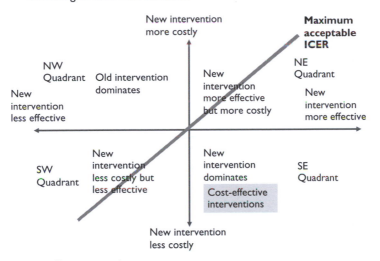

Figure 16.1 The cost-effectiveness plane

Note that the CER is usually presented as a range. The range is generated from the sensitivity analysis and reflects the uncertainty underlying the assumptions made in the estimation of both costs and outcomes.

Applications of economic evaluation nationally and internationally

In recent years it has become fashionable to make comparisons (in 'league tables' or rankings) between health care interventions in terms of their relative cost-effectiveness, in cost per life year, cost per QALY gained or cost per DALY. However, league tables frequently compare ICERs from studies that have computed these ratios using different methods and assumptions including choice of comparator, choice of discount rate, time horizon and population sub-group (Gerard and Mooney 1993). The methodological differences among studies may influence the ranking of the studies and therefore decisions made using a league table may not always reflect differences in the relative value for money of interventions. However, there have been attempts to gain greater consistency in economic evaluation methodology. In addition, league tables generally do not include measures of the uncertainty of the cost-effectiveness estimates. In spite of these issues, economic evaluation has been used to ration health services by influencing the design of a variety of essential packages of care in developed and developing countries as the following examples show.

The World Bank's 1993 World Development Report (WDR)

In 1993 the *World Development Report* (WDR) (World Bank 1993) presented a global priority-setting exercise which led to recommendations about essential public health and clinical services packages for low- and middle-income countries. The WDR used DALYs to measure the burden of various diseases, and advocated a minimum (or 'essential health') package of public health interventions and clinical services that should be financed by public resources. A 'good buy' was deemed to be one which is both cost-effective and addresses a large burden of disease. Table 16.5 presents the

Table 16.5 Cost-effectiveness of the health interventions (and clusters of interventions) included in the minimum package of health services in low-income countries

Country group and component of package	Cost per DALY ($)
Public health	
EPI Plus	12–17
School health programme	20–25
Other public health programmes (including family planning, health and nutrition information)[a]	[b]
Tobacco and alcohol control programme	35–55
AIDS prevention programme[c]	3–5
Clinical services	
Short-course chemotherapy for tuberculosis	3–5
Management of the sick child	30–50
Prenatal and delivery care	30–50
Family planning	20–30
Treatment of STDs	1–3
Limited care	200–300

Note: cost per DALY is rounded to the nearest $

a. Includes information, communication and education on selected risk factors and health behaviours, plus vector control, disease surveillance and monitoring.

b. The health benefits from information and communication and from disease surveillance are counted in the other public and clinical services in the health package. The health benefits from vector control are unknown consumption; if such prevalence were to rise, the potential benefits would be larger.

c. Excludes treatment of STDs, which are in the clinical services package.

Source: Adapted from (World Bank 1993)

essential package of public health interventions developed for the WDR. From high-income countries there are only a few such examples. A scheme that attracted considerable interest and debate was the 'Oregon Plan'.

The Oregon experience

In 1989 the US state of Oregon launched an initiative to ration treatment under the Medicaid scheme. The aim was, under a fixed budget, to provide the most efficient services to the largest number of people, rather than providing less efficient services to all. The approach developed a league table which ranks health care interventions in terms of their gains in health-related quality of life. Since 1989 several lists have been developed allowing some flexibility for change and improvement of methodology. For example, in the version that was implemented in 1994, 565 treatments were listed and only these treatments were reimbursed by Medicaid. Notably, the public has been involved in this process and preferences and values of community committees were incorporated into the complex process of ranking of treatment outcomes (Ganiats and Kaplan 1996).

During public discussions the approach was criticized for a variety of methodological, ethical and political reasons:

1 Is it justified to use preferences of non-Medicaid recipients to prioritize services for the poor?
2 Are the methods used to attach utility weights reliable? Different methods yielded different weights.
3 As recipients of Medicaid are mainly the poor and among them women and children, does the rationing discriminate against those who are most vulnerable and need care most?
4 Do politicians have a mandate to ration health services, before other sectors of expenditure such as defence or space exploration come under similar close scrutiny?

Proponents of the scheme have argued that rationing occurs in all health care systems, though mostly invisible and implicit, whereas attempts such as the Oregon Plan make rationing explicit and visible. They also emphasize that the Plan had increased access to care for many recipients. As the debate demonstrated, economic evaluation for priority-setting involves complex political and ethical issues and is not merely a technical exercise.

NICE – the National Institute for Health and Clinical Excellence

The National Institute for Health and Clinical Excellence or NICE is a special health authority of the NHS in England and Wales. Given that the NHS has a limited budget NICE attempts to assess the cost-effectiveness of potential expenditures to establish whether or not they represent 'better value' for money than treatments that would be neglected if the expenditure took place. NICE uses the QALY to measure the health benefits delivered by a given treatment regime. Theoretically it might be possible to draw up a table of all possible treatments sorted by increasing the cost per QALY gained. Those treatments with lowest cost per QALY gained would appear at the top of the table and deliver the most benefit per pound spent and would be the easiest to justify funding for. Those where the delivered benefit is low and the cost is high would appear at the bottom of the list. Decision-makers would, theoretically, work down the table, adopting services that are the most cost-effective. The point at which the NHS budget is exhausted would reveal the cost-effectiveness threshold. In practice this exercise is not performed, but a threshold has been used by NICE for many years in its assessments to determine which treatments the NHS should and should not fund – £20,000–30,000 per QALY gained, although, in practice, the threshold for rejecting technologies has been found to be in the range of £35,000 to £48,000 (Devlin and Parkin 2004).

The Copenhagen Consensus

A final example is the Copenhagen Consensus, which attempts inter-sectoral priority-setting and thus needs to use CBA. The goal of the Copenhagen Consensus project is to use CBA to set priorities among a series of proposals for confronting 10 great global challenges. These challenges, selected from a wider set of issues identified by the United Nations, are: civil conflicts; climate change; communicable diseases; education; financial stability; governance; hunger and malnutrition; migration; trade reform; and water and sanitation. A panel of economic experts was invited to consider these issues. The panel was asked to address the 10 challenge areas and to answer the question, 'What would be the best ways of advancing global welfare, and particularly the welfare of developing countries, supposing that an additional £50 billion of resources were at governments' disposal?' The 2004 meeting found that combating HIV/AIDS had a very high rate of return and should be at the top of the world's priority list. About 28 million cases could be prevented by 2010. The cost would be £27 billion, with benefits almost 40 times as high. See www.copenhagenconsensus.com for further details.

Activity 16.3

In your view, how could the use of economic evaluations in your setting be encouraged?

Feedback

You might wish to consider both the demand and supply of economic evidence. For example, with respect to the former, decision-makers could be encouraged to acknowledge the importance of considering the economic consequences of their decisions. And with respect to the latter, are there enough health economists and others with relevant training and expertise so that decision-makers can trust the results of studies that are performed?

Some perceived advantages and disadvantages of economic evaluation

As a decision-making tool that helps allocate scarce resources to programmes that maximize societal economic benefit, CBA compels analysts to study the full economic impact of all potential outcomes of an intervention. Expressing the results of this comprehensive analysis in purely monetary terms makes it possible to compare different programmes having different health outcomes, or health programmes to non-health programmes. Furthermore, the identification of all resource requirements (costs) and benefits of an intervention or programme allows analysts to examine its distributional aspects (e.g. who will receive these benefits and who will bear the costs). The major limitation of CBA is the empirical difficulty associated with assigning monetary values to benefits (e.g. extended human life, improved health and reduced health risks). Besides the complexity of various methods designed to value these benefits, analysts usually confront controversy over the appropriateness of attaching a certain monetary value to human life.

Measuring the cost per unit of *health outcome* in CEA/CUA circumvents the need to make an explicit valuation of human life. Nevertheless, when decisions are to be made as to whether to implement a life-saving intervention based on its cost-effectiveness measure, policy-makers must make the *implicit* decision as to whether the investment is worth the lives it will save. CBA makes this consideration *explicit*. Finally, as in any other study, the results of an economic evaluation are only as good as the assumptions and valuations on which they are based. Understanding the implications of analysis assumptions and methods is essential for a correct interpretation of results.

Activity 16.4

Answer true or false to the following questions:

1 CEA is used widely in public health to evaluate alternative programmes or policies to gain the maximal health outcome for a given level of resources.
2 A CEA would be useful for an organization to determine the return on investment from a health programme.
3 For a CEA to be useful in comparing two different programmes, common health outcomes must be employed.
4 The results of a CEA evaluating a vaccination programme designed to reduce infant mortality in a developing country could be used by a programme manager in the UK for evidence of the programme's cost-effectiveness.

Feedback

1 True.
2 False. A CBA measures health outcomes in monetary terms and should be used to determine the return on investment for a particular health programme.
3 True.
4 False. The risk factors and exposures of vaccine-preventable diseases among children in the developing world are different than those experienced by children in developed nations, which would result in dissimilar outcomes that should not be compared.

Ten questions to ask of any study – the Drummond checklist

As a decision-maker in the health sector, you may find yourself in the position of receiving an economic evaluation on the basis of which you may be expected to take some action. The following questions were drawn up by Drummond and Stoddart in a 1985 article, and they have stood the test of time. These questions provide a framework for assessing the results of any economic evaluation (see Drummond et al. 2005).

1 Was a well-defined question posed in answerable form?
   a) Did the study examine both costs and effects of the service(s) or programme(s)?
   b) Did the study involve a comparison of alternatives?
   c) Was a viewpoint for the analysis stated or was the study placed in a particular decision-making context?
2 Was a comprehensive description of the competing alternatives given?
   a) Were any important alternatives omitted?
   b) Was (should) a 'do-nothing' alternative (have been) considered?
3 Was there evidence that the programmes' effectiveness had been established? Was this done through a randomized, controlled clinical trial? If not, how strong was the evidence of effectiveness?
4 Were all important and relevant costs and consequences for each alternative identified?
   a) Was the range wide enough for the research question at hand?
   b) Did it cover all relevant viewpoints (e.g. those of the community or society, patients and third-party payers)?
   c) Were capital costs as well as operating costs included?
5 Were costs and consequences measured accurately in appropriate physical units (e.g. hours of nursing time, number of physician visits, days lost from work or years of life gained) prior to valuation?
   a) Were any identified items omitted from measurement? If so, does this mean that they carried no weight in the subsequent analysis?
   b) Were there any special circumstances (e.g. joint use of resources) that made measurement difficult? Were these circumstances handled appropriately?
6 Were costs and consequences valued credibly?
   a) Were the sources of all values (e.g. market values, patient or client preferences and views, policy-makers' views and health care professionals' judgements) clearly identified?
   b) Were market values used for changes involving resources gained or used?
   c) When market values were absent (e.g. when volunteers were used) or did not reflect actual values (e.g. clinic space was donated at a reduced rate) were adjustments made to approximate market values?
   d) Was the valuation of consequences appropriate for the question posed (i.e. was the appropriate type, or types, of analysis – cost-effectiveness, cost–benefit or cost–utility – selected)?
7 Were costs and consequences adjusted for differential timing?
   a) Were costs and consequences that occurred in the future 'discounted' to their present values?
   b) Was any justification given for the discount rate used?
8 Was an incremental analysis of costs and consequences of alternatives performed? Were the additional (incremental) costs generated by the use of one alternative over another compared with the additional effects, benefits or utilities generated?
9 Was a sensitivity analysis performed?
   a) Was justification provided for the ranges of values (for key parameters) used in the sensitivity analysis?

b) Were the study results sensitive to changes in the values (within the assumed range)?

10 Did the presentation and discussion of the results of the study include all issues of concern to users?

   a) Were the conclusions of the analysis based on some overall index or ratio of costs to consequences (e.g. CER)? If so, was the index interpreted intelligently or in a mechanistic fashion?

   b) Were the results compared with those of other studies that had investigated the same questions?

   c) Did the study discuss the generalizability of the results to other settings and patient/clinic groups?

   d) Did the study allude to, or take account of, other important factors in the choice or decision under consideration (e.g. distribution of costs and consequences or relevant ethical issues)?

   e) Did the study discuss issues of implementation, such as the feasibility of adopting the 'preferred' programme, given existing financial or other constraints, and whether any freed resources could be used for other worthwhile programmes?

Other criteria to consider when making decisions

While the emphasis of this chapter is on value for money – that is, whether a health policy should be adopted and not who pays for it – if the object is to decide how to spend public funds, economic evaluation is only one of at least nine criteria relevant for priority-setting in health. Cost alone matters, as do the capacities of potential beneficiaries to pay for an intervention. The other criteria that may affect priorities include horizontal equity and vertical equity (discussed in Chapter 17); adequacy of demand; and public attitudes and wants. Two criteria, whether an intervention is a public good and whether it yields substantial externalities, are classic justifications for public intervention, because private markets could not supply them efficiently, just as in other sectors.

Poverty and risk of impoverishment from ill health may also influence priorities; so do the budgets available, and the decisions of how much to make available for buying interventions. Finally, the effectiveness of an intervention and, therefore, the degree to which it deserves priority, depend on how far it is culturally appropriate or acceptable for the population it is intended to benefit. Identical interventions, technically speaking, may lead to different degrees of use or compliance in different population groups, and information and incentives may be needed to achieve the full potential outcomes.

Summary

In this chapter you have looked at the process of combining costs and outcomes using different types of economic evaluation. You have also read about issues arising from the use of economic evaluation in priority-setting of health services at different levels (local and global) and different income levels (low- and high-income settings). You also looked at some of the pros and cons of economics evaluation. Before finishing we reviewed some of the other criteria, in addition to cost-effectiveness, that are often used when health care decisions are made.

References

Devlin N and Parkin D (2004) Does NICE have a cost-effectiveness threshold and what other factors influence its decisions? A binary choice analysis. *Health Economics* 13:437–52.

Drummond MF *et al.* (2005) *Methods for the economic evaluation of health care programmes* (3rd edn). Oxford: Oxford University Press.

Ganiats TG and Kaplan RM (1996) Priority setting: the Oregon example, in Schwartz FW, Glennerster H and Saltman RB (eds) *Fixing health budgets: experience from Europe and North America.* New York: Wiley.

Gerard K and Mooney G (1993) QALY league tables: handle with care. *Health Economics* 2(1):59–64.

Hirth RA *et al.* (2000) Willingness to pay for a quality-adjusted life year: in search of a standard. *Medical Decision Making* 20(3):332–42.

Hutubessy RC, Baltussen RM, Torres-Edejer TT and Evans DB (2002) Generalised cost-effectiveness analysis: an aid to decision making in health. *Applied Health Economics and Health Policy* 1(2):89–95.

Laupacis A, Feeny D, Detsky AS and Tugwell PX (1992) How attractive does a new technology have to be to warrant adoption and utilization? Tentative guidelines for using clinical and economic evaluations. *Canadian Medical Association Journal* 146(4):473–81.

Murray CJ, Evans DB, Acharya A and Baltussen RM (2000) Development of WHO guidelines on generalized cost-effectiveness analysis. *Health Economics* 9(3):235–51.

World Bank (1993) *World development report 1993.* Washington, DC: Oxford University Press.

World Health Organization (2001) *Macroeconomics and health: investing in health for economic development,* report of the Commission on Macroeconomics and Health, http://whqlibdoc.who.int/publications/2001/924154550x.pdf.

Further reading

Dalziel K, Segal L and Mortimer D (2008) Review of Australian health economic evaluation – 245 interventions: what can we say about cost effectiveness? *Cost Effectiveness and Resource Allocation* 20(6):9.

Hutubessy RC, Baltussen RM, Torres-Edejer TT and Evans DB (2002) Generalised cost-effectiveness analysis: an aid to decision making in health. *Applied Health Economics and Health Policy* 1(2):89–95.

Neumann PJ (2004) Why don't Americans use cost-effectiveness analysis? *American Journal of Managed Care* 10(5):308–12.

Williams I, McIver S, Moore D and Bryan S (2008) The use of economic evaluations in NHS decision-making: a review and empirical investigation. *Health Technology Assessment* 12(7):iii,ix–x,1–175.

Yothasamut J, Tantivess S and Teerawattananon Y (2009) Using economic evaluation in policy decision-making in Asian countries: mission impossible or mission probable? *Value Health* 12(Suppl 3):S26–30.

SECTION 6

Equity

Promoting equity and the role of government   17

Stephen Jan and Virginia Wiseman

Overview

For most people, when they think about economics, they associate it with the objective of efficiency. You will recall from Chapters 1 and 7 that efficiency is essentially about getting the greatest health gain from a finite set of resources. However, as a society we are also concerned about *equity*, which is the fairness by which resources, health and health care are distributed. Equity is an important area of economic analysis because of its usual prominence as a policy objective, its frequent incompatibility with efficiency objectives and the implications it has for the allocation of resources. Governments regularly play a role in the provision, financing and regulation of health services with the aim of promoting equity as well as addressing different forms of market failure. We will only scratch the surface of equity but expect that by the end of this chapter you will be in a stronger position to understand some of the popular language and key debates in this area.

Learning objectives

After working through this chapter, you will be able to:

- describe the relationship between equity and equality
- distinguish between horizontal and vertical equity
- outline the different definitions of equity as applied in the health sector
- explain potential trade-offs between equity and efficiency
- consider the pros and cons of government intervention in the health care sector

Key terms

Equity. A policy objective which seeks to establish fairness in the allocation of resources. It is often, though not exclusively, defined by an objective based on equality in the distribution of health, health care or access to health care across population groups.

Equity–efficiency trade-off. The usual conundrum in which policies aimed at achieving a more equitable share of resources often are not the most efficient options and thus result in less to share overall.

Horizontal equity. Equal treatment of equals (e.g. equal access for equal need).

Resource allocation formula.   A formula that uses indicators of the relative need for health services to guide resource allocation decisions in an effort to achieve equity of funding across geographic areas.

User fees.   Formal out-of-pocket expenditures incurred by patients at the time of health care use.

Vertical equity.   Unequal (but fair) treatment of unequals (i.e. individuals who are unequal should be treated differently according to their level of need).

Equity as a concept

Equity is subjective in so far as it will mean different things to different people and there is no uniquely correct way of defining it, although it is fundamentally about fairness and justice. Key to the discussion of equity in the health sector is that the concepts of fairness and justice are distinct from the philosophical concept of *egalitarianism*. *Equity is different to equality.* While equity is about fairness, this may or may not mean the equal sharing of a good. It may for example be deemed fair that a disadvantaged group in society receive a greater share of resources. For example, resource allocation formulae used in countries such as Australia and Canada to distribute health care resources often include 'weightings' to reflect the higher health needs of particular population groups such as indigenous people or rural/urban populations. In this case equity does not translate into everyone receiving equal shares of a good or service. Another example is the use of equity 'weights' in cost-effectiveness analysis (CEA) to revalue consequences such that greater weight is given to the health gain of one group or individual in relation to another. Some economists have proposed 'equity-weighted Quality Adjusted Life Years (QALYs)' (Dolan and Olsen 2001). It is argued that in order to reduce inequalities in health, then QALY gains could be distributed initially to those who would be the most worse off if left untreated. We will look more closely at this issue of positively discriminating in favour of the disadvantaged – namely 'vertical equity' – below.

Equity in practice

Within the health sector, equity tends to be interpreted very generally as providing a basic level of health services to everyone. The problem is that this definition is not specific enough when one is trying to actually implement some policy on equity in health care. A more specific and usable equity criterion is needed. In this section we will explore some of the different ways equity has been operationalized in health care.

Horizontal and vertical equity

Horizontal equity is about ensuring that people in equivalent circumstances are treated the same. Vertical equity is about treating individuals (or communities) who are unequal differently, in a way that is seen to be commensurate with their relative disadvantage. Of course, how this is determined is very much a matter of contention and central to many public policy debates. Let us now tease apart these principles and explore how they might be applied in practice.

Horizontal equity

There are three popular ways of defining horizontal equity in health care:

* equal access to health care for equal need;
* equal use of health care for equal need;
* equal health care expenditure for equal need.

Equal access for equal need is often defined in terms of people with the same level of need who face the same level of barrier to health care taking into account distance, cost and any language or cultural issues that may limit access to services. *Equal utilization for equal need* requires that policy-makers ensure that not only do those with the same level of need have the same level of access but that they actually use the same amount of services. *Equal health care expenditure for equal need* implies that if two individuals have the same level of need then they should be allocated the same amount of health care expenditure.

The concept of *need* underlies each of the above definitions of equity. It is commonly defined in terms of variables such as standardized mortality ratios, socioeconomic status and rurality. Measures of self-reported health have also been used. Need is used to assess the level of health disadvantage experienced by particular groups or individuals. The goal of horizontal equity is ultimately about ensuring that people with the same level of disadvantage are treated no differently.

Vertical equity

In contrast to horizontal equity, vertical equity is to do with treating people differently when the level of need among them differs – i.e. trying to lessen the gap between the 'haves' and the 'have nots' through preferential treatment of the latter. It has been referred to as a form of 'positive discrimination' to promote equity in health services. For example, consider a village where there are some rich people and some poor people. An outbreak of disease afflicts both groups. As a minimum you might first aim for some horizontal equity by making drugs available to all who are sick (equal treatment for all people who are sick). However, upon closer inspection, you begin to notice that the rich are doing much better as they have time and money to come to the clinic, adhere to therapy and consequently recover more rapidly and suffer fewer complications. So you might then start to worry about vertical equity – unequal treatment of unequals (e.g. the poor might need to be given more help to purchase drugs and adhere to treatment). One option may be to specifically target poorer individuals by subsidizing their medicines. This measure would seek to lessen the gap in outcomes between rich and poor – a vertical equity measure. It could be argued that the objective here is ultimately 'equal health' although it is debatable how achievable this is. We will come back to the goal of equal health in a moment after considering some policies to promote vertical equity.

Activity 17.1

Do you think equality of health is a feasible goal?

Feedback

There is a range of reasons why equality of health is often impossible to achieve. You may have thought of the following ...

a) Many factors influence health in addition to health care. In some instances, what health services can do to affect the levels of health in populations or communities may be quite limited.

b) Genetic differences between people mean that complete inequality of health is simply impossible.

c) There is no consensus on what is meant by 'good health'.

d) Equalizing health might be considered paternalistic since it may restrict individuals' lifestyle choices which often have an impact on health.

e) If no more resources are to be made available to health services to achieve this goal, then to achieve equal health some people's health will need to improve and some deteriorate.

There are various policies in health care that aim to provide a disadvantaged group in society with a greater share of available resources. You have already learnt that in some countries resource allocation formulae used to distribute health care resources often include 'weightings' to reflect the higher health needs of particular population groups such as indigenous people or rural communities. In this case equity does not translate into everyone receiving equal shares of a good or service. Instead, it means that certain disadvantaged groups receive a greater share of funding based on the weights used. Other examples include exemptions on user fees and progressive payment scales for social health insurance levels. Such policies that target disadvantaged groups in this way represent the application of vertical equity. Let us now look at two of these policy initiatives – including their strengths and weaknesses – in a little more detail. While you read, think about your own country and how vertical equity might (or might not) be reflected in health care financing and provision.

Resource allocation formula in South Africa

This case study is based on a paper from South Africa (McIntyre *et al.* 2002) that explores how resource allocation formulae can be used to pursue vertical equity goals. Resource allocation refers to the process by which available resources are distributed among competing needs. Resource allocation formulae use indicators of the relative need for health services in different geographic areas to guide resource allocation decisions.

For most resource allocation formulae, the main driver is the population size of each area – the more people you have, the more resources you will get. This is known as your *base population*. However, this on its own would not be a fair way of distributing resources as we know that some groups have greater needs (e.g. pregnant women, older people, indigenous populations) or simply live in geographical areas that are costly to service. For this reason adjustments are often made to the base population to account for these kinds of factors. Indicators of the relative need for health services in different geographic areas are used to 'adjust' the allocation of resources across geographic areas. These indicators might include maternal and infant mortality rates, the size of the population covered by private health insurance, socioeconomic status and so on.

In the study, the authors explored the feasibility of developing a broad-based area deprivation index and its implications for the allocation of health care resources across geographic areas in that country. Results showed that 'the formula currently used by the National Treasury to allocate resources between geographic areas biases allocations towards less deprived areas within the country. The inclusion of the GID [a general index of deprivation] within this formula dramatically alters allocations towards those areas suffering from human development deficits'. The results highlight 'the importance of considering deprivation in resource allocation mechanisms if vertical equity goals are to be promoted through resource allocation, particularly within decentralized health systems'. The authors further conclude that 'while there are considerable debates around the concept of equity and which definition of equity is most appropriate, the vertical approach is arguably the most appropriate means of effectively and speedily achieving equity gains in South Africa given that it recognizes that different groups within our society have very different starting points and therefore require differential treatment.

(McIntyre *et al.* 2002)

User fee exemptions in Cambodia

User fees have been implemented in many countries despite widespread criticism, especially concerning their equity implications. One vertical equity strategy has been to exempt the poor from paying these fees. But exemption schemes can be problematic as the following excerpt from a paper by Jacobs *et al.* (2007) illustrates.

Two important messages can be gained from this case study of user fee exemptions. First, 'in the Cambodian context, user fee exemption schemes need to be underpinned by a range of interventions that will enable the poor to seek health care in a timely fashion and in a way which will minimize the likelihood of increasing economic vulnerability. The fourfold increase in hospitalization rates (from 8/1000 to 32.5/1000 population) among the poor who were exempted from hospital fees by providing entitlement cards, indicates that such cards should become standard practice for exemption schemes'. The second important finding from the Cambodian study was 'that identification of the poor for exemption from user fees and reimbursement of transport costs did not guarantee free care as the FEP [fee exempted patients] incurred both direct costs (out-of-pocket health care expenditure) and indirect costs. In terms of direct costs, FEP incurred an average of US$4.3 for the illness episode leading to hospitalization, lower than the US$15.3 incurred by PP [fee paying patients]. Despite receiving health care free at the point of delivery, and incurring relatively smaller direct costs associated with the hospitalization, only 7% of the FEP claimed to have sufficient cash to pay for all costs, compared with 51% of PP. Because of a lack of collateral necessary to secure a loan, and a failure to repay previous debts, 1 in 11 FEP in need of cash could not access any source of credit or loan ... One ethical question that needs to be addressed is whether outstanding debts as a result of care seeking in the private sector should be considered an eligibility criteria [for exemption].

(Jacobs *et al.* 2007)

Both of the examples above highlight the importance of vertical equity as a goal of health systems. They also highlight that vertical equity is often more complicated to implement than horizontal equity as it involves some difficult judgements about how to meet different needs differentially. Judging the extent of differences in needs is no easy task and there is much debate over *who* should make these judgements – should it be the responsibility of society at large, health professionals, patients, special interest groups or politicians? This partly explains why health care policy up to this point in time has tended to focus on the pursuit of horizontal equity.

Comparing definitions

The objective of reduced inequalities in health is often espoused by governments and by international organizations such as the World Health Organization (WHO), but as we saw earlier in this chapter it has a number of serious limitations. How do our other definitions fare? Let us now take a closer look at equality of access, utilization and expenditure.

Activity 17.2

Can you think of any problems with measuring equality of access?

Feedback

Equality of access requires that for different communities:

a) Travel distance to facilities and services is the same.
b) Transport and communications services are the same.
c) Waiting times are the same.
d) Patients are equally informed about the availability and effectiveness of treatments.
e) Charges are the same and ability to pay is the same.

Because of these difficulties, health care planners will often resort to 'use' as an indicator of 'access' to health care. But there are important differences between utilization and access that we must be mindful of. Equal access for equal need is about providing individuals with the *opportunity* to use services. Individuals may choose to comply with treatment to different degrees and this will result in different patterns of utilization, even among those with the same health needs. Some people will go to see a doctor or nurse and others will not. We know that religion, culture, gender, age and education all have a bearing on treatment-seeking behaviour.

Activity 17.3

Equality of expenditure also has some limitations. Can you think of any?

Feedback

This presents a problem in so far as spending the same amount on different individuals might result in differences in outcomes because of, among other things, differences in the cost of services between groups or areas. This has not stopped the widespread use of equality of expenditure. Its popularity largely stems from the relative ease with which inputs can be measured and monitored.

One critical issue to bear in mind at this point is that you will get a different policy outcome depending on what definition of equity you choose to apply. Each definition has its own strengths and weaknesses. Different definitions also have different data requirements. More complicated definitions, such as those that include some measure of vertical equity, may require routinely collected survey data that does not exist in all settings. Definitions must also be easily interpreted by policy-makers and managers, as well as being palatable to members of the general public.

Equity and health care financing

In terms of international comparisons of equity in health care finance, some general findings can be drawn from the literature. Most notably, the degree to which a health care financing system is regressive or progressive depends on the mix of financing sources. As a general rule, those systems based on social insurance and which rely more on direct and general taxes tend to be more progressive. Those that are based on private insurance and rely more on direct user payments tend to be more regressive. Donaldson *et al.* (2005) reach the following broad conclusions about equity and health care financing:

> Regarding fairness with which health care systems are financed, largely publicly financed systems in developed countries, especially those predominantly tax-financed, are the most successful at meeting equity objectives … Predominantly private health care systems appear less equitable. While public finance cannot ensure equity in principle and private finance does not preclude it, in the real world it is clear that publicly financed systems are likely to do better in the pursuit of equity. This may well be because the reason that many health systems *are public* is precisely because of the importance placed on equity objectives.
>
> (Donaldson *et al.* 2005)

In setting economic objectives, most health care systems will want to pursue both efficiency and equity goals. Efficiency is rather more straightforward in the sense that there is a general consensus around what it means and how it can be measured. Equity is a somewhat trickier concept to pin down, as we have seen from its varied definitions. In the next section we will turn our focus to examining how equity and efficiency are often involved in a trade-off.

Potential trade-offs between efficiency and equity

Although the notion of allocative efficiency is elusive, it represents a logical policy goal (at least for many economists!). However, it needs to be borne in mind that policies aimed at achieving this type of efficiency can often conflict with equity. Below are just three examples but you can probably think of others.

- *Example 1:* income can be transferred from people with high incomes to those with low incomes through taxation to achieve a more equitable distribution of wealth. Taxing people's income from employment, however, reduces their incentive to work and save and as a consequence introduces inefficiency.
- *Example 2:* a dollar taken from a wealthy person through income redistribution policies does not generally end up as a dollar in the pocket of a poorer person. The resources used in collecting these taxes could be used in alternative ways to produce goods and services of higher value to the economy.
- *Example 3:* arguments for the centralization of health services are often made on efficiency grounds. For example, there may be a number of primary care clinics each servicing a local population in a district. Closing down some of these clinics and centralizing services could avoid duplication of services and allow for greater shared costs. The equity argument would be that geographical access to services might be reduced as some people would have further to travel.
- *Example 4:* the introduction of user fees is a commonly cited example of the potential trade-off between equity and efficiency in health care. It is argued that imposing such charges can address the problem of consumer moral hazard by deterring the frivolous use of health services. On the flip-side, however, user fees are also reported to impose heavy burdens on poorer groups and can therefore be inequitable.

The examples above illustrate that equity and efficiency can be at odds with one another. Let us now take a moment to think about how one might compare the size of the relative trade-off between these two important goals of health systems. Below is an excerpt from a study by James *et al.* (2005) that explores how different 'weightings' can be attached to equity and efficiency criteria and how this in turn impacts upon the prioritization of different health care interventions.

In this illustration, we take five interventions for different health problems in a low-income country context:

1 Treatment of multi-drug resistant tuberculosis (TB).
2 Quinine for complicated malaria cases.
3 Oral rehydration therapy (ORT) for minor diarrhoeal ailments.
4 Inpatient care for acute schizophrenia.
5 Manipulation and plastering for simple fractures.

These are compared in terms of how they rate in terms of cost-effectiveness, severe health conditions and poverty reduction (see Table 17.1). The first step is to determine how each of these interventions scores in terms of the efficiency and equity criteria used. The number of categories in this example for cost-effectiveness (very cost-effective, cost-effective and not cost-effective) and severe health condition (very severe, severe and not severe) is three. Two categories are specified for poverty reduction (a positive or neutral effect). Note that the scores given in the table are only for illustrative purposes, although they are based on broad evidence (for instance, WHO-CHOICE estimates of cost effectiveness).

Table 17.1 Comparison of interventions for different health problems

Intervention	Score		
	Cost effectiveness	Severe health conditions	Poverty reduction
Treatment of multi-drug resistant TB	Cost-effective	Very severe	Positive
Quinine for complicated malaria cases	Very cost-effective	Very severe	Positive
ORT for minor diarrhoeal ailments	Very cost-effective	Not severe	Positive
Inpatient care for acute schizophrenia	Not cost-effective	Severe	Neutral
Manipulation/plastering for simple fractures	Very cost-effective	Not severe	Neutral

It is assumed here that: maximum (1) and minimum (0) scores are equivalent across different criteria. For example, 'very cost-effective' (for cost-effectiveness), 'very severe' (for severe health condition) and 'positive' (for poverty reduction) all achieve a maximum score of 1. Secondly, it is assumed that category intervals are linear. Thus, for example, the difference between 'very cost-effective' and 'cost-effective' is identical to that between 'cost-effective' and 'not cost-effective'.

We continue by defining the prioritization score of a health intervention A, PRS_A, as:

1 $PRS_A = \alpha$ [equity] + $(1-\alpha)$ [efficiency]

where the efficiency score is measured here in terms of its cost-effectiveness, and equity is further defined as:

2 Equity = β [severe health conditions] + $(1-\beta)$ [poverty reduction]

[The prioritization score (PRS) is therefore a score calculated using a combination of the efficiency and equity scores weighted for their importance.]

Using this simple framework, we can explore the effect of different weighting options. It is important to note, though, that the weights attached are purely illustrative as are how each intervention scores in each of the criteria. Here, we reflect three particular weighting possibilities:

Pure efficiency rating. Here, only the efficiency criterion of cost effectiveness is considered, thus COST EFFECTIVENESS = 100%, SEVERE HEALTH CONDITIONS = 0%, POVERTY REDUCTION = 0%. This is reflected by setting $\alpha = 0$.

Equal weights to efficiency and equity. Further assuming that severe health conditions and poverty reduction are given equal weights, this gives an overall weighting of: COST EFFECTIVENESS = 50%, SEVERE HEALTH CONDITIONS = 25%, POVERTY REDUCTION = 25%. This is reflected by setting $\alpha = 0.5$ and $\beta = 0.5$.

Greater weight to severe health conditions. Further assuming that cost effectiveness and poverty reduction are given equal weights, this could give an overall weighting of: COST EFFECTIVENESS = 20%, SEVERE HEALTH CONDITIONS = 60%. POVERTY REDUCTION= 20%. This is reflected by setting $\alpha = 0.8$ and $\beta = 0.75$.

The implications of these different weighting of efficiency and equity criteria on prioritization decisions are illustrated in Figure 17.1.

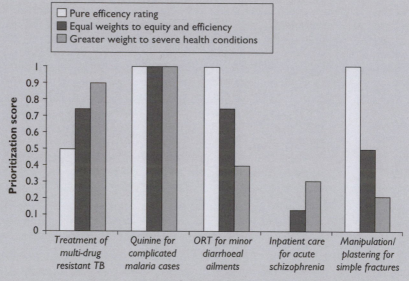

Figure 17.1 Impact of different weights for equity and efficiency criteria on prioritization decisions

This example shows the importance of appropriately accounting for both equity and efficiency concerns in prioritization decisions. For instance, whilst treatment of multi-drug resistant TB is only ranked fourth out of the five interventions under pure efficiency considerations, it is given a much higher priority if the policymaker is concerned with the equity criteria of severe health conditions and poverty reduction. Similarly, inpatient care for acute schizophrenia is given more relative importance if the policymaker is particularly concerned with combating severe health conditions.

Whilst this example is purely illustrative, it does show how one can use criteria to guide the priority-setting process. In particular it enables the policymaker to clearly see the implications of tradeoffs between efficiency and different equity concerns on prioritization decisions.

(James *et al.* 2005)

Many other equity criteria could potentially offset efficiency when prioritizing health care. Another equity principle that has received considerable attention in the health economic literature is the 'fair innings' approach. It is based on the premise that the elderly may be regarded as having a lower priority since they have had a 'fair innings' (Williams 1997). According to this approach, if health care resources are to be distributed fairly then every person should receive enough health care to give them the opportunity to live in good health for a 'normal' span of years. What constitutes a 'normal' span of years is often defined as 'life expectancy at birth'. The equity weights depend on community preferences. This notion of 'intergenerational' equity or, as some prefer to call it, 'age-based rationing' requires greater discrimination against the elderly than would be the case if only efficiency criteria were used based on, for example, cost-effectiveness rankings. Invoking this concept raises a number of practical challenges including the following. In summary, reaching agreement on 'appropriate' equity criteria to guide the allocation of scarce resources can raise many difficult questions. How should equity weights be generated (i.e. should there be different weightings depending on age, gender, race, socioeconomic status, etc.? What size should the relative weights be? Who should decide on their size? What mixture of qualitative and quantitative methods should be used to generate these weightings?).

Role of government

As well as minimizing the impact of market failures, governments often intervene in the health sector for other reasons – principally equity ones. While equity is not strictly a form of market failure, it is an important additional objective to efficiency. Governments regularly play a role in the provision, financing and regulation of health services with the aim of promoting equity. According to Mills and Ranson (2010), the precise role of government depends on the ethical basis of a health system. The authors explain what they mean below.

It is important to note that although economic arguments [i.e. market failures] provide justification for state involvement, they do not necessarily imply that the state should itself provide health services (as opposed to contracting others to provide it). A key change in recent decades has been the recognition that the state need not provide services itself directly, but instead could play an enabling role … An important influence on this position is the recognition that in many countries the state has failed in its policies to provide public services, including health services, for everyone.

These arguments derive from a number of strands of economic thinking, notable among which are public choice theory and property rights theories. The former argues that government officials are no different from anyone else in pursuing their own interests…. The result is that the public sector is wasteful because politicians and bureaucrats have no incentive to promote allocative or technical efficiency … Property rights theorists argue that the source of inefficiency in the public sector is the weakening of property rights … In the public sector there is little obvious threat to an enterprise if staff perform poorly; hence, incentives for efficient performance are weak.

These theories underlie what has been termed the "new public management," which seeks to expose public services to market pressures, without necessarily privatizing them (Walsh, 1995). Such approaches change the nature of state involvement, with policies of opening up services to competitive tender or putting services out to contract on a competitive basis, introducing internal markets where public providers have to compete for contracts from public purchasers, devolving financial control to organizations such as individual hospitals, and spinning off parts of government into separate public agencies (such as an agency to manage government health services).

... in practice the actual role of the state in any particular country is shaped by a wide variety of influences. Most notable are the history of state involvement in health services and the rationale for its involvement over time, the extent to which private providers and insurers developed early in the history of the health system and thus were able to play a prominent role, and the attitude of the medical profession to an increased state role ... One key issue has been the extent to which the state took on itself the responsibility for providing services to the whole population, or instead concerned itself only with the poor and indigent.

(Mills and Ranson 2010)

Government intervention in the health sector can lead to certain inefficiencies that must also be considered. Here are some examples.

- Financing government programmes requires diverting money (resources) from other areas of the economy. This is usually done by levying taxes on people's incomes or on the sale of goods, creating losses to producers and consumers. If the loss is very large then the intervention may not be justified.
- Besides programme costs, there are administration costs involved in every government action. For example, there is no such thing as a cost-free transfer. If you want to take money from one group of people and give it to another group then you have to pay the lawyers who draft the law, the civil servants who administer the transfer and the police and lawyers who enforce the law. This means that the gaining group will gain a smaller amount of money than the amount that is taken away from the losing group.
- You ought to assume that politicians and civil servants act in their own interests in the same way that patients and doctors are assumed to act in theirs. This means that due to an asymmetry of information between the general public and civil servants, the latter does not always do as the former would like. For one thing, some civil servants try to expand their own department because this increases their power and prestige. They will press for this even if it is not beneficial to society, although civil servants may have an ethical code that constrains their actions just as doctors do.
- As for the provision of services, it may be difficult to replace the coordinating powers of market forces with a large number of independent decisions made by a group of civil servants.

In concluding this section it is important to bear in mind that the role of the state in health care is dependent on a complex range of historical, political and economic factors. Even with perfectly operating private markets for health services and health insurance, there will always be equity arguments for government intervention.

Summary

Equity is an ethical principle. It is based largely on value judgement in the same way that efficiency and its desirability is also a value judgement. Health care systems all around the world are in the business of pursuing a fair distribution of health care. The problem is that this definition is not specific enough when one is trying to actually implement policy on equity in health care. It tells us nothing about the steps planners and health professionals can take towards a more equitable health system.

There is widespread support for equality of access which recognizes that individuals may have different preferences for health and health care. Even though it is more feasible than equality of health, ensuring equal opportunity to use resources is no easy task. Many cultural, financial and geographical barriers must be overcome.

It is wise to remember there is no one universal equity goal that is aspired to by all health systems around the globe. It is however generally accepted that publicly financed health care systems tend to do better on equity grounds compared to those based on private insurance which rely more on direct user payments.

References

Dolan P and Olsen JA (2001) Equity in health: the importance of different health streams. *Journal of Health Economics* 20(5):823–34.

Donaldson C *et al.* (2005) *Economics of health care financing: the visible hand.* Basingstoke: Palgrave Macmillan.

Jacobs B, Price NL and Oeun S (2007) Do exemptions from user fees mean free access to health services? A case study from a rural Cambodian hospital. *Tropical Medicine and International Health* 12(11): 1391–401.

James C *et al.* (2005) Clarifying efficiency-equity trade-offs through explicit criteria, with a focus on developing countries. *Health Care Analysis* 13(1).

McIntyre D, Muirhead D and Gilson L (2002) Geographic patterns of deprivation in South Africa: informing health equity analysis and public resource allocation strategies. *Health Policy and Planning* 17(Suppl):30–9.

Mills A and Ranson K (2010) Design of health systems, in Merson MH, Black RE and Mills A (eds) *International public health.* Sudbury: Jones & Bartlett.

Williams A (1997) Intergenerational equity: an exploration of the 'fair innings' argument. *Health Economics* 6(2):117–32.

Further reading

Donaldson C *et al.* (2005) *Economics of health care financing: the visible hand.* Basingstoke: Palgrave Macmillan: 85–6.

Jan S *et al.* (2005) *Economic analysis for management and policy.* Maidenhead: Open University Press: 179–98.

Mills A and Ranson K (2010) Design of health systems, in Merson MH, Black RE and Mills A (eds) *International public health.* Sudbury: Jones & Bartlett: 513–51.

Mooney G and Jan S (1996) And now for vertical equity: some concerns arising from Aboriginal health in Australia. *Health Economics* 5(2):99–104.

Glossary

Actuarially fair premium A premium that is set so that the expected payouts equal the premiums paid by the insured (plus the cost of administration).

Adverse selection When a party enters into an agreement in which they can use their own private information to the disadvantage of another party.

Agency A situation in which one person employs another to act on their behalf.

Allocative efficiency A situation in which the factors of production have been allocated so as to reflect what people demand (i.e. demand matches supply). Social welfare is maximized as MB = MC in all markets and there can be no substitution between markets to increase welfare beyond its current level.

Annualized costs The annual share of the initial cost of capital equipment or investments, spread over the life of the project – usually modified to take account of depreciation.

Asymmetry of information A market situation where all participants do not have access to the same level of information.

Average cost-effectiveness ratio (ACER) Ratio of the difference in cost to the difference in effect of a single intervention against its baseline option (e.g. no programme or current practice).

Balance of payments (BOP) Measure of currency flow between countries.

Benefit-cost ratio (BCR) Ratio of total monetized benefits divided by total costs. Indicator used in cost–benefit analysis (CBA).

Budget line A line on graph representing all the possible combinations of two goods that can be purchased at given prices with a set budget.

Capitation payment A predetermined amount of money given to a provider per member of a defined population to deliver specific services.

Cardinal scale A scale that provides measurements with quantifiable differences.

Ceteris paribus The assumption that all other variables remain unchanged.

Co-insurance The percentage of a medical bill that the insured must pay, after deductibles and co-payments are met. Some insurance schemes have co-insurance without deductibles and co-payments.

Community financing Collective action of local communities to finance health services through pooling out-of-pocket payments that can include a variety of payment methods such as cash, in-kind and partial or delayed payment.

Community rating Insurance premiums that are based on the pooled risk of a community. All individuals in the community pay the same premium, regardless of claims experience or personal level of risk.

Complement A good that is often needed when consuming another good. For instance, sugar can be seen to be a complement to tea.

Constant dollars Also known as constant currency, these correspond to values that have been adjusted for inflation, and so reflect the 'real' or actual purchasing power.

Consumer surplus The difference between what a consumer actually pays for a good and the maximum they would have been willing to pay for it. In a sense it represents the 'profit' to a consumer.

Contingent valuation A technique used for assessing people's willingness to pay by asking 'Would you pay for this product if it were offered at this price?' for the same good at different price levels.

Co-payment A specified amount the insured must pay for each received service that can vary by service.

Cost–benefit analysis (CBA) An economic evaluation technique in which outcomes are expressed in monetary terms.

Cost-effectiveness analysis (CEA) An economic evaluation technique in which outcomes are expressed in health units such as life years saved.

Cost–utility analysis (CUA) An economic evaluation technique where outcomes are expressed in health units that capture not just the quantity but quality of life.

Cross price-elasticity of demand The percentage change in quantity demanded of a good divided by the percentage change in the price of another related good.

Cross-subsidization A situation arising when the funds of different population groups' risk pools are pooled.

Current dollars Current dollars or currency refers to the actual dollars spent, without adjustment for inflation.

Deadweight loss The loss in allocative efficiency occurring when the loss of consumer surplus outweighs the gain in producer surplus.

Deductible A fixed amount of a health care charge that the insured must pay before the insurer begins payment for all or part of the remainder of the costs.

Demand curve A graph showing the relationship between the quantity demanded of a good and its price when all other variables are unchanged.

Diagnosis-related group (DRG) Also known as health care resource groups (HRGs) these are casemix classification schemes which provide a means of relating the number and type of acute inpatients treated in a hospital to the resources required by the hospital.

Diminishing returns to scale A situation when a proportionate increase in all inputs yields a less than proportionate increase in output.

Direct cost Resources used in the design, implementation, receipt and continuation of a health care intervention.

Disability adjusted life year (DALY) A measure of health based not only on the length of a person's life but also their level of ability or disability.

Discount rate The rate at which future costs and outcomes are discounted to account for time preference.

Discounting A method for adjusting the value of costs and outcomes which occur in different time periods into a common time period, usually the present.

Discrete choice experiments A technique used for assessing people's willingness to pay by determining how they rank different attributes (convenience, quality, price) of a service.

Diseconomies of scale Technological conditions under which long-run average cost increases as output increases.

Economic (productive) efficiency A situation in which a producer cannot produce more without increasing cost.

Economic evaluation Compares the costs and consequences of alternative health care interventions to assess their value for money.

Economic growth A positive change in the level of production of goods and services of a country over time.

Economic profit This is total revenue minus total cost, distinct from normal profit.

Economies of scale The conditions under which long-run average cost decreases as output increases.

Economies of scope The conditions under which long-run average cost decreases as the range of production/services expands.

Efficiency A general term used to describe the relationship between inputs and outputs. It is concerned with maximizing benefits with the resources available, or minimizing costs for a given level of benefit.

Equity A policy objective which seeks to establish fairness in the allocation of resources. It is often, though not exclusively, defined by an objective based on equality in the distribution of health, health care or access to health care across population groups.

Equity–efficiency trade-off The conundrum in which policies aimed at achieving a more equitable share of resources often are not the most efficient options and thus result in less to share overall.

Experience rating Insurance premiums are based on the claims experience or risk level, such as age, of each insured group.

Externality The cost or benefit arising from an individual's production or consumption decision which indirectly affects the well-being of others.

Fee-for-service Payment mechanism where providers receive a specific amount of money for each service provided.

Financial (budgetary) cost The accounting cost of a good or service usually representing the original (historical) amount paid – distinct from the opportunity (economic) cost.

Financial intermediary An agency collecting money to pay providers on behalf of patients.

Fixed cost/input A cost/input of production that does not vary with the level of output. The time for which at least one input cannot be changed actually defines the short run.

Formal sector employees Members of the population that are employed with a taxable income.

Fragmentation A situation whereby there are many financing schemes which operate as separate risk pools with limited cross-subsidization.

Fund pooling The collection of funds that can be used for financing a given population's health care so that contributors to the pool share risks.

Goods The outputs (such as health care) of a production process that involves the combining of different resources such as labour and equipment.

Gross domestic income (GDI) Measures the income from all economic activities that take place within a country, and includes wages, profits, rents and interest.

Gross domestic product (GDP) The total value of goods and services produced within one year in a country. It is concerned with the output produced in a specific geographic location, regardless of the nationality of who produces it (e.g. a foreign-owned company).

Gross national income (GNI) GNI is GDP plus income earned by a country's citizens from abroad, minus income earned in that country by foreign citizens.

Horizontal equity Equal treatment of equals (e.g. equal access for equal need).

Human capital approach An approach that uses wages to measure the value of productivity lost through illness.

Income elasticity of demand The percentage change in quantity demanded of a good divided by the percentage change in population income.

Income effect Demand for a good falls as its price rises in order for an individual to have enough income available to buy other goods.

Incremental analysis A comparison of the difference in costs with the difference in consequences.

Incremental cost-effectiveness ratio (ICER) Ratio of the difference in costs between two alternative programmes to the difference in effectiveness between the same two interventions.

Indirect cost The value of resources expended by patients and their carers to enable individuals to receive an intervention.

Inferior goods Goods for which demand decreases as income increases.

Intangible cost The cost of discomfort, pain, anxiety or inconvenience.

Interval scale A scale that provides measures with quantifiable differences that does not have a true zero, for example a temperature scale.

Law of diminishing marginal utility A hypothesis that states that as consumption of a good increases so the marginal utility (extra benefit gained) decreases.

Long run A decision-making time frame over which quantities of *all* inputs to production can be varied.

Macroeconomics The study of the performance and functioning of the economy as a whole.

Marginal analysis An examination of the additional benefits or costs arising from an extra unit of consumption or production of a 'good'.

Marginal cost The change in the total cost if one additional unit of output is produced.

Marginal cost-effectiveness ratio (MCER) Ratio of the difference in cost and effect resulting from the expansion or contraction of a programme.

Marginal utility The change in total utility derived from a one-unit increase in consumption.

Market demand Horizontal summation of all individual demand curves to represent the aggregate demand for a particular good within a market.

Market equilibrium A situation where the price in a given market is such that the quantity demanded is equal to the quantity supplied.

Market failure A situation in which the market does not result in an efficient allocation of resources.

Microeconomics The study of decisions taken by individual consumers, households and firms and the way in which these decisions contribute to the setting of prices and output in various kinds of market.

Monopoly power The ability of a monopoly to raise price by restricting output.

Moral hazard A situation in which one of the parties to an agreement has an incentive, after the agreement is made, to act in a manner that brings additional benefits to themselves at the expense of the other party.

Natural monopoly A situation where one firm can meet market demand at a lower average cost than two or more firms could meet that demand.

Net benefit The benefits of an intervention minus its costs.

Net present value (NPV) Total monetized benefits minus costs. An indicator used in CBA.

Non-rival A good or service that can be consumed simultaneously by everyone.

Normal goods Goods for which demand increases as income increases.

Normal profit The return a firm receives from inputs such as a director's role in organizing and running the business. This is part of the firm's opportunity cost.

Normative economics A strand of economic analysis which seeks to make recommendations about how the world *should* be – i.e containing value judgement. For example, a study which concludes that drug A is more cost-effective than drug B is a normative analysis.

Operational efficiency See technical efficiency.

Opportunity (economic) cost As resources are scarce, an individual in choosing to consume a good, in principle, chooses the good which gives to him or her the greatest benefit and thus he or she forgoes the consumption of a range of alternative goods of lesser value. The opportunity cost is the value of the benefit of the *next best* alternative.

Outcome A change in health status as a result of the system processes (in the health services context, the change in health status as a result of care).

Out-of-pocket (direct) payment Payment made by a patient directly to a provider.

Output The good or service that is the result of the production process (in the case of health services, the service that is delivered).

Overhead cost Costs that are not incurred directly from providing patient care but are necessary to support the organization overall (e.g. personnel functions).

Pareto efficiency A situation in which there is no way of making any person better off without making someone else worse off (a point on the production possibilities frontier).

Patient sovereignty A situation in which patients can judge the costs and benefits of health care; bear the costs and receive the benefits of health care; and purchase those treatments where benefits exceed the costs.

Perfect competition A market in which there are many suppliers, each selling an identical product and many buyers who are completely informed about the price of each supplier's product, and there are no restrictions on entry into the market.

Pigouvian tax A tax that is set to internalize the cost of negative externalities.

Positive economics Economic statements that describe how things *are*. For example a study that measures the change in health care expenditure for a particular country over time is a positive analysis.

Price discrimination This occurs when a firm offers the same product at different prices to different people.

Price elastic A change in price produces a more than proportionate change in quantity demanded.

Price elasticity of demand The relative responsiveness of the quantity demanded of a good to a change in its own price. The percentage change in quantity demanded divided by the associated percentage change in price.

Price elasticity of supply The percentage change in quantity supplied of a good divided by the percentage change in the good's own price.

Price inelastic A change in price produces a less than proportionate change in quantity demanded.

Price taker A supplier that cannot influence the price of the good or service they supply.

Principal A person on whose behalf an agent acts.

Producer surplus The difference between the amount that a producer receives from the sale of a good and the lowest amount that producer is willing to accept for that good.

Production function The functional relationship that indicates how inputs are transformed into outputs in the most efficient way.

Production possibilities frontier A line on a graph that shows the boundary between the combinations of goods that can be produced and those that cannot with the resources available.

Progressive A financing mechanism is described as progressive if it consumes an increasing proportion of income as income rises.

Public good A good or service that can be consumed simultaneously by everyone and from which no one can be excluded.

Purchasing power parity (PPP) Exchange rate that equates the price of a basket of identical traded goods and services in different countries.

Quality adjusted life years (QALY) A year of life adjusted for its quality. A year in perfect health is considered equal to 1.0 QALY.

Ratio scale A cardinal scale that has a true zero, for example length.

Recurrent cost The value of resources with useful lives of less than one year that have to be purchased at least once a year.

Regressive A financing mechanism is described as regressive if it consumes a decreasing proportion of income as income rises.

Resources These represent inputs into the process of producing goods. They can be classified into three main factors: labour, capital and land. Different goods would generally require varying combinations of these factors. Resources are generally valued in monetary terms.

Returns to a factor This measures the addition to output as one factor to production is increased.

Returns to scale This measures the addition to output as the scale of operations increases in the long run so that all inputs can be varied.

Revenue collection The raising of funds either directly from individuals seeking health care or indirectly through governments or donors.

Risk aversion The unwillingness of an individual to take on an identified risk.

Scale efficiency A situation where the provider is producing at an output level such that average cost is minimized.

Sensitivity analysis The process of assessing the robustness of the findings of an economic evaluation by varying the assumptions used in the analysis.

Shadow price The true economic price of a good that reflects its value to society.

Short run A decision-making time frame within which at least one input (the fixed input – see above) cannot be varied.

Social cost The total cost associated with an activity including both private costs and those incurred by society as a whole.

Substitutes Goods that can be used in place of other goods (e.g. tea and coffee are seen as substitutes).

Supply curve A graph showing the relationship between the quantity supplied of a good and its price when all other variables are unchanged.

Supplier-induced demand The demand that exists beyond what would have been asked by consumers if they had been perfectly informed about their health problems and the various treatments available.

Technical (operational) efficiency A point at which a producer cannot produce more output without using more of at least one input.

Time preference People's preference for consumption (or use of resources) now rather than later because they value present consumption more than the same consumption in the future.

Total (economic) cost The sum of all the costs of an intervention or health problem.

Transaction costs Costs of engaging in trade – i.e. the costs arising from finding someone with whom to do business, of reaching an agreement and of ensuring the terms of the agreement are fulfilled.

Underwriting The insurer's process of reviewing insurance applications, deciding what coverage to offer and determining the applicable premiums based on the health status of the applicant.

Unofficial payments Spending in excess of official fees, also called 'under the table' or 'envelope' payments.

Utility The happiness or satisfaction an individual gains from consuming a good. The more utility an individual derives from the consumption of a good, all else being equal, the more he or she would be willing to spend his or her income on it.

Variable cost/input A input/cost of production that varies directly with the level of output.

Vertical equity Unequal (but fair) treatment of unequals (i.e. individuals who are unequal should be treated differently according to their level of need).

Welfare (or social welfare) The economic criterion on which a policy change or intervention is deemed to affect the well-being of a society. In general, this is assumed to be determined by aggregation of the utilities experienced by every individual in a society.

Willingness to pay (WTP) The value an individual places on reducing a health problem or gaining an improvement in health.

Index

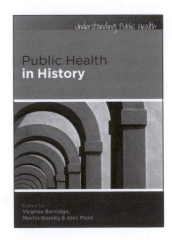

PUBLIC HEALTH IN HISTORY

Virginia Berridge, Martin Gorsky and Alex Mold

9780335242641 (Paperback)
2011

eBook also available

This fascinating book offers a wide ranging exploration of the history of public health and the development of health services over the past two centuries. The book surveys the rise and redefinition of public health since the sanitary revolution of the mid-nineteenth century, assessing the reforms in the post World War II years and the coming of welfare states.

Written by experts from the London School of Hygiene and Tropical Medicine, this is the definitive history of public health.

Key features:

- Case studies on malaria, sexual health, alcohol and substance abuse
- A comparative examination of why healthcare has taken such different trajectories in different countries
- Exercises enabling readers to easily interact with and critically assess historical source material

www.openup.co.uk

OPEN UNIVERSITY PRESS
McGraw - Hill Education

Understanding Public Health Series

Series editors: Ros Plowman and Nicki Thorogood, London School of Hygiene & Tropical Medicine.

Throughout the world, there is growing recognition of the importance of public health to sustainable, safe and healthy societies. The achievements of public health in nineteenth-century Europe were for much of the twentieth century overshadowed by advances in personal care, in particular in hospital care. Now, in the twenty-first century, there is increasing understanding of the inevitable limits of individual health care and of the need to complement such services with effective public health strategies. Major improvements in people's health will come from controlling communicable diseases, eradicating environmental hazards, improving people's diets and enhancing the availability and quality of effective health care. To achieve this, every country needs a cadre of knowledgeable public health practitioners with social, political and organizational skills to lead and bring about changes at international, national and local levels.

This is one of a series of books that provides a foundation for those wishing to join in and contribute to the regeneration of public health, helping to put the concerns and perspectives of public health at the heart of policy-making and service provision. While each book stands alone, together they provide a comprehensive account of the three main aims of public health: protecting the public from environmental hazards, improving the health of the public and ensuring high quality health services are available to all. Some of the books focus on methods, others on key topics. They have been written by staff at the London School of Hygiene & Tropical Medicine with considerable experience of teaching public health to students from low, middle and high income countries. Much of the material has been developed and tested with postgraduate students both in face-to-face teaching and through distance learning.

The books are designed for self-directed learning. Each chapter has explicit learning objectives, key terms are highlighted and the text contains many activities to enable the reader to test their own understanding of the ideas and material covered. Written in a clear and accessible style, the series is essential reading for students taking postgraduate courses in public health and will also be of interest to public health practitioners and policy-makers.

Titles in the series

Analytical models for decision making: Colin Sanderson and Reinhold Gruen
Controlling communicable disease: Norman Noah
Economic analysis for management and policy: Stephen Jan, Lilani Kumaranayake, Jenny Roberts, Kara Hanson and Kate Archibald
Economic evaluation: Julia Fox-Rushby and John Cairns (eds)
Environmental epidemiology: Paul Wilkinson (ed)
Environmental health policy: Megan Landon and Tony Fletcher
Financial management in health services: Reinhold Gruen and Anne Howarth
Global change and health: Kelley Lee and Jeff Collin (eds)
Health care evaluation: Sarah Smith, Don Sinclair, Rosalind Raine and Barnaby Reeves
Health promotion practice: Maggie Davies, Wendy Macdowall and Chris Bonell (eds)
Health promotion theory: Maggie Davies and Wendy Macdowall (eds)
Introduction to epidemiology, second edition: Ilona Carneiro and Natasha Howard
Introduction to health economics, second edition: Lorna Guinness and Virginia Wiseman (eds)
Issues in public health, second edition: Fiona Sim and Martin McKee (eds)
Managing health services: Nick Goodwin, Reinhold Gruen and Valerie Iles
Medical anthropology: Robert Pool and Wenzel Geissler
Principles of social research: Judith Green and John Browne (eds)
Public health in history: Virginia Berridge, Martin Gorsky and Alex Mold
Understanding health services: Nick Black and Reinhold Gruen

Forthcoming titles:

Sexual health: a public health perspective: Kaye Wellings, Martine Collumbien, Wendy Macdowall and Kirstin Mitchell
Conflict and health: Natasha Howard, Egbert Sondorp and Annemarie ter Veen (eds)
Making health policy, second edition: Kent Buse, Nicholas Mays and Gill Walt
Environment, health and sustainable development, second edition: Emma Hutchinson and Megan Landon (eds)

Introduction to Health Economics

Second edition